THE
LAST ASSASSIN

Also by Peter Stothard

Thirty Days

On the Spartacus Road

Alexandria

The Senecans

THE
LAST ASSASSIN

THE HUNT FOR THE KILLERS
OF JULIUS CAESAR

PETER STOTHARD

WEIDENFELD & NICOLSON

First published in Great Britain in 2020 by Weidenfeld & Nicolson
an imprint of The Orion Publishing Group Ltd
Carmelite House, 50 Victoria Embankment
London EC4Y 0DZ

An Hachette UK Company

10 9 8 7 6 5 4 3

A CIP catalogue record for this book is
available from the British Library.

ISBN (Hardback) 978 1 4746 1315 6
ISBN (eBook) 978 1 4746 1317 0

Typeset by Input Data Services Ltd, Somerset
Printed in Great Britain by Clays Ltd, Elcograf S.p.A.

MIX
Paper from
responsible sources
FSC® C104740

www.weidenfeldandnicolson.co.uk
www.orionbooks.co.uk

To Ruth

CONTENTS

MAIN CHARACTERS

ASSASSINS

CASSIUS PARMENSIS (c75–30 BC): Poet, playwright, naval commander, longest surviving assassin of Julius Caesar. Epicurean. Executed in retirement in Athens.

GAIUS CASSIUS LONGINUS (c86–42): Philosopher, politician, general, joint leader of the assassins. Husband of Marcus Brutus's sister. Epicurean. Committed suicide after first defeat at Philippi.

MARCUS BRUTUS (85–42): Orator, politician, idealist, general, joint leader of the assassins. Son of Caesar's mistress, Servilia. Committed suicide after second defeat at Philippi.

DECIMUS JUNIUS BRUTUS (c83–43): General, military innovator, closest friend to Caesar among the assassins. Killed on orders of Mark Antony while in flight to join Brutus and Cassius.

GAIUS TREBONIUS (c92–43): General for Caesar, editor and anthologist of Cicero. Tortured by Dolabella. First of the assassins to be killed.

PUBLIUS SERVILIUS CASCA (c84–42): Senator, People's Tribune. Striker of the first blow in Caesar's assassination.

TILLIUS CIMBER (c80–42): Impetuous naval commander. Embittered by failed petition to Caesar on behalf of his exiled brother.

PONTIUS AQUILA (c80–43): Independent-minded banker, soldier, aide to Decimus Brutus. Angered by the confiscation of his land for Caesar's mistress, Servilia. Killed in battle against Mark Antony.

LUCIUS MINUCIUS BASILUS (c80–43): Military aide to Caesar. Frustrated by lack of promotion. Killed by his slaves during the Proscriptions against the assassins.

QUINTUS LIGARIUS (c80–43): Supporter of Pompey in the civil war against Caesar. Spared by Caesar after persuasion by Cicero. Hunted under the *Lex Pedia*.

SERVIUS SULPICIUS GALBA (c80–c43): Officer for Caesar. Insulted by Caesar's affair with his wife and a disputed debt. Hunted under the *Lex Pedia*.

PACUVIUS LABEO: (c85–42): Lawyer close to Marcus Brutus. Committed suicide at Philippi.

DECIMUS TURULLIUS (c75–31): Assassin and naval commander with Cassius Parmensis. Executed on Octavian's orders in Cos after the battle of Actium.

SUPPORTERS

MARCUS TULLIUS CICERO (106–43): Orator, philosopher, politician. Sympathiser with the assassins. Enemy of Mark Antony. Executed on orders of Antony and Octavian.

SEXTUS POMPEIUS (67–36): Younger son of Caesar's last rival, Pompey the Great. Independent naval commander. Joined by Cassius Parmensis and defeated by Octavian in one of the great sea battles of antiquity.

QUINTUS HORATIUS FLACCUS, Horace (65–8): Poet. Supporter of Marcus Brutus. Fighter at Philippi. Subsequently crosses to the side of Octavian.

SERVILIA (c100–c40): Mother of Marcus Brutus, lover of Caesar. Wealthy and influential operator in the assassins' cause.

PORCIA (70–43): Wife of Marcus Brutus and daughter of Caesar's enemy, Cato. Powerful spur to the assassination.

AVENGERS

CAIUS JULIUS CAESAR OCTAVIANUS, Octavian (63 BC–14 AD): Adopted son and heir of Julius Caesar. Prime mover of the hunt for the assassins through the *Lex Pedia* and the terror of the Proscriptions. Future Emperor Augustus.

MARCUS ANTONIUS, Mark Antony (83–30): Heir to Caesar's cause until the arrival of Octavian. Initial negotiator with Cicero of an amnesty for the assassins. Drawn by Octavian down a competitive course of vengeance.

MARCUS AEMILIUS LEPIDUS (c89–c13): General for Caesar, aristocrat. Third member of the Triumvirate that avenged Caesar's death. Removed before the final confrontation between Octavian and Mark Antony.

LUCIUS ANTONIUS (c75–c39): Brutal younger brother of Mark Antony. Destroyer of Parma. Defeated by Octavian in the siege of Perusia.

PUBLIUS CORNELIUS DOLABELLA (69–43): Dissolute street agitator for Caesar. Sometime son-in-law of Cicero.

BLACK SEA

THRACE

Dyrrachium
Apollonia

MACEDONIA

Philippi

THASOS

Melas
Gulf

Nicomedia

Nicaea

BITHYNIA

GREECE

CORCYRA

Actium

LEUCAS

CEPHALLENIA

AEGEAN SEA

LESBOS

Troy

Pergamum

Sardis

Smyrna

Ephesus

ATHENS

Corinth

SAMOS

Miletus

Myndos

COS

RHODES

CRETE

PROLOGUE

THE MONSTER ON THE PATH

Epicurus, detail from *The School of Athens*, Raphael (1509–11)

From a half-closed window the hills of Athens rose ragged against the haze. The fires down below belonged to those who had not been in the city long. The summer dawn was crackling with the sound of sometime soldiers – and of cicadas and of birds awaking high amid pale-painted marble, the light crunch of lizards on leaves, a thin curtain of noise.

The night wind still blew out to sea, soon about to turn as the land warmed and the day winds began. The last thin scent of sulphur rolled off the Acropolis slopes.

Cassius Parmensis was in bed in a small house behind a boarded door. He was a sailor, poet and playwright and Athens was being good to him. For the last surviving assassin of Julius Caesar, a year after his last battle, this ever more crowded city was arguably the very best place of retirement. Every dawn was a surprise. Athenian dawns were some of the most perfumed and orange-pink. It was small wonder that so many people came here.

Parmensis, named for his family's home in Parma, near where Italy then met Gaul, had been one of the lesser wielders of the daggers on the Ides of March, one of the common herd of conspirators, not a Brutus, not the other more famous Cassius, those men who were dead and already entering history. While, like others in the conspiracy, Parmensis was a writer of history himself, his name was not yet a part of it.

In his early forties, he was old enough respectably to retire. But, at a time when Caesar's angry heir ruled supreme, he could not return to Italy, not to Rome, not to his once fertile home between the Rubicon and Po rivers. In the streets below the Acropolis, Parmensis had new admirers, a few former brothers-in-arms, even some readers for his poems and plays.

Fourteen years after the assassination that had failed to change the world, Athens was still a favoured place for writers, for dissidents and theorists, for stubborn dreamers, recent veterans who wrote of battles lost and old soldiers who told them how they could have won. Through its past it offered a kind of asylum.

Words and swords still stood side by side in the battle to be remembered. Particularly towards the end of a man's life the writing of a poem might mean more than all the killings and failures to kill. A great last act might be more than just the end of a play. His new home suited well the remaining hopes of Cassius Parmensis.

Athens, like so many of its night-time visitors, was a city whose best years were behind it, a sheltered home for many other Romans like himself, men of the navy and the minor arts, educated citizens who, while they had not themselves been prepared (or asked) to thrust their daggers into Caesar's corpse, preferred some sort of freedom to any sort of one-man rule. The best ideals of ancient

Greece, however hazy, stood out brightly against what their own country had become.

Athenians were fickle. They might unite to fight Romans or divide and back one Roman side against another. That had long been their way. But every cultured man felt better in the city where the works of Homer were first put in writing, the city of Aeschylus, Euripides, Socrates and Plato. Parmensis himself followed the philosophy of Epicurus, famed for his Athenian garden, dead for more than two hundred years but influential in Athens and far beyond. The poet from Parma who became a sea captain never claimed originality. He did like to be consistent. He was thorough. That was what ships and poetry demanded.

His last fight at sea had been at Actium, the year before, 31 BC, two hundred miles to the north and west of Athens, the last battle of the civil war that began with the daggers of Parmensis and his fellow assassins. This last battle had been between the two leaders of what was once a single alliance, those who had stuck to the cause of Caesar beyond his death before ending by fighting each other. Men who cared little for politics (a large number even in Athens) occasionally asked him how this had happened. It was easy to explain but not always easy to understand.

Mark Antony, Caesar's veteran brother-in-arms, and Octavian, Caesar's young great-nephew, had together defeated the leading assassins at Philippi in eastern Greece. That was the hard part. Then they had moved on to a war against each other on the west side. The prize was the supremacy that Caesar seemed to have bequeathed. It was like a mad game of chequers where the last black pieces, having conquered the white, go black-on-black. Actium was the last corner of the board.

Parmensis had fought at Actium for Antony and Cleopatra, for Caesar's friend and the fabulously wealthy queen who had been the mistress of Caesar and Antony in turn. He had no great love for those he had served, only a very great loathing of the 'the divine Caesar's son', the title that Octavian, who after Actium could also become emperor of Rome, had long ago given to himself.

This battle of the last black pieces had been barely even a fight. That was clearer in retrospect even than it had been at the time. Cleopatra had fled from Actium at the first whiff of defeat. Antony, a shadow of the man who helped Caesar conquer Gaul, had meekly followed her. Once worshipped as a god at Athens, he had become more like a dog.

Parmensis had afterwards lived quietly through the year of Octavian's last moves to imperial power, the year in which the last remnants of opposition were hunted down and destroyed. He recognised the dangers to himself from the moment he arrived in Athens. He did not know how very close the danger was.

He knew about fear, its ubiquity, its necessity, its smell, and was gradually getting to know more. For the past fourteen years he had felt safest at sea. When he was commanding men at war around Cyprus and Sicily, ramming and boarding Octavian's ships, or following the voyages of Homer's Odysseus as a poet might prefer to say, he was almost secure. On land, as night turned to dawn, he was much easier prey if his predator so chose.

Not only had Octavian defeated all his enemies: Cassius Parmensis had fought for each of those enemies in turn, in the navies of Caesar's killers and then, with varying zeal, for each of the rivals who wanted to stop a dynasty of Caesars. As civil war turned to peace Parmensis was for the first time alone.

He might possibly be safe in Athens among the mass of refugees and losers in the wars. His death ought hardly to be a priority for the new sole ruler of the Roman world. It would merely bring a stuttering story to an end.

And yet, that end might be no small thing. Octavian might desire and demand it. As a playwright Parmensis saw professionally the purpose of endings. He had ample time to reflect.

In Athens he could read his own poetry, and that of his friends, in what was almost peace. The city around him was the best place anywhere for buying words, in Latin and in Greek, ancient and modern, easy replacements for all the papyrus rolls he had lost on his campaigns. He could read the epics of Homer and the great tragedies, the *Iliad* on anger, the *Odyssey* on survival, Aeschylus on vengeance, Sophocles and Euripides on mothers murdering their children in revenge. He had by his hand the best plays written in Latin, by the master of comic darkness, Titus Maccius Plautus, born not far from Parma, by Marcus Pacuvius and Lucius Accius, tragedians but neither of them as good as the Greeks. Parmensis was writing tragedies of his own.

One was a *Brutus*, not about his dead fellow assassin but about rape and suicide in the early history of Rome. Another was a *Thyestes*, part of the most vicious vengeance cycle in the Greek myths that came before the beginning of history. Thyestes was the brother of Atreus, both men rival claimants to the throne of Mycenae, not far from Athens to the west: Thyestes was tricked by Atreus into eating his own children, an act that unleashed a chain of killings until the goddess Athena, *dea ex machina* in her own city, brought the cycle to an end.

This was the art of civil war. In the Greek dramas of Agamemnon, Clytemnestra and their daughter, Electra – and those of child-murdering Medea and Tereus, Thracian rapist of his wife's sister, and many more – lay few lessons of forgiveness, far more screams, curses and the cutting of tongues. A comedy by Plautus exposed the reality of chains, collars and whips. Every play was in its own roll made from papyrus reeds, each one about a foot high, all the columns of text leaning to the right, toppling and tumbling in the strange way preferred by scribes, horror falling upon horror.

In Athens Parmensis was a reader and a writer rather than any longer an actor in great events. All around him in the summer of 30 BC the view was changing. The land might as well be sea, its storms stirring in every direction as if from nowhere. Literature was as changeable as the rest of life. Alongside their Euripides, Homer and ancient Latin, the poetry sellers for students offered popular new Latin words from Virgil, Varius and Parmensis's fellow fighter, Horace, greater poets than he, as everyone agreed, also much greater at surviving.

The only one of these he knew personally was Horace, not

well but well enough. The two men, tied by youthful loyalties and buoyed by old ideals, had been on the same side against Octavian and Antony. Horace had fought alongside Caesar's assassins on land at Philippi, north and east of Athens where Greece met Asia, in the blood and dirt when so many heroes died. But twelve years had passed since then and Horace had been swiftly seduced into the service of Caesar's son; he was already becoming as feted and famed as Parmensis was not.

The Athenians themselves were turning. This had been the city most enthusiastic for Brutus and Cassius. The senior killers of Caesar had once been compared to the city's own greatest heroes and remembered in marble. Instead, in the sculpture gardens around the Acropolis there were new monuments to the mercy of the young Octavian Caesar, bright against those older stones.

That massive charioteer in charge of four giant horses was slated to be a new tribute to Octavian's admiral, Marcus Agrippa: it still represented a neighbouring king and Olympic champion, but not for much longer. Agrippa was Octavian's closest friend, the man who had prosecuted assassins in the courts of Rome before taking to the seas and winning bigger battles for his master. Athenians who had paid tax to Brutus and Cassius, danced with Cleopatra, watched Antony marry the goddess Athena, claimed barely to remember them.

Parmensis could have run from Athens but he preferred to wait. Nowhere would be safe from betrayers and everywhere would be less comfortable. Near his house, on every day that came, he could pass the remains of Epicurus's gardens, paying homage to the Greek philosopher who had taught every Roman of taste how to avoid the fear of death and how, once that fear was banished, every other part of life was enhanced.

Julius Caesar's last assassin knew his Epicurus well. So had Caesar himself, and Marcus Tullius Cicero and Gaius Cassius and other dead men in his story. Critics said that philosophy was drifting into self-absorption, the search for mere contentment through self-control, forgetful of disintegrating control over government.

But a philosophy of calm, with no fear of punishments in an under-world, was seen by Epicureans as a help to anyone, within a society and within oneself.

Parmensis had been a public man. He had lived a public, prac-tical life. But just as important for any follower of Epicurus was knowing that preparedness for death was the principal purpose of living; that rejecting the fear of death was a skill of logic, a lesson that could be learnt; that after death there was no self to be harmed, therefore neither a reason to fear nor an entity about which fear was possible. Only the material was real. Any gods were infinitely far away. He knew all that. He absolutely knew it.

But then again, like all student Epicureans, Parmensis knew that knowledge was not enough. There was something about being human that maintained old prejudices, the sense of the supernatural and the fear of the unknown, strong against all the power of reason. He had seen long and agonising exits from life. Not everyone could die as quickly as Caesar had. The only remedy for doubt was repe-tition and more repetition, the chanting that was the reinforcement of logic in pupils' minds. Classes in outstaring death were another good reason for living in Athens.

Beneath the fading dawn the ground was pale and grey. Rome had parks; Athens had only ground. The silver under an olive leaf was a startling colour in the summer in the hillside gardens where nothing else grew. For refugees ready to eat grass there was no grass. In the woods beneath the sweating pines and dusty oaks the orchids were gone. The air was filled with scent of fading herbs. Above the ground were only dead leaves, beneath them the bulbs and tubers that would show life again in October.

All of Caesar's other assassins were dead. It was hard to be abso-lutely sure but it was hard to be absolutely sure of anything. Gaius Trebonius was the first to die, terribly, horribly tortured, his head kicked against a wall for sport; Decimus Turullius was the latest. There were so many deaths from vengeance in between. The brave drunkard Tillius Cimber was probably dead. Parmensis couldn't be sure.

Turullius was the last victim whose fate he knew. A minor Roman on the day of Caesar's death, he too became a captain of ships. Together they had repaired floating hulks, built and rebuilt, extorted a useful fleet for the assassins from the treasuries of the Greek islands. After the loss of Brutus and Cassius at the brutal twin battles of Philippi, they had taken their ships into the service of Octavian's menacing enemy at sea, Sextus Pompeius, son of Julius Caesar's rival and son-in-law, Pompey the Great. These were family wars as well as wars of ideas and the world. After Sextus's defeat, pursuit and execution, he and Turullius had turned to Antony for a final chance of victory.

Since then Turullius had been executed too, the most recent of so many, on the Greek island of Cos, charged by Octavian's men with cutting down wood from a sacred grove to build a mast. Everyone knew that this had not been his capital crime. While Octavian still had the top assassins in his sights, he had made his need for vengeance clear. But when the victor was closing on the last of his father's killers he preferred to give other reasons to kill. The job was almost done. The new message was peace and healing.

A full list of the assassins might have been of nineteen men, or twenty-three, sixty, eighty. Octavian did not know. Parmensis did not precisely know. The plot to kill Caesar had been hasty as well as a long time coming, its method and ideals a mixture of the new as well as very old. So much was so hazy. Only one thing was clear. Caesar's grip had been like a gaoler's. Although the assassins had all been desperate to escape, freedom from captivity had not brought the different freedoms that they sought.

While counting numbers had hardly mattered before Caesar's last appearance at the senate on the Ides of March, secrecy had been essential, only barely successful enough. Betrayal was a risk as late as the first blows, when Tillius Cimber, heavy and clumsy, his petition in his hand, had tugged at Caesar's toga, when Servilius Casca had thrust his dagger. Or so it was said. Maybe it was the other Casca. There were so many Cascas. Parmensis had not seen all the acts. Was Marcus Brutus next? Probably not; he was a fastidious assassin. Or was it Decimus his more military distant cousin, or Gaius Cassius, the true leader of the conspiracy as many claimed, although leadership, once the dictator was dead, was what had been lacking most?

Parmensis had struck his own dagger blow but whether it was on the body of Caesar or one of his fellow killers he could not be sure. No one could be sure. All that most witnesses remembered, as though the act were an hour ago, was the blood on so much fine linen, the streams of red on white, like the misty end of a drinking party, no not quite like that. What it was like then was nothing like what it became.

He could not begin to order the names of those who had used their weapons while the seats of the senate hall were filling, fourteen years before, when so many eyes were turned elsewhere. By contrast he could name with naval precision the order in which the conspirators had themselves been killed. There was quickly a clear list of those, not necessarily complete or the same as those who had done the killing but definitively of those deemed guilty.

Some were gone within a year. Gaius Trebonius, a very literary senator, was tortured to death by one of Julius Caesar's most dissolute creatures, Publius Cornelius Dolabella, at the Asian port of Smyrna. Dolabella was a slug, a sot, a charmer and a shameless changer of sides; Parmensis had found himself both for and against him at different times.

Pontius Aquila, a banker not so well known, was killed fighting Antony in the swamps of Mutina not far from Parma, a great prize for any soldier who could claim the deed. Decimus Brutus, Caesar's friend and deemed the greatest traitor of them all, died a few weeks later at the hands of a Gallic chief looking for favours from Rome and probably finding them.

At first there was supposed to be an amnesty for all the conspirators but soon there wasn't. He knew exactly why. It was complicated. He could explain it when anyone asked. It was a common question.

On the afternoon of the assassination Antony had been as diplomatic at Rome as he had been a devastating fighter in Gaul. He soon agreed a deal. Octavian was different. He wanted a hunt for his father's killers, one by one, whatever it took. So did the voters of Rome and Caesar's soldiers. Antony followed. There was soon a list of assassins, a court, laws to protect the hunters. Those wanting a quieter life found the quiet harder to find.

Most knew only a part of what was happening. Battles were fought whose combatants knew nothing of other battles on which their fate depended. Speeches were delivered, edited and reedited. Only afterwards did a whole story come, though not the whole that Parmensis would have written himself.

There were gaps, so many spaces between what was known and what was hidden. Parmensis did not know what was in the gaps. Maybe no one knew. Antony and Octavian were divided and united in turn, uniting to kill and steal from other Romans, dividing to kill and steal from each other. Parmensis stayed at Rome, and then in the Italian countryside and then out at sea, watching and fighting and writing to Marcus Tullius Cicero before Cicero too, a sympathiser but not an assassin, was killed, his head severed by a hesitant soldier, his hands and tongue nailed high in the Forum. Understanding was hard. In the last hours of Athenian night to count further down the list was simpler.

Sickly Quintus Ligarius had hated Caesar because Caesar had pardoned him. He was no proud aristocrat. Like Cicero, he had made his own way up the ladder of life and all the more prized such status as he had. Caesar's notorious clemency could destroy a man's dignity; it was quite a common cause for hate. Ligarius had two brothers. Their names were entered on varying lists of those to be killed, either for what they had done or for what could be stolen from them, some to be slaughtered in the streets, others dragged from hiding places in ovens and rivers. There were many such stories.

Then came the two battles at Philippi, twenty days apart, thirty months after the assassination: those at least were fixed dates and facts, in a fixed place on the Roman road from Greece to Asia. Gaius Cassius, soldier, sailor, scholar, was panicked to take his own life

but lucky enough to take it before Octavian could take an avenger's pleasure. That was during the first battle, the critical day, when
Romans killed Romans as never before.

After the second round at Philippi, Marcus Brutus killed himself
too. Brutus was so stern a man, a poet too, a son of Caesar's lover, Servilia, maybe Caesar's own son, some said, so strange a story,
his family tracing itself back to the earliest years of Rome's glory,
his mind haunted by the ghost he called his evil genius. Parmensis
had an evil genius too, a conscience maybe or a madness. Studying
Epicurus did not always stop the fear of phantoms one could see.

Publius Servilius Casca, striker of perhaps the only fatal blow
among all the wild wielders of daggers, died fighting. Lucius Tillius
Cimber, ever keen on his next job and his next drink, disappeared.
Pacuvius Antistius Labeo, Brutus's lawyer friend in a time when law
had failed, dug his own grave on the same day. Thousands died at
Philippi, hundreds of them from the first families of Rome. Soldiers
hunted Caesar's killers tent by tent until slowly the noise of war was
stilled and vengeance, that darkest power of the human spirit, had
vanquished all else.

Afterwards the great cause of the assassins prospered best at sea.
Parmensis had known many days of hope under sail, on land many
fewer until there were none. After Actium quiet came eventually to
every field and bay of battle. Even his own home towns, Parma and
its beleaguered neighbours, gained the peace to rebuild, slowly and
as best they could, what had been so savagely lost.

His friend Turullius was quietly killed for cutting the wrong
trees. And finally there was Parmensis himself, the last assassin, still
waiting with his poetry and plays beside him, a tragedy about the
mythical Thyestes, lured into banqueting on the flesh of his boys,
a play about the not quite as mythical, Lucretia, who was raped
opposing an early tyrant of Rome and avenged by Brutus's most
famous ancestor, Marcus Junius, a hard act for any hero to follow.
Vengeance lived at the heart of art, and was maybe more under-
standable there.

Also on the shelves were his epigrams, written out in pages of columns more crooked than his plays, short lines, long lines, lines leaning this way and that, some of them about Octavian, his satires on the bakers, pimps and money-lenders in Caesar's much-vaunted family tree. These poems might have been a mistake. Without them the new tyrant of Rome, fully successful where Caesar had almost been, might have forgotten him. They were not his finest work but they were at least words he could take to the gods if he died and got the chance to get his story in first.

But, of course, he did not think that. No, he did not think anything like that. An Epicurean could not countenance such nonsense. He did not believe in taking one's words to gods. Even if gods were to exist, they would not care about him or about Octavian. The self-styled 'son of the divine Caesar' knew that his human decision alone had made Caesar a god after the Ides of March. Octavian knew that the deification was a political act, a piece of propaganda beside so many other pieces. Yet he might still be nervous of poems about his human past.

Poetry was as flexible as history but more durable. In Athens men still spoke of his one-time neighbour in Gaul, the poet Helvius Cinna, killed after Caesar's funeral by a Roman mob who mistook him for a forgettable politician, Lucius Cornelius Cinna. There would soon be many poems about the past fourteen years. Poet to poet, man of Gaul to man of Gaul: that would be one good way to tell the story. Cinna would be the start; Parmensis would be the end of it. In a world made of words he would die a writer's death.

The time for poetry alone was not, however, quite yet. Octavian was not celebrating victory by reading. Nor, as his own court poets claimed, was he reordering the east or reconquering empire. He was not invading Parthia or Britain. He was still avenging Caesar, ridding Rome even of the hall where Caesar died. He was still overseeing the last deaths of those he deemed his father's betrayers.

Down below the crowds heaved and another day began. The wind began to blow from the sea. Up above, behind barred doors as the cicadas cried to the slowly rising sun, came Parmensis's last fear, a dark, dishevelled, bearded giant coming for him step by crunching step. He called his slaves and asked if anyone else had seen the monster. They said no. He returned to sleep. There were dried leaves and flowers, pungent aniseed and other seeds, for nightmares.

He saw the monster again. He called for a lamp. He called his slaves to stay beside him. The fear returned. Soon afterwards Octavian's emissary came.

ONE

THROUGH CAESAR'S COUNTRY

Caesar and the Crossing of the Rubicon, Francesco Granacci (1493–4)

In the wild January of 44 BC, Julius Caesar's last January alive, a man waving farewell to his home in Parma would never see its walls again. A town of low brick markets and barracks, built less than a century before, would be the rubble of civil war before he or his fellow travellers could return. *Parmenses miserrimos*, most wretched people of Parma, would be the message to Rome, leaving no more words to be said. For some this was a routine trip. In the coming weeks there would be little that was easy or routine.

To those leaving for the capital there were the usual outlines against the sky at their backs, the look-out tower, the half-built temple, warehouses for millet and wool, all slipping into the winter distance as they always did. Grey mist sank into black-streaked mud. Behind them lay the watery tracks to Mantua and Cremona, the wooden palisades along the River Parma itself, the shifting River Taurus, the edgeless tracks to their farms. Ahead of these wealthy Parmenses, not yet the most wretched of a wretched place, lay the first of the two roads south, the *Via Aemilia*, one-hundred-and-fifty miles through flat land and flooded forest to the sea. After that they would take the *Via Flaminia*, the second road west over the mountains to the madness of the greatest city of their time.

Travellers like these were soldiers and soldiers' sons. Parmensis was a soldier poet before he became a sailor. Poets and sailors of Parma were rare, soldiers common. They were not naïve. They knew how to look after each other in dangerous ground. They prized their land linked to the sea, the communication to the world beyond that a coastline allowed.

Their home was then called Cisalpine Gaul, the part of Gaul on 'this side of the Alps', as the Romans saw it, soon to be made a part of Italy. Their roads were means of war as well as ways to walk, means to vote at Rome, to buy and sell, dominate and be dominated as well as highways on which to be drawn to Rome by slaves, or by mules, as Parmensis would have been. They knew of civil war and something of what to expect if it came again, but not the enormity of what would come.

Cassius Parmensis was around thirty years old. Julius Caesar, the great man of his time, was almost thirty years older, and this was Caesar's country as well as his own. Caesar had long settled his retired soldiers here. His first Cisalpine colonists had grown rich from pigs and grain on Parma's wide spreading fields. The wealth of the latest veterans was the gold of the other Gaul from the other side of the Alps, plunder which their commander had distributed to the most loyal. The town took its name, it was said, from the *parmula*, the small round shield with which its first founders fought off the

Gauls. No one had ever fought and conquered Gauls as Caesar had.

Only a year before Caesar had settled there his Twelfth Legion, known as the Thunderbolt, in gratitude for its grim service against his enemies at home and abroad. The lightning flash, a bright scar across their long infantrymen's shields, was still their sign of honour. Caesar had recruited thousands of fresh soldiers from the town and from the plains of the River Po behind it. Five years before, he had given Roman citizenship to all free men in Cisalpine Gaul and had elevated their leaders to the senate. In his latest act of power, the conqueror of Gaul, his dignity disabling his will to be a mere citizen again, had accepted for himself the dictatorship of Rome – not for a temporary crisis, as others had in the past, but for the rest of his life.

This was some of the news waiting for the men from Parma. Caesar was part of it all. Ten years before there had been a question in a popular poem: was Caesar a white man or a black man, a good man or a bad man, womanly or manly in bed. The poet then said he didn't care. Carelessness had since become more dangerous.

Shallow lakes spread to left and right. Water-birds flocked amid massive clouds in the grey sky. It was easier to describe a homeland when it was fading into the fog and the past. Parmensis knew his fellow men of Parma, those with deep roots in the town, the newcomers who had made it their home, their shifting loyalties to their own past and their hopes. They were independent men, in a total population of probably no more than five thousand, men of the frontier, their lightning shields never far from their left arm. They did not trust ancient aristocrats from other places; they did not trust the voters of the modern mob of Rome.

They revered Julius Caesar and they feared him – but only broadly speaking, as a man might speak when there were no ears to listen bar those of wild boars and eagles. Caesar had long ago forged ahead into the pathless wastelands of thought where few could follow. Caesar was a ruthless politician, a not very revered high priest, a peerless killer and commander, a plain-writing historian of his own life. Not every Parmensis on the *Via Aemilia* felt the same about him. Cassius Parmensis, from one of the founding families of the town, with a nearby village bearing the Cassius name, was not himself sure what he felt.

By the first midday the men from Parma could see in the distance a yellowing plateau of rock, like a broken column on the watery plain. There were nuts and porcupine quills to pick, hot springs in which to bathe. By the evening they were in Mutina, the twin colony to Parma on the Scultenna river forty miles closer to the coast, almost identical at their birth in 183 BC. That was the year when Hannibal died, Rome's greatest adversary, the Gauls' greatest ally, not killed in battle but hunted and betrayed faraway after his defeat.

Each of the thousand pioneer settlers in Parma had received around five acres, eight *iugera*, each *iugerum* defined by how much a pair of oxen could plough in a day. In Mutina the allotment had been smaller, five *iugera*, but in most other respects the risks and rewards in the two would-be towns were the same. Later their lives divided. During the vicious class struggles of the seventies, between the established and the excluded, the rich and the rest, the hopeful poor of Mutina had been besieged by the army of the young aristocrat, Pompey, a brutalising experience that Parma had been spared. Mutina's defender then was Marcus Junius Brutus whose son thirty-three years later seemed still committed to the populist side.

The travellers crossed the low, wooded islands of the River Rhenus, through the streets of Bononia, once the capital of the Gallic Boii, Hannibal's allies whom the Romans had displaced. A *boius* had since become a joke word for a slave who chafed at his chains, a *boia* the word for a Boian woman, her vagina, her jewellery and a punishment collar. *Boius est, boiam terit,* wrote Plautus, the pioneer genius of Roman comedy born only a few miles down the road. He's a Boian, he wears out his chain: behind the mockery there was always an undertone of nervousness. Next came Claterna where travellers could divert to the Etruscan pottery-makers of Arretium. Neither town meant much to the men from Parma but a reason to move on. The border with Roman Italy, the Rubicon river, lay ahead, and with it memories shared by all.

The Rubicon flowed between red rock banks just beyond the end of the *Via Aemilia.* It was nothing like the Po or even the Scultenna or Rhenus. It was a fine line drawn by a map-maker not a force of nature. In crossing the Rubicon five years earlier Caesar had begun his civil war, breaking the law to bring his troops home from his province. The Thunderbolt legion led the way. Behind him Parma and Mutina were platforms for that war, possessions, prizes.

His enemy – no longer merely a rival – was the same Pompey who in 77 BC had besieged Mutina, known to his admirers but not to Caesar as Pompey the Great. Throughout their lives Pompey and Caesar had shared both political causes and the closest family connections. In the end Pompey's principal support had come from the traditionalists of the senate further south, Caesar's from the more radical. But *Optimates* and *Populares* were increasingly antique terms, the best and the popular, sometimes identified only by shades of purple on a toga, different dyes from costly crushed sea-snails of the east, lighter for reformers, darker for conservatives, club badges more than signs of belief.

This Pompey had a surviving son, a man in his early twenties yet not to be seen as lesser because his father was Great. The latest news from Spain showed that Sextus Pompeius was a power in himself. Caesar did not yet have a son except with the Egyptian queen, Cleopatra, currently in Rome but useless for a Roman dynasty. Caesar, it was said, kept his most paternal love for Marcus Brutus, son of the father of the same name whom Pompey had executed after the siege of Mutina. In the previous year he had made him Rome's governor of all Cisalpine Gaul. Marcus Brutus had been popular in Parma. Parmensis might find out more about the latest Marcus Brutus when he arrived in Rome.

In sight of Ariminum, the last and richest town before the mountains, the road turned down the coast, then sharply right and changed its name. The *Via Flaminia* was the high route to Rome, past a giant silver ridge of caves, home of bears and bats, as much a natural boundary as the Po river, as much a boundary as the Rubicon was not. In the winter of 44 BC, just as in that same season of 49 when Caesar crossed, there was water in the Rubicon and every stream. In the summer, as every traveller knew, the winter beds were dry.

There had been four years of war after Caesar's crossing. On the one side was Pompey, the fabulously rich conqueror of the East, master of the seas, and the lesser of two evils for the traditionalists of the Roman senate. On the other was Caesar whose money and power came from populism at Rome and the conquering of Gaul. They were friends who had become enemies, who had fought together against shared foes and found their most famous hostility in each other.

The two men fought for the last time at Pharsalus in Greece before Pompey lost his last battle, fleeing down the coast of Asia to the shallow waters of Egypt to be stabbed at the bottom of a small boat, in full sight of his wife and Sextus, his son, perhaps an unnecessary humiliation. Caesar was sorry when he saw the head that had been hacked off on the nearest beach, ready to be remembered ever after in poems and pictures.

As the *Via Flaminia* rose above flooded forests the pace slowed and the traffic increased. The road narrowed over long bridges, sometimes hardly more than stepping stones, with tall reeds on either side. Nature vied with its invaders. Men vied with birds and with each other.

Above in the darkening sky, and on every repeated journey almost as constant, the marsh birds flew, in clouds and waves, tall-standing storks, giant cranes and grey herons, the messengers of local gods, bittern and night heron in the near distance, and further away the white tailed eagles with wings once used for brushing floors, great bustards, pelicans as tall as a man.

Nothing was different from any other time. Some saw their future in flights of birds; some believed the priests who watched on their behalf. Parmensis saw merely birds, sometimes harbingers of bandits but nothing more. He was as accustomed to seeing the same coastal starlings, as to seeing the same stars, the ravens lumbering slowly, the same target practice for boys, the same hail-laden clouds skidding through the sky, woodcock walking around a copse rather than taking the trouble to fly, the owls at the perfect height to hit a marching man, every marsh bird panicking when a hawk flew.

The embankments became higher, built on arches like aqueducts. A man on one side had no sight of his friend or enemy on the other. At the rougher track to the town called Fulginiae travellers could turn towards Perusia, the exuberant town of the Etruscans, the closest ancient civilisation to Parma. They could cross the tumbling Tiber, kick the grey volcanic ash that fell from the cliffs, stumble into rock tombs that opened in the rains. They could buy from some of their world's finest craftsmen in bronze. Or they could continue to Rome.

This was the road of rumours – of gossip, poems, pamphlets that were as important to the men of the provinces as were the mutton and millet of Mutina which moved in the other direction. Caesar was dictator-for-life: no one knew what would happen when he was dead. While Caesar might have been Parma's preferred dictator, some thought it better to have no dictator.

They phrased that thought as a series of questions – about what was possible, when, how, at what cost and, most importantly perhaps, what was the right thing. Cassius Parmensis was beginning to acquire a philosophy that offered answers. And as soon as anyone had a philosophy he could call himself a philosopher. That was a common claim of his times. Thought lived in poetry and plays. Many of those by whom Parmensis's life and name would later be defined were poets – in their own minds if not always in the minds of their readers.

Thought was nothing if it was not practical. Parmensis knew the lessons which Epicurus, uniquely two and a half centuries before, gave equally to slaves, women and men. First apply logic; secondly, when the logic was clear and unassailable, repeat the result, ruthlessly, over and over again, until the last bit of doubt was banished. A successful argument in itself was not enough. It had to be assumed into the mind.

Those who succeeded in absorbing the thought of Epicurus as

their own were free from the wounds of life. They knew that birds did not bring prophecies from the gods whatever the priestly college of augurs might claim. They knew that everything everywhere was material, that what men called spirits were thin layers sloughed off the surface of things, liable to deceive the unknowing but no more real for that. Practised Epicureans were no longer afraid of death. They were ready for death instead, permanently. They could do anything. They could live better than anyone.

At a time when the site of Parma was still a home to Gauls and Rome had no philosophy of its own, the Athenian master had left behind a specific cure for life's most desperate disease, a chant as well as an argument. Philosophy lived longer in words that were remembered. That was one reason why a man such as Cassius Parmensis might want to be a poet.

Death is nothing to me.
What is dust does not perceive, and what does not perceive is
nothing to me.

After that the teachers recommended a pause.

Death brings neither pleasure nor pain.
The only thing that is bad for me is pain.
Thus, death is not bad for me.

Pause. Repeat.

If in doubt – or if at the end of a long journey, slipping through the tanneries and graveyards before the walls of Rome – the student could repeat and repeat. Epicurus's advice about public life was, where possible, to avoid it. Equality for women and slaves was important and only within a walled garden, away from the bounds of convention, could this be achieved. But Epicurus also prized peace and free speech and would surely have had advice at a time of dictatorship imposed for one life and maybe more.

Parmensis had friends and family in Rome who had given this matter much thought. There was Gaius Cassius Longinus, the most prominent of the Cassii of the time; Marcus Brutus was Gaius's brother-in-law. Both were men of the mind. But philosophers did not have all the answers. All people made choices. Thoughts did not choose. The travellers entered Rome, crossed the Field of Mars, skirted the forest of marble and ivory behind Pompey's Theatre and made for the brown stones of the Palatine. Not only would they fail to see the walls of their home town again, no one would. In the wars after the Ides of March they would be among the first casualties.

2

PARMENSIS AND THE
FIRST ASSASSINS

Cassius Parmensis, Giuseppe Bertoluzzi (c1830)

Parma was a town on a plain by the banks of a mild-mannered stream. Rome was a city of hills above a river that in January was a wild wave and was prone to flood at any time. The last miles from the *Via Flaminia* passed the shallow Quirinal and Viminal hills before turning out its travellers at the foot of the steep Capitoline. Above them the temple of Jupiter stood guardian over the Forum, the place of politics, where the Roman people listened to their leaders, sacrificed and rioted, actions as unpredictable as the torrent.

There was the entrance to the great sewer, the *Cloaca Maxima*, which carried any waters from the Forum to the Tiber that were not required. Then came the Palatine hill, later to give its name to every place called a palace. Broad enough for streets, near to the river but not too close, it was already the favoured home for the powerful and those who sought power.

Gaius Cassius Longinus was married to Marcus Brutus's sister; he was slightly older than Marcus Brutus, although Brutus was fuller in himself and had the grander position of authority. In the great brown houses of the Palatine hill it was important to remember both fact and deception. Gaius Cassius was not only slighter in status and appearance; he was sensitive, pale-faced, weak-eyed, unpredictable and prone to anger. Only the boldest nicknamed him 'the date' for his youthful fruit-trading adventures in the eastern deserts. He had a long history of giving good advice that others ignored. He avoided alcohol but might easily take offence at any time, and not just with a middle-ranking member of his family from faraway Parma.

In 44 BC Gaius Cassius was a junior praetor, ranked second in the second level of Roman officials; Marcus Brutus, though younger was the senior praetor. Both roles were just below those of the consuls but Cassius, barely satisfied with the praetorship at all, believed that they should have been reversed in his favour. He blamed Caesar. Caesar joked that his face was too pale to be trusted.

Small matters mattered. The Cassii were an ancient family, not the grandest but as conscious of their present dignity as schooled in their past. Their first consul, Cassius Viscellinus, almost 500 years before, proposed giving land to the poor, was charged with currying favour and put to death by his peers for aspiring to make himself king. Some said that his own father had led the prosecution, proof that in times of trial fatherland should come before family. For the sake of Rome, varyingly expressed and argued, Gaius Cassius was considering whether Caesar should share his ancient ancestor's fate.

Ruling Rome was a family affair. Horror at unchecked rule was fused to the Cassii's own sense of themselves, not just the rejection of illegitimate tyranny by a single usurper but legalised monarchy too. Every arm of power should be constrained by another: the senate, the consuls, the courts and juries, the junior magistrates, the people's tribunes, the people in their own assembly. The questions of who and how many should govern Rome that winter, the hints and rumours in the halls, were from their own family history. The argument about the dictator, for killing him or not, came within the circles of the city where Parmensis was invited only by his name. It was closed to those without connections, hard to comprehend even by those who had.

Gaius Cassius was a soldier, sailor and philosopher or, as he preferred sometimes, a philosopher first. He read and spoke fluently in Greek, more readily than most on the Palatine, most readily when the subject was a deep passion. He had lived for four decades and in each of them Rome had become even more of an empire, less and less like the city state, remembered and imagined, of his ancestors. Twice Caesar had successfully intervened to impede his rise through the rungs of public office. It hardly needed to be said that Caesar's interventions against Cassius, however motivated, were successful; he had the overwhelming power. The man who had rolled the dice to cross the Rubicon controlled everyone's luck.

That was the power that made Cassius an Epicurean like his cousin from Parma. He adopted this very practical Greek theory at the same times as Caesar had grabbed every lever of Roman rule. At first he had reacted to Caesar's supremacy by withdrawing from politics: that was what Epicurus had recommended as a wise man's prime self-protection. And then he had begun to consider what level of lawless tyranny justified its removal by force.

Cassius hated Caesar but he knew he needed reason to kill him. Arguments had to compete like men at arms. Cassius had studied Greek in the independent island of Rhodes. At its university he had learned the disciplines of abstract thought just as he had learned the power of oratory to persuade. Rome's expansion threatened Rome's best ideals. That was increasingly, uncomfortably, clear. If a modern imperial city could not be governed in the old ways, he was asking how it could or should be run.

Autocracy was an affront, both in word and fact. Under the rule of one man all others were slaves. A senator should be free – and able to tell others that they were free too. Even autocratic clemency, Caesar's generous sparing of the suddenly weak, clashed with individual freedom for Gaius Cassius. To owe a man one's life was a philosophical problem in itself.

After the crossing of the Rubicon he had fought for Pompey against Caesar. Off the shores of Sicily he had almost destroyed Caesar's fleet. After Caesar's victory he had been pardoned. Cassius's first thoughts of killing Caesar came immediately after Caesar, at Brutus's request, had spared his life. Cassius was married to Brutus's sister.

Those very first thoughts of assassination had almost become fact. All need for agonising argument would then have gone. By the banks of the Cydnus river in the far north-east of the Mediterranean Cassius had begun a bold but too hasty attempt on Caesar's life. Caesar, not knowing his luck, had survived by mooring his boat where he was not expected. A successful assassin would need more thought, better plans.

Both the thought and the conspiracy were hard. Epicurus had taught the power of friendship's bonds but not whether it was right to treat a dictator as a friend. The answer might depend on how bad the dictator was – or was likely to become. The whole populace of Rome might be deemed friends whom an Epicurean should aim to spare from tyranny. Pursuit by logic took hours and days even for those determined and trained.

On the Palatine there were many more men thoughtlessly wanting to be Caesar's friend, an offence to a committed philosopher, good sense to those who simply wanted to get on. Anxiety about status was everywhere rising, just as the power of office was falling. Caesar had raised the number of the lesser praetors, respecting the sons of ancient families, but all had to be his allies. The lists of consuls for Caesar's years had been full of famous names but none who would be famous men.

An assassin needed allies. Brutus was a thinker who might also conspire. He was a man darker than Cassius, one who looked inward, his eyes deep set, his hair styled like the knowingly handsome, his

jaw suggesting obstinacy indulged. His philosophy was not that of
Epicurus but of the more traditional schools. More than any new
thinking he revered his place in the history of Rome. He never considered the virtue of protecting his peace of mind behind garden
walls.

Brutus owed his life to Caesar twice, some said. He had chosen
Pompey's side, though less keenly than Cassius, and been forgiven.
He was also the son of Caesar's mistress, Servilia, the mother, by
her second husband, of Cassius's wife. Perhaps he was even Caesar's
own son, so desperately had Caesar enquired after his safety as the
bodies lay unburied after Pompey's final defeat. Perhaps he was
embarrassed about Servilia, who was barely fifteen years older than
himself, keenly protective of her family and more passionate for
Caesar than for either of her husbands.

An undoubted truth, even clearer in Rome than in Parma, ever
clearer in those February days, was that every topic of conversation, from sex to moneylending (at which Brutus was a notorious
extorter), from religion to legionary food supply, would come to
encompass Caesar sooner or later. Some of those conversing would
be killers if they could find each other, a place and a time.

* * *

That time had to be soon. The newly declared dictator-for-life was
about to leave Rome – for the conquest of the Parthians in the farthest east. The date was set for three days after the Ides, a propitious
time sacred to Jupiter and set by the calendar of the moon. The
immediate questions, spoken and unspoken, were of what and why
and what after.

Caesar's own motives were clear. Conquering the Gauls – a total
conquest not just a deal to pay tribute – had not been enough. It
had made him neither satisfied nor safe. If Rome was to be ruled,
it had to be ruled from the east as well as the west. His dead rival,
Pompey, had won his greatest glory in the east, the pearls and gold
for his triumphs, the peoples who still paid tax to Rome. His other

dead rival, Marcus Licinius Crassus, despite his Palatine house with its pioneering columns of marble, his legendary wealth, and with Gaius Cassius advising uselessly at his side, had been humiliated and murdered by the Parthians. Alexander the Great had conquered in the east. For Caesar this was unfinished business, repetition, reinforcement and revenge, some of it unfinished over centuries.

Caesar's preparations to leave included settling the government of Rome while he was set to be away, the appointment of provincial governors, consuls and other magistrates for three years ahead. Such control of the future was a gift to him, delivered in a law proposed to the people by Lucius Antonius, the youngest brother of Mark Antony, Caesar's fellow consul for the year.

There was much talk of the Antonii that year. Their other brother, Gaius Antonius, one more of Caesar's praetors, was the least sophisticated of the three but maybe the most dangerous. Their mother was Caesar's cousin. All of them, for all that they lacked wealth and were no counterweight to Caesar, were men of insinuating influence in Caesar's Rome.

Those on the Palatine who were set to benefit from this future planning already saw some attractions in it. Gaius Cassius himself was due to govern Syria after he had completed his duties as praetor. Brutus's close and younger cousin, Decimus, also one of the very closest men to Caesar, another son in the eyes of some, was to rule Parma, Mutina and every other town of Cisalpine Gaul: after that, in 42 BC, he would be consul.

Another winner would be Gaius Trebonius, no aristocrat but a commander for Caesar through many campaigns. A year earlier he had allegedly discussed with Antony the killing of Caesar in Gaul, a rumour that had cost him nothing. A literary man too, he would take the wealth of Asia. For the ebullient, bull-necked consul, Mark Antony, Caesar's finest commander when sober, the legions of Macedonia lay ahead.

One question for Cassius and Brutus was whether honours under Caesar were honours worth having. Good character appeared to play less and less a part in winning them. That appearance mattered as much as fact.

Caesar's tame thug, Publius Cornelius Dolabella, minor heir to the great family of the Cornelii, rapist of everywhere he governed and many whom he met, would be a first beneficiary, a replacement for Caesar as consul as soon as Caesar had left for his Parthian war, the beneficiary of another extension of dictatorial patronage. Dolabella was shorter than an ambitious man liked to be. He had lost more money, more street battles, more ships in battle than he had ever won. But nothing seemed to dent Caesar's confidence in his creature. Caesar's confidence was all that counted.

Others of the dictator's party saw only lost hopes. Lucius Minucius Basilus, a praetor of the previous year, was one of the many minor men who thought they should be major, whom Caesar had paid off and passed over. Basilus had no province to plunder. Publius Servilius Casca and his brother were poorer than they thought Caesar should have allowed them to be. Tillius Cimber, impetuous and a notorious drunk, believed that he was overdue a pardon for his brother, Publius.

Quintus Ligarius, like Publius Cimber, had stuck with Pompey's cause longer than was wise for his future. He had endured a lengthy exile, Caesar's open abuse as 'an enemy villain' and the ignominy of a pardon without prospects. Decimus Turullius had been an aide to Tillius Cimber. Pontius Aquila had seen his land near Naples given to Caesar's mistress: he had refused to rise to his feet for Caesar's triumph, a mocked man by the dictator from that point on.

Some of these names lived only in the gossip of the baths and banquets. Basilus had almost captured the great chieftain, Ambiorix, when campaigning in Gaul, but had failed in the last strike. Perhaps Caesar, for all his sympathy, had never fully forgiven him. Servius Sulpicius Galba was one of many grandees whose wives Caesar had seduced. Others were themselves the gossipers. Galba had also disputed with Caesar about money and about a lost election for the consulship of 49 BC which, he believed, Caesar should have done more to help him win. While the steam rose and wine flowed he was not afraid of letting these arguments be known.

Those were the men with personal complaints. But even those with no hopes of preferment or fears of exclusion might think that the Parthian war should be directed from the Capitoline in Rome, not Rome from Caesar's camps in Parthia. The lawyer Pacuvius Labeo, like Decimus, was a wealthy philosophical friend of Marcus Brutus. For Caesar to be dictator-for-life was an outrage to lovers of the old ways of government. Some of those ways might seem dated but not all were dead. This dictator was setting the fate of Rome as though he was one of the Fates himself.

Cassius Parmensis had no known hopes of his own high advancement. But the absence of hope affected more than those who were themselves deprived. Senators in the city had reluctantly accepted many of the novelties of Caesar's supremacy, his bright golden throne, his new personal priest and temple, his suddenly ubiquitous statues, the steep marble noses, tight-cropped ears and receding hairline which the knives of sculptors had made so closely to match the man. To a younger man from Parma these may have been shocks.

The people's hopes, much more importantly, were different. The mass of Romans in the tight-packed homes around the Palatine and beyond, their number rising at this time towards a million, were hardly shocked at all. Their city was ever more filled with new shrines as well as human newcomers. Brown stucco walls were becoming backdrops to bright marble. Old temples were extravagantly restored. Trusting Caesar to feed and support them, most citizens gave hardly a glance to the images of their dictator sprouting in the narrow streets around the Forum, only the first of them worthy of comment, their successors merely urban furniture or items of fun.

Cassius Parmensis could have restricted himself to disapproval of Caesar, to the philosophical, the poetic or merely the personal distaste of an independent provincial. If nothing changed he was set to be a *quaestor*, the lowest rung on Rome's ladder of honours.

Instead, for reasons not fully known, probably not even at the time and by himself, he came closer to what, quietly, secretly and in code, was an expanding conspiracy to kill.

* * *

There was a strange incident at the end of January when someone put a laurel crown with a white band, a colour of royalty, on one of Caesar's more conspicuous stone heads. If this was a joke about the dictator's aspiration to be king, the subject did not find it funny. Another joker called Caesar 'Rex'; the dictator joked back that he was 'not Rex but Caesar'. It was a dry quip: one of Caesar's distant family names was Rex, the Latin for king, but not everyone knew that and no one could be sure.

Incipient monarchy unsettled all sides. When senators came to offer new honours and titles they expected Caesar to stand to receive them not merely to slouch back in his throne. Cassius had voted against the honours but even the more obsequious of the powerless expected their obeisance to be accepted with grace. When Caesar failed that test, he might or might not have known the depth of the offence.

At the festival of the Lupercalia in February there were many Roman citizens with roots outside Rome who packed the city for the display, the feasting at public expense, the sight of almost naked young men lashing women in a drunken procession between fig trees. Caesar watched from his golden throne above the Forum, his purple toga billowing and the laurel crown on his head. Mark Antony, perhaps a bit fat, grand and old for the naked running, was experienced enough to note the people's delight when he joined the race.

The festival began in a cave at the foot of the Palatine and celebrated the suckling of Romulus and Remus there beside a fig tree by a she-wolf, the best loved story of the city's foundation, the source too for the idea that there be two rulers, one checking and balancing the other. At the beginning as at the end, principle and practice had failed to meet. Romulus had killed Remus; successors had followed his example; and yet the principle was still alive.

This was a popular show. The men wore mud and goatskin loin cloths. The women bared their legs for the whips of the runners, a spectacle exclusive to Rome on the day of Lupercalia, itself maybe worth the trip from Naples or Parma. It was a festival of breathlessness and nightmare, sex and myth, demons kept at bay by winter flowers.

Antony showed himself a master of theatre that day. He had the family nose of the Antonii, not the grandest of families but usefully related to Caesar and allegedly to Hercules, the nose of an ancient Roman, aquiline, hooked like an eagle's beak. If for the Lupercalia he also looked like a Hercules, paunchy but muscled beneath a thin coarse coat, that was not by accident. He was as ready to wear a low-slung broadsword like a club as to run naked with a goat-whip. He ended the wildness of the day by climbing up to Caesar and offering a golden crown. Caesar refused it and received tumultuous applause.

Three times Antony repeated the offer. Three times Caesar repeated his refusal. Watchers asked whether this was a long gaze into a past or a preview of a future. Caesar must have known that it was about to happen. But, as to what the two men wanted to happen next, acceptance or rejection, public acclaim as king or for not being king, it was hard to be sure. What Caesar wanted when he returned from Parthia was a matter on which well-informed men could disagree. It was all too clear the extent of his present domination.

Yet to the voters in the streets of Rome Caesar's was not an onerous domination, not a tyranny except for those devoted to politics and its theories. The people's assemblies, the P in the city's SPQR, still passed the laws and elected their chosen men to public office. *Senatus Populusque Romanus*, the Senate and the Roman People: that was still the symbol of the system and, since it was necessary to be present in person to cast a vote, the people who lived in Rome itself had much more power than citizens in Parma or elsewhere down the Roman roads.

Pompey was dead but huge ranks of his supporters in his war against Caesar had been pardoned. Pompey's younger son, Sextus, was still a power in Spain in the spring of 44 BC, successfully defending himself against Caesar's generals, for some a focus of a different future for Rome. Other supporters of the Pompeys, still alive in Syria, had caused Caesar's nephew, Lucius, to be killed by his own troops. There was no absolute and remorseless pursuit, no vengeful terror.

Hundreds of thousands of Gauls had died but dictatorships of the past had devastated many more Roman lives than Caesar had. Everyone over forty, from Parma to the Palatine Hill, remembered that. The dictator Sulla, Pompey's mentor, had murdered thousands of Romans.

Conspirators risked the charge of disproportion. One of Cassius's bitterest complaints against Caesar was the seizure of some lions he had been saving in Greece for a gladiator show. That was a loss of dignity which, while as important for Roman senators as life itself, was not death itself. The compliant and complacent, and those who were self-interested with sound reasons, understood that there were many worse fates than rule by Caesar.

* * *

Cassius Parmensis had to be careful what he heard and said as he passed from house to house, giving his formal greetings, gaining promises in return. Discussing Caesar's right to rule might still bring risk. Although surveillance was in no way onerous, privacy was rare too. Slaves were everywhere and might have more than one master.

In the conspiracy's early days history and philosophy were safer subjects than the latest political news. Battles lost or won or half-forgotten, lines from epics or tragedies, where and with whom a man was working or sleeping: all could be clues to something more. To make best sense of conversation at Rome it was necessary to know the codes.

The philosophy of Epicurus was just one of those codes. As a choice for the Cassii it had sometimes seemed almost perverse since public life, which the Cassii embraced as ancient duty, was notoriously nothing to Epicurus. That was not just because he lived in Athens when the city was past its greatness but because Epicurus believed politics at any place and time to be unnecessary disturbance to a life of peace and contentment.

It seemed strange that Epicurus was becoming fashionable to men for whom politics was life itself. Speaking to his own community in his own garden, he had advocated life in obscurity, the enjoyment of small things, the happiness of the individual. This was when Alexander of Macedon was about to begin the career that would make him 'the Great' and Athens forever a backwater.

Long dead, Epicurus still spoke across Greece, Italy and beyond, to Parma, the Peloponnese and on the roads to Parthia. In Caesar's Rome his voice had never been louder. A new version of his thought in verse, *De Rerum Natura,* On the Nature of the World, was circulating. The work of Epicurus, and of Lucretius, his Latin interpreter, was useful for thinking about politics in difficult times, less dangerous precisely because it was, on the surface at least, disconnected from practice.

This disconnection was a disguise. In his dedication to the poem Lucretius referred to what he saw as a rare state of present emergency. Law and justice had always been issues alongside pleasure and pain in the philosophers' garden. If political argument invaded their calm, they were not mere theoretical abstractions. Justice, said Epicurus, was a contract. It was an agreement neither to harm nor be harmed, necessary for enjoyment of the full benefits of living together, also requiring rules to keep the misguided in line. It was a material thing, as close as a concept could be to the atoms that made the world.

Justice was a question of advantage. If a politician were wise he would recognize where his advantage ended, have limited desires and no need to engage in prohibited conduct. For the unwise – and there were always many of those – there was the tossing of the dice for war or peace. Laws that promoted happiness were just; those that did not were not. But then there were the hard cases. Caesar's way with law and dice was the current hardest case.

3

CICERO'S STAGE,
PORCIA'S PEOPLE

Portia Wounding her Thigh, Elisabetta Sirani (1664)

Between the new images of Caesar around the Forum that were almost godlike and the many older portraits of generals and orators, the merely reverential, there was only one statue of a Roman woman from history rather than myth. Her name was Cornelia Africana, maybe all the more influential in 44 BC for being a rare face in the crowd, her body leant back in a chair, right hand on her lap, the left over her shoulder, relaxed as the men in marble rarely were.

She was the daughter of Publius Scipio Africanus, the victor over Hannibal, but the fame that won her portrait was as the 'mother of

the Gracchi', Tiberius and Gaius, two out of only three survivors of
her twelve children, aristocratic revolutionaries who had lost their
lives challenging the privileges of their class almost a hundred years
before. Her statue, copied as a model for centuries to come, recognised this mother as a great mentor to her sons, encouraging and
financing their aims to redistribute public land to the poor.

Cornelia Africana deliberately set herself as an example. Even
her use of two names marked her out from her peers and successors. The very grandest woman might normally have only one name
while the men in their families marked their history and status by
three or four. Marcus Brutus, weighing the hardest decision of his
life, had not only a powerful mother, Servilia, but a wife too in the
frail but potent tradition of Cornelia Africana.

Porcia had only one name but she was the very determined
daughter of a great enemy of Julius Caesar. She was the first member
of the club that became his honorary assassins, urging the deed that
they could not do themselves. Her father was Cato Uticensis, last
leader of Pompey's cause at Utica in Africa when Pompey himself
was dead. Her great-great-grand-father, Marcus Porcius Cato the
Censor, had been a famed and often lonely upholder of old Roman
values, also a supporter of Roman citizenship rights in Parma and
Mutina.

Porcia, like Cornelia before her, became famous for her part
behind the scenes when violence was judged the only means to good
government. Like Servilia she was fervent in protecting her family's
interest. The preparations for the Ides of March began almost as a
domestic plot.

* * *

It was hard to judge who would join a conspiracy to kill Julius
Caesar, who might, and who would never join. There were lists of
names in every category, drawn first from neighbours and family
and then from those who sought to join them in distinction.

Marcus Tullius Cicero, Brutus's competitor in oratory and

philosophy, was a possible name on every list, the 'woulds', the 'mights' and the 'nevers'. Rome's finest speaker, its best known master of constitutional argument, a strategist much consulted by the greatest men of Rome, if he were to join a plot he would grace it.

Cicero was a priest too, one of the leading members of the bird-watching college of augurs. He prized his tokens of acceptance in the highest society. But he knew always that he was a man of the middle ranks, the first of his family to be a senator, to be consul, a *novus homo*, a new man, a status that made him cautious. He was twenty years older than Brutus and Cassius, six years older than Caesar and somewhat weary of the world. He was a sceptical priest even by the standards of his day.

Cicero's starting point – in life and thought – was very different from that of Brutus, a noble of old Rome, and of Porcia too, their families traceable to the city's defining years. Brutus and Porcia stood for history, directly in its line. Cicero was an interpreter of their history, its thinker, urged by his friends to write Rome's past from its beginnings to his own day. He was the philosopher of what Porcia's people had become, grappling all his life with the problem of power, its justification and its limits.

Cicero, his critics said, was liable to say more than he did, a dangerous trait in a conspirator. He wrote as though writing always came first. Yet he was obsessive in pursuing a target, as many enemies had found to their cost. He had brutally suppressed a revolution in his one year as consul twenty years before, ordering the strangulation of Antony's mother's husband. He might act decisively if called upon again.

He might also discover the truth even if he were not consulted. His massive house on the north-west Palatine slope, purchased with legal and political favours, was a regular place for swapping news, gossip and verbal justifications. It would be dangerous to offend him.

Gaius Cassius might be the best to make the approach. He was a close friend to Cicero and, if Cassius was for killing Caesar, Cicero might hear, agree and come to the party too. But yet again, when the planning began, Cicero's willingness to join a conspiracy of others was still deemed low, the danger of alerting him too great. Even if he found out, he might prefer not to know.

Pleasure and peace of mind are won by virtue, justice and right: thus Cassius had written to Cicero at the end of the previous year. His question was whether the just man should risk his own peace of mind for the peace of others. For Cassius, the Epicurean, the answer was yes. Cicero, the student and teacher of all Greek thought, preferred clarification of the question.

Cicero was fascinated by the thought of Epicurus. He was not, however, persuaded by it. He echoed the enthusiasm for Lucretius of his erratic brother, Quintus, but never saw Quintus as much of a guide to life. He tried to protect Epicurus's Athenian garden when it was under threat from builders but this was hardly a major concern. The Roman Epicureans were fundamentally irresponsible, always too prone to promote personal over public good: the would-be developer of the garden was the very man to whom Lucretius had dedicated his poem. That seemed a poor sort of solidarity.

Excessive calm was a public danger. If men waited for an emergency before they left their gardens for politics they would have too little experience for it. Their materialism was more than an atomic theory of the physical world; it suggested a false belief that anything important could be measured and weighed. Their morality was suspect even when their arguments were not.

Epicurean meant something more immediate, specific and proudly practical to Gaius Cassius. He had the enthusiasm of a late convert. He believed that he already had the experience. Caesar was a clear threat to the public good, exactly the kind of threat to which a man should come out of his garden and respond. Otherwise there was no purpose to the peace of the garden.

When Cassius first adopted Epicurus's ways of thinking, his commander, Pompey, had just lost to Caesar a decisive battle at Pharsalus that he should have won. This had been a shock, a reason for him to re-evaluate the views he shared with Brutus and Cicero and so many. Thought had been his excuse for temporary retirement. Brutus had used that same time for making money. Gaius Cassius had used his time better, he believed.

If Cicero were too sceptical to trust in a conspiracy to kill, there were others, highly committed followers of Caesar, who, for personal more than philosophical reasons, seemed better prospects. Decimus Brutus, like Marcus Brutus, was almost a son to Caesar, maybe a real son, certainly one of his most trusted generals in Gaul. He was not the brightest and almost because of that not one who would lightly let a father down. But Decimus was hostile to dictatorship, knew the dictator all too well, and maybe thought that his commitment had been taken for granted, stretched too far.

Gaius Trebonius was also a strong candidate. In addition to killing Britons and Gauls for Caesar, he was known as a man open to argument. He understood Caesar's ambition and was an authority on the thoughts of Cicero without the hesitant flexibility of Cicero himself.

Trebonius was a persuader. He had made an anthology of Cicero's best lines, a great resource for those who liked to seem more learned than they were, for whom words were signals of intent not ways of advancing argument. Like Cassius, he had considered assassination before. He had a governorship in Asia ahead of him but grudges behind him, an unsettled mind and perhaps the intent of a plotter.

Cassius Parmensis was in the places where dozens of names were quietly moved from list to list, 'woulds' to 'mights', 'nevers' to 'woulds', where motives were quietly analysed and exchanged. More openly, it was safer to talk about philosophy which, like the weather or the unreliability of slaves, was a subject for everyone.

There was nothing necessarily suspicious in discussing the finer points of Greek teaching. Epicureans were fashionable; they included Caesar's father-in-law and other grandees. Peace of mind was the key to keeping death's terrors at bay, life as good as it could be. Politics was no place for peace of mind but virtue in government might be necessary for such peace. To discuss that was not subversive in itself.

What had to follow the talking was practical choice, what was the prime aim, what was to be done. Killing Caesar could lead to civil war. Even the sound of the words seemed like civil war. One man might say that civil war destroyed all virtue of any kind, another that enduring tyranny was worse. Statilius, an influential Epicurean of the Palatine, was just one who rebuffed Brutus's intimation of his plot. He rejected the lure of any personal upheaval on others' behalf.

Another on the list of 'mights', Marcus Favonius, Pompey's closest aide till the last day of his life, placed civil war at the top of any list of pain to be avoided; he too heard the philosophical code words and gave the wrong answer. The Epicurean, Statilius, said that the wise should not bear anxieties on behalf of the stupid. Brutus's philosophical lawyer, Quintus Antistius Labeo, was more welcoming.

Theory disguised a range of intents. When Brutus spoke he followed his own philosophical path. He adhered to fundamental ideas of liberty, free speech and service to a public that should be grateful. He picked from the authority of Plato and others from the academy of Athens. He believed in ideas, ghosts and a spirit world, an older world. He spoke plainly and expected to be heard. He was easier to hear; his arguments were more familiar and many did hear and agree.

Caesar once said that he feared thin philosophers more than fat generals. Both Cassius and Brutus sought arguments for everything. In a present emergency even the most self-protecting Epicurean could and should, Cassius thought, be politically engaged. Brutus relied more on the exemplary sacrifices of the past. One necessity was absolutely agreed. However justified, and whatever the mixture of argument, subversion had necessarily to be secret. Cassius and Brutus were becoming unalterably subversive.

Cicero perhaps was too – or perhaps not. It was hard to decide. Many a recruitment conversation returned to his name. He would have been their finest recruiter. He had words to move any man. He could make even a dictator cry. Admirers still remembered the case of Quintus Ligarius, a beneficiary of Cicero's pleading to Caesar for pardon of some gross acts of treachery on behalf of Pompey's sons. There was no defence from the facts; Cicero pleaded instead the universal virtue of avoiding vengeance. Caesar conceded with tears in his eyes.

Almost twenty years before, in 63 BC, Cicero had used his powers as consul to seek and destroy the conspiracy of Lucius Sergius Catilina, a rebel aristocrat in the tradition of the Gracchi. But he was too much the intellectual now to be a candidate for an assassin's cause against Caesar. He talked too much and could see all sides of every case. He was a proud augur who also knew that augury was nonsense. That was the problem with theory. Cicero's pre-eminence lay in providing the subtleties of justification for anything. Minor minds were maybe better when a deed had been decided.

Ligarius was a better prospect than the lawyer who had saved him. Cassius Parmensis too was a minor mind. He did not understand all that was said around him. He was hardly alone in that and the plot had not been concluded yet.

* * *

For several more weeks it remained safer to discuss dead court cases and what a great Greek philosopher might have said than to begin in the practicalities of the present. The questions were still whether direct action was to be preferred to passive acceptance, whether being moral was a good in itself or only if it were a means to good ends. Cassius wrote to Cicero. Cicero replied.

Assassination was an awesome act. But so too was allowing the battered republic to die. An assassination of one man might lead to a civil war. Thousands of other men might die. But failure to assassinate might bring more death or more lives that were little different from death. One choice had to be the greater evil. Textbooks would help decide.

Cassius and Brutus, buoyed by variant ideals, committed each other to the final plot. Final candidates to join them included thoughtful opponents of one-man rule, men with a grudge and simpler men like Ligarius, pardoned by Caesar for supporting Pompey and hating themselves for it. There were some who had

fought for Caesar and resented the favours given to those who had
not. Decimus Brutus, despite his coming governorship of Cisalpine
Gaul, did, indeed, feel insufficiently appreciated and joined too.

Gaius Trebonius, guide to the thought of Cicero, had, like
Cassius, planned his own assassination plot against the dictator in
Gaul, at the gateway to Spain, a year before. Or so it was whispered.
Trebonius was still known as Caesar's closest confidant but not to
those who knew him best. Suggestions were safer than certainties
until the final days. Brutus and Cassius welcomed Trebonius. They
needed a firmer list but it was changing all the time.

One fact was certain from the start. Whoever were the killers
and the plotters they would be the same men. Assassination would
not be a job for slaves or soldiers. It would be a political act – for
politicians alone. Direct and brutal violence, followed by the swift-
est possible effort to restore normality, was what the killers claimed
to crave. This could not be a matter for contract.

The quietest question was who, if anyone, should be killed in
addition to Caesar. The plot tumbled into existence for a while without an answer to whether Caesar alone should die or his long-time
fighting friend and fellow consul, Mark Antony too, or maybe more.
Mark Antony's whole family was close and dangerous, his brutal,
rabble-rousing brothers, Gaius and Lucius, their mother Julia, who
was Caesar's cousin, his fierce populist wife, Fulvia, another fervent
heir to Cornelia Africana. Cassius wanted Antony dead in order to
stop a new dictator replacing the old. He saw monarchy as the target. Brutus disagreed. He saw only the monarch.

Brutus was both the calmer and the vainer man, better known
and trusted than Cassius, much more conscious of his image and
his legacy. He hated tyranny more than he hated Caesar. He wanted
one dead body only. He kept his family tree as a work of art on his
wall. He wanted to be a heroic tyrant-slayer, like the great Greeks
whose marble statues stood in Athens, not a mere killer of rivals, a
continuer of Pompey's war, the leader of a bloody coup.

His wife, Porcia, lived in her own heroic history. She too saw
symbols more than solutions. The future was a mirror of her past.

Her father had always worn the darkest purple to show his commitment to the old ways. He preferred the most theatrical painful suicide to accepting Caesar's pardon in defeat. Porcia's marriage to Brutus, only a few months later, was an almost equally flamboyant gesture of independence and defiance.

Cato Uticensis, as he became known by admirers, had stabbed his stomach with his sword, alone at night beside a battlefield in Africa, fainting with pain, waking to find a doctor sewing the wound, tearing out his own intestines to make his intention clear. It was a story of courageous failure but, two years later and on the bigger stage, Porcia saw that Cato could still win. Caesar would die alone in ignominy and she herself could be part of the assassination story, by advising, helping, doing everything that she could.

Porcia famously stabbed herself in the thigh to prove to her husband her ability to keep his secrets, her courage under torture if the need came. Or so it was said. Much attention was given to what Porcia said and why she said it. She had her own family propagandists. Her story, like her father's, was created to survive. Porcia was an assassin in her own mind. Her motives almost immediately fascinated and beguiled. Some gossiped about her problems with Brutus's mother Servilia, Caesar's lover, who hated any rival for her son's affection. Porcia's people had always much to say.

Her husband, Brutus, had not supported Cato to the end at Utica but he had written an eloquent, loyal defence of him, so much so that Caesar himself had written an anti-Cato in reply, alleging incest and love of drink and other challenges to an irritant reputation for virtue. When politics was crazy, close and personal, Porcia followed. Porcia mattered in the public business of Rome, more than Servilia, maybe even more than Fulvia, for whom Antony was her third highly political husband.

Cassius had fewer concerns for image. He was the more practical. He saw the immediate dangers in leaving Antony alive to inherit the system that Caesar had created. But he was weaker in the counsels of the Palatine. Like Antony, he was the poorer man in a political system that demanded wealth. He was not a moneylender like

Brutus. He had been teased even for trading in dates during his dramatic escape from the Parthians. He had lived more and thought more. He was angry. He felt cheated. He had more experience of frustration and failure.

Cassius accepted Brutus's view that Antony be saved. Probably he saw no choice. If he had insisted on killing Antony, Brutus might have withdrawn. Brutus's sense of himself in history was essential both to recruitment of assassins and how the plot would be seen when the deed was done. The assassination of Julius Caesar had its place in history before it happened. Porcia's sense of her family intensified Brutus's own. In March 44 BC it was wise for a visitor from Parma to remember that.

* * *

The wise visitor might also have noted what the people of Rome thought. But that was a question of the 'second order', as philosophers were learning to say. Its answer was not one that they wanted to hear; that the people of Rome in March 44 BC were no more discontent than usual, regularly consulted, very regularly flattered, happy to listen to speeches on the Field of Mars behind the Forum where their favour and disfavour were made clear. They had lost little political power under Caesar; they still passed the laws and elected officers of the state. Whatever the assassins might claim, they were not acting for the rights of the popular assembly. It was the authority of the Palatine over money, prestige, war and peace that they sought to restore.

Porcia and the rest of the plotters felt that they knew the popular interest better than the populace did itself. Cicero and his followers deplored the excesses of the Lupercalia. Porcia would have stayed at home on the day. A man from Parma, new to the old songs and sexual licence of the streets, might better note Caesar's hold over his troops and over the poor. Greek lessons on liberty were deceptive when the voters and soldiers were not taking them.

Cassius Parmensis fell into a plot hatched in code and

philosophical controversies whose instigators agreed on little but the need to kill Caesar and the time and place for the deed to be done, the Ides of March, the senate house in the theatre of Pompey, chosen by Caesar himself for the last meeting of the senate before he left for Parthia. Cicero remained outside. Brutus was the chief persuader; assassination was the right thing to do and he was the one trusted to know when and how and why.

The final days of talking were fraught, the betrayal of so large and variously shared enterprise at times almost inevitable. Those who survived by secrecy became obsessed by it. Almost forty years before, the greatest plot against Rome in its history had remained a secret for an unconscionable month before a hundred thousand men, women and children had been massacred by Asians, in dozens of different towns, on the orders of the Black Sea king, Mithradates. How to avenge them? Pompey had delivered the answer to that. How had no one heard of the horror in advance? That was harder to understand – but encouraging too.

The noise of conspiracy grew louder. Alongside the codes came public graffiti and anonymous letters with explicit calls for the killing. The lawyer Labeo fell to an appeal from Brutus to his conservative legal principles. Ligarius was told by Brutus that the time of the assassins was a bad time to be sick. He replied that if the plan was one worthy of his friend he was no longer sick; he would join the party. Bucolianus and the Caecilii brothers followed faithfully as the risks rose all around them.

One of the readers of the state auguries, a more influential figure in Rome than any mere soothsayer, had told Caesar to beware the Ides of March. Caesar had merely laughed at Spurinna the *haruspex* of caution. There were rumours that Caesar's wife and friends had noted other bad messages from the gods: that his new temple had collapsed, that the horses he had dedicated to the Rubicon were weeping in their meadows; that a bird with a laurel in its beak had been torn apart by other birds in Pompey's theatre.

On the night before the Ides Caesar had dinner with his trusted friend, Decimus Brutus, unthreatening talker and reminiscer of shared battles. Decimus persuaded him that his duty to attend the senate took precedence over fears of falling masonry, sick horses, angry birds and a *haruspex*. He called the next morning to check that Caesar's mind remained unchanged.

4

ASSASSINATION DAY

The Death of Caesar, Jean-Leon Gerome (1867)

The morning of the Ides of March was dark behind the Capitoline hill. Pompey's theatre was a palace for the summer, its plane trees bleak and purposeless against the cold, its twin groves shading what at the end of winter needed no shade, watered by splashing streams unappreciated until the heat came. Only in the unbuilt sites to the east, beside the flooding banks of the Tiber, was the grass green as it was always green, *viridis* in Latin, a word used too of the rain-filled sky.

Behind the hall where the senate was set to meet stretched a vast complex for pleasure and curiosity, completed only ten years before on the prime place where the people voted in the Field of Mars, showing on its walls plundered wonders once known only to those with houses on the hills of the rich. In Pompey's theatre there was no brown stucco, no cheap volcanic rock like that of the Forum. There was marble like gold, paintings for those who might never have seen a painting, reds from river mud, purples from the shells of distant sea, a riot of theatrical images, whores and monsters, human savages and animals massed for sacrifice.

In a second section rows of ivory-white seats soared into the sky, the theatre itself. Pompey's gift to the city was still a thing of wonder for any visitor to Rome, a short walk from the Forum around the Capitoline, almost a new hill, flying tiers of red and grey arcades, stage-sets with secret doors into painted forests, seats for 10,000 living spectators and hundreds of the bronze and marble dead. On a sacred day fountains sprayed perfumed mist into the dusty air. There was nothing like it in Parma, nothing like it anywhere in Italy or even in the East from which most of its ornaments, and all of the scents, had come.

Spectacular in a place of spectaculars there rose a heroic statue of the man whose achievements it both celebrated and mocked. When the senate met in its hall in his theatre, Pompey the Great, as naked as a god, still welcomed those in whose name he had fought against Caesar. Four years earlier, the man himself, supported by Brutus and Cassius and most of Rome's aristocratic elite, had stood between Caesar and dictatorship. In March 44 BC only his image, its right hand unnaturally outstretched, its right thigh against the palm tree of victory, its left hand holding the globe of conquest, lay between Caesar and the seats of those who wanted their own power restored.

Pompey's legacy to Rome was a triumphant gift of one man. It held his own portrait bust in pearls, kings' crowns of pearls, onyx cups and drinking bowls, a moon of solid gold on a gambling board of gem stones, statues of gods from three continents, the stuff of the greatest triumph that had ever passed through the city's streets. Many kings had been unwilling contributors, the greatest of them Mithradates of the Black Sea, a not quite adequate revenge for his terrorist massacre, so inexplicably kept secret, of so many Romans in a single day in 88 BC.

The theatre was not quite a temple to Pompey. A prominent shrine to Venus the Victorious, at the far end beyond the auditorium, kept the propriety that this extraordinary place was a part of Roman tradition, still a sacred site where the senate might properly meet, several hundred of its members already gathering for a lengthy agenda. There was a shrine to Virtue too. Some senators still saw themselves as virtuous Pompeians, either out of old loyalty, distant admiration, nostalgia or hope.

Pompey, once called *adulescentulus carnifex*, the teenage butcher, for his brutality to defeated enemies, first known as *Magnus* because he looked a bit like Alexander the Great, had been no simple traditionalist. For senators who wanted a return to the old republic, with powers balanced between annually elected consuls, themselves and the people, SPQR, Pompey had been merely the better of two bad men. He had become a symbol of Roman tradition nonetheless, despite his theatre that displayed, as nothing had ever done before, the traditions of everywhere.

If the loser at the battle of Pharsalus had been the winner Rome's government might have been little different from what the conspirators were now determined to end. Men argued the case. Pompey had been as much an emperor-in-waiting as Caesar became, maybe more. Brutus and Cassius had merely moved from one man's sole command to another whom, four years later, they were waiting to kill.

That move had been embarrassingly fast for men of principle. Brutus had betrayed Pompey to Caesar even while accepting Caesar's pardon, revealing that his defeated commander could soon be hunted down in Egypt. Once Pompey was a headless corpse no one would ever know what sort of monarch he might have been. Every pretence was possible.

By contrast it was all too clearly known what path Caesar had chosen. He abused almost any enemy as a Pompeian. Aside from the realms of rhetoric, memory and theory, there was that very practical difference between what a living man had become and what a dead man had failed to become. A dictator was a present danger: someone who merely might have been a dictator was not.

Caesar was about to face an act of public civic cooperation, a proper response to autocracy perhaps, even when it was a cooperation to kill. In deliberate distinction from the object of their plot, the assassination was not to be the work of one man alone. As they waited for the dictator's arrival every man in the plot had a dagger concealed within the white linen folds of his toga. A sword in the hand of a single well-trained Roman, though much more certain in effect, would have less likely avoided detection. There was security as well as symbolism in numbers.

The assassins' only swords were in the hands of a band of gladiators owned by Decimus Brutus and about to be displayed in a theatre show. For more than an hour the lesser plotters watched their leaders while all awaited their victim. There were strengthening rumours that he might stay at home. Caesar's wife, Calpurnia, might have won her domestic battle with Decimus. An Epicurean would prefer to call this human intuition than divine intervention: it would be a disaster whatever it was called.

Worse than rumours of cancellation or delay were rumours of the plot itself. As many as eighty men may have known of it. Not even Brutus and Cassius themselves knew how many. Hatred of Caesar held only some of them together.

In the morning they had celebrated the coming of age of Cassius's son, a first shave and a ritual commitment to the future. Even among their intimates at the feast it was uncertain how many knew. Fear of the unknown was more justified than any fear of the act itself. If the senate had been meeting in an ancient temple on the Forum, even the most devoted Epicureans might have feared the gods at such a time; in a place of theatre there was only but always stage-fright.

Brutus and Cassius calmly conducted their praetors' business as they sat on the benches, in togas and red shoes, adjudicating disputes, agreeing which cases to take and which not. A disappointed litigant shouted that he would appeal Brutus's judgement to Caesar himself. Secretaries sat at the side with wax tablets to record the coming debates.

The noise rose around the veined marbled walls. Brutus retorted to the complainer that Caesar would not stop him ruling under the law. Nearby were the Casca brothers, Publius and Titiedius, whom Cassius Parmensis had heard and overheard. Publius was shuddering. Buconianus, with his brother Caecilius, was behind and out of sight. In front of them all was Tillius Cimber carrying an open petition as well as his hidden weapon.

Outside was a lone conspirator with a single task of his own. Gaius Trebonius had tried to attract Antony into his plot to kill Caesar a year before. This time his job was merely to distract him and ensure that he did not arrive with Caesar. Antony was often drunk, a bulging-veined brawler then who did not need a sword. In a senate house without guards Antony was the most likely figure to rise in Caesar's defence.

This diversion was perhaps not hard: in only three days Caesar would be on his way to Parthia and Antony would be the senior consul in Rome. There were many plausible and urgent issues to raise and Trebonius was the right man to raise them. First, he was the only assassin who had himself been consul, in the previous year, a year of glory for a man whose family had never had a consul before. Secondly, he was angry that his consulship, granted by Caesar, had been ruined on its last day; his colleague had died and Caesar had made a mockery of Trebonius's achievement, appointing the shortest-serving consul in Roman history to join him for a few comic hours.

Caesar's joke had become a common joke at the expense of Trebonius, his family and his future glory The election had taken place during votes for the lowest officials. In the consulship of Gaius Caninius Rebilus nothing had happened, barely even a breakfast. Cicero swung between laughter and tears. Those who climbed the greasy *cursus honorum* at Rome liked their arrival at the summit to be greeted as though they were Porcia's people. To those who did not know Trebonius his reason for joining the assassins might have seemed as trivial as Cassius's lost lions: it was not trivial to him.

As time stretched out and away, the news came of Caesar's departure from the Forum and imminent arrival. Escorted by ceremonial lictors to clear the curious among the crowd, he had passed the site where his own great marble halls were planned soon to soar from their foundations. His litter, born by slaves not soldiers, was at Pompey's steps. Caesar understood fear and preferred not to have the permanent military protection that made a man afraid. Whatever their reasons for betrayal, Trebonius and Decimus, who between them had won one of the most critical battles of the war against Pompey, had done their initial work to destroy their former commander. The dictator-for-life was at the door to his death – and he was alone.

It was just before noon. Caesar was surrounded by petitioners as he stepped down. The same *haruspex* who had told him to beware the Ides of March, was told by the dictator that 'the Ides had come'. Caesar acted as a man with no more than his normal cares, receiving and writing notes. A written prediction of the plot was given to him, received with impatience rather than scepticism, and stuffed away unread.

The next petitioner was a senator whom Brutus and Cassius feared might expose them. After him came the brawler, Tillius Cimber, pretending to request mercy for his exiled brother, pulling at the purple of Caesar's toga, dragging it from his shoulder so that one of the Casca brothers could strike the first blow, probably the only fatal blow. Why, this is violence!, Caesar shouted. *Ista quidem vis est!*

Buconianus swiftly followed from behind, Gaius Cassius from the front, pulling their daggers from the linen over their left arms. Caesar hurled Casca back: Casca, you vile thing, what are you doing? The frustrated Lucius Basilus was there somewhere. Casca called for help in Greek. Somewhere else in the press of men, as the conspirators pierced the flesh of Caesar and each other, was Cassius Parmensis.

Marcus Brutus stabbed Caesar's thigh and took a wound on his own hand. When Caesar saw him he cried out in Greek *kai su teknon*, a line varyingly interpreted over the coming decades, centuries and millennia as 'even you my son', or 'up yours and see you in hell'. Caesar still tried to escape but, blinded by blood, he tripped and fell, taking his final stab wounds as he lay already dead on the lower steps.

Only two men, Gaius Calvisius Sabinus and Lucius Marcius Censorinus, neither of them well known, had attempted a defence. They, and the pen in Caesar's own hand, were all that remained of the vast mass forces that had protected and idolised the dictator.

The assassins waited for the plaudits which would surely come. No praise came. Minutes passed. Still no praise came. Instead there was the rush of men escaping a trap, then a dull, stunned calm. Instead of dragging Caesar's body to the Tiber where a tyrant would rightly have belonged, the killers hesitated.

There was no one left to speak to. In minutes the space had changed. The body, no more than an oyster spewed from a man's throat, stayed where it fell until three of Caesar's domestic slaves arrived to bring their master home. The theatre of Pompey was soon as empty as it was silent.

* * *

There were never more assassins of Julius Caesar than in the crowd that gathered on the Capitoline hill a few hours later. With the building sites and parade grounds of the Field of Mars behind them, with the Forum in front, they had pride in their daggers, their blood-stained clothes and their achievement. Even those new to the plot became heroes to each other, heroes most of all to Cicero, who put words to their deed and bestowed approval like a benediction. They would always share this day. The Caecilii brothers, Rubrius Ruga, Sextius Naso, Marcus Spurius, Tillius Cimber, Quintus Ligarius,

Pontius Aquila and Decimus Turullius all took their place under a dark winter sky.

Beyond the assassins' cloud of certainty the world was hard to see. Marcus Brutus, his hand still bleeding, went down briefly to the Forum and spoke about political principle in his dry Greek style. This was the speech he had hoped to make to an admiring senate. A praetor, Lucius Cornelius Cinna, another relative of Caesar, stripped off his robe of office and said that the dictator had deserved his death: this was a mistake though not immediately for him. Decimus Brutus was thanked and praised, both for his gladiators and his betrayal. New supporters climbed the steep hill from the temples of Concord and Saturn, professing various forms of sympathy, remembered republicanism for some, urgent interests for others.

Dolabella ranted against the man to whom he owed most of what he had. He wanted the consulship which, if Caesar had stayed alive for three more days, would already have been his. He needed the assassins to back him. He knew that there were other obstacles in his way than the absence of his patron. He was barely more than thirty years old, around the same age as Parmensis, too young to be a consul under the law: Caesar had made men care less for the law that set such rules but without him the order of the old might be restored.

The Mamertine prison had sometimes been a more likely home for Dolabella than the temple of Concord that stood beside it. There was the long-time enmity of Antony (and not just for an ill-judged affair with his wife), obstructive priests, hostile creditors threatened by his battles for the abolition of debt, relatives of some 800 men whose lives had been lost in one such campaign, his own debts and bankruptcy, the twisted legacy of a life of offence. He put on the glowing purple-striped regalia of a consul, neither too dark nor too light, still stinking from its stale salt die, never an easy garment for a short man: he climbed breathless to the Capitol.

Others disappeared. Some who had merely kept watch on Caesar's supporters, men who might have defended him but did not, were happy to be known as assassins. Some who had killed were not. Names and numbers fell from lists. Marcus Favonius, the Epicurean who had preferred the good of bad government to the evil of civil war, was as enthusiastic as anyone who had been an assassin himself. Lucius Minucius Basilus received one of the first excited notes from Cicero ('Congratulations! I rejoice. I adore you') before disappearing to the edge of history. Some changed their stories; some had their stories changed. Imagination became memory.

Cassius Parmensis remained an assassin. The assassins' story was about to include the brutal destruction of his home town, none of whose citizens had played the slightest part. The people of Parma had suffered before for their place on the road beyond the Rubicon into Cisalpine Gaul. A town safe when Caesar fought Pompey would be obliterated in the wars when Caesar was dead. *Parmenses miserrimos*, Decimus would write to Cicero in a letter destroyed after its opening words.

Meanwhile, as the news spread, the people of Rome were still quiet. Bars and bathhouses closed. Slaves barred their masters' doors. Men brought money-chests to the ancient temple of the twins, Castor and Pollux, divine protectors of the senate, the city and themselves. The calmer sought in the same temple a dentist or a pack of powder for their face. Life in the Forum limped on through the fear. The distant legions did not yet know what had happened. Caesar's veteran soldiers in the streets did not intervene in what they did not yet understand.

The assassins held their hopes, the done deed still an extraordinary thing, its delivery an all-changing fact. The men faithful to Caesar were surely those fearful now, Mark Antony, who had taken on the clothes of a slave and sought his safety at home, most fearful of all. Fear was everywhere. The night of the Ides was cold on the Capitoline. A fire might seem to be in either celebration or mourning. No one yet knew which purpose would be the more popular.

There was a legion on Tiber's island, a place of two bridges, one street between them, and temples to Aesculapius, the god of good health, and to Iupiter Iurarius, the Jupiter who kept men to their promises. Some eight thousand men there had been loyal to Caesar and were still awaiting the reward in money and land for that loyalty: they were commanded by his military deputy, the slight, diplomatic patrician, Marcus Aemilius Lepidus.

The assassins discussed this threat with their first full sense of unease. They saw detachments of guards arriving in front of the treasury and at the rostra where a speaker might rouse a crowd. Brutus descended to try to rouse a crowd before the soldiers were in place. He failed. Self-congratulation most notably failed.

Lepidus assembled his men. The assassins retreated. Decimus's gladiators, an uneasy guard for the liberators of a republic, would have been nothing against such a force if it chose to avenge its dead master.

The talking continued. Antony, they heard, had visited Caesar's wife and taken money and papers. Brutus and Cassius asked for a meeting with Lepidus and Antony together. The rest of the assassins should join them. Cicero should speak. There was worry about what Antony would say. Lepidus, after first thoughts of vengeance would probably swing the way of the wind – if he or anyone else could ascertain where was the wind.

Cicero himself arrived. He congratulated and he warned. He said that it didn't matter what Antony said. The word of a terrified man was worthless. He argued for an immediate meeting of the senate instead. With one consul dead and the other in hiding, the two praetors, Brutus and Cassius had the power to call it.

Cicero wanted to legitimise the assassination, giving Lepidus orders that he would obey. Those who had led the killing wanted to negotiate behind closed doors. The discussion of aims and tactics, practice and principle, was less coded than on the Palatine hill but little different in decisiveness from what it had been before.

Thick, dark clouds gathered. Dust choked the air. To the south in Sicily Mount Etna had erupted but in Rome it was possible only to see the brutal sky as a portent. Opinions differed of what the gods might be saying. Thunderous rain fell. Lightning lit the political stage below.

* * *

Cassius Parmensis knew many poems of night, of other cold nights of siege and assault, most of them in Greek. He chose Latin poetry himself, national plays and epics, squibs of abuse. Not everyone could switch between languages like Brutus, Cassius and Cicero could.

'Nocte intempesta nostrum devenit domum: Late in the night he came down to our house.' Parmensis was writing about the enemy of an older Brutus, a clash from the beginnings of the history of Rome, from when the temple of Saturn, its marble pitted and cracking in the Forum below, was bright and young.

'Nocte intempesta nostrum devenit domum'. It was not much of a line, loose, ponderous, too many long syllables, even a bit comic, but it said much about what had just happened and was still happening. It was noted by Rome's most discerning collector of lines, Marcus Terentius Varro, a senator who proudly called himself a Pompeian, a former general who was twice pardoned by Caesar, a wealthy anthologist and antiquarian who collected everything that mattered to him.

The Romans had removed kings before, not just generals who behaved like kings but a royal family, the Tarquins from lands not far from Parma, Etruscans who in the distant, but undeniably real past, had handed the title, rex, down the generations. That was until one of them had made a mistake and the republic began. The mistake was a rape and Parmensis, with Varro reading closely, had begun to write a play about it.

The heroine was the wife of a good Tarquin prince, Lucretia, who aroused the lust of a bad one and stabbed herself to death. The hero was Junius Brutus, avenger of Lucretia, first consul of the new republic, the ancestor claimed by Parmensis's fellow assassin, Marcus Brutus, who on the evening of the Ides of March had just made a warmly (but not very warmly) received speech about liberty.

In the twisted streets around the Forum some of the many statues of the ancient Brutus were still wreathed with placards reading 'Brutus are you dead or are you bribed and why are you not living at this hour?'. Those who had conspired against Caesar were not alone in wanting him dead and designating his killer.

Names transcended past and present, truth and fiction. Names made characters, both those stirring around him and those in papyrus rolls. Odysseus had a sense of what it was to be Odysseus; Atreus what it meant to be Atreus, Medea to be Medea, Brutus to be Brutus. Characters in art, in history and in the streets of Rome below him were much the same. Then and now might elegantly be linked in his play.

The view from the Capitoline was studded with reminders of the Tarquins; the Field of Mars, new marble floating on moonlit water, had been their legendary domain, the temple of Jupiter on the hill itself their gift to the City, the Tiber island the mud-piled relics of their discarded possessions, their last harvest it was said. The vast palaces of the Palatine, still visible in parts, their terraces wider than any street, were massive remembered facts of how kings concentrated power, minatory prophecies that they might return. The fear that Caesar was about to found a royal dynasty of his own was one of the few around which all of the assassins had united.

The cries of Lucretia echoed across the centuries. Tarquinius Superbus, the last king of Rome, had won his throne by murder and feared that his own rule would end the same way. Snakes and rams, dogs and vultures were messengers of his doom. The snakes barked; the dogs spoke. Cicero might mock such superstitious belief – and in his newly completed book on prophecy mocked heartily – but Tarquin's terror was for Parmensis closer to the public mood.

Lucretia had been raped while her husband, Collatinus, was away at war. It was a family rape. Collatinus was a Tarquin. Superbus's son Sextus was either inflamed by Lucretia's beauty or irritated by her marital fidelity, a virtue proved a few weeks before when a band of brothers had ridden back from a battle to check on their wives and found all but Lucretia taking full advantage of their freedom.

Lucretia had admitted Sextus to her house even though it was late and she was praying for her husband's safety. Sextus was the king's son. How could she not? At first she successfully kept this nocturnal suitor from her bed, turning down advancements in her royal career, his love, his demands for her obedience, everything until he threatened to rape her, kill her and leave her body in bed with a dead, black slave who would be announced as her lover. At this she succumbed, only to summon next day her father and husband, first to confess her story and then to stab a dagger into her heart.

Junius Brutus became her avenger. Till then he had been known as Brutus the Stupid but this stupidity, he revealed, was merely a pretence to protect himself in a treacherous court. He roused the people at the injustice done to Lucretia. The Tarquins were forced to flee. The date of the royal flight, the *regifugium*, the last week of February, was deemed the end of the Roman year.

Collatinus and Brutus became the first consuls of the republic, the first to share power so that there be no rule by one man again. After an awkward interval, the innocent Collatinus was also expelled, leaving Brutus, newly transformed from the Stupid to the Wise, in a partnership with an innocuous colleague, as the pathfinder for the new era. When Tarquinius Superbus attempted to reclaim his throne his army was destroyed with the help of Castor and Pollux, gods in the guise of cavalry men.

Cassius Parmensis had dramatic plans. *Nocte intempesta nostrum devenit domum*: first the rape, then its aftermath. The temple of Castor and Pollux, stark in the middle of the Forum, commemorated the very battle of Lake Regillus, ten miles to the south-east, where the twin gods helped Rome defeat Tarquinius Superbus for the last time. A spring in the Forum provided water for their horses. Varro preserved the line for purposes of his own.

Parmensis's playwright predecessor, Lucius Accius, had already taken on the story. Modern poetry could improve it. With a few refinements a new *Brutus* could be revived as the first rejection by Romans of the kings, the parading of Lucretia's body a parody of whatever was planned for Caesar's. In truth the fall of the Tarquins was less a citizen uprising against tyranny than a palace coup that went wrong, a coup by one side of a royal family against another. It was a perfect subject for Parmensis nonetheless. A man from Parma was close to the Etruscans. He knew and could adapt the story. History in verse ran to different rules from facts in prose, as Cicero himself had said – in prose.

Parmensis could perhaps help Cicero too. The great man needed a tame poet. As consul almost twenty years before, he had seen a revolution coming and brutally suppressed it, pursuing its conspirators to the death, declaiming against them in the Forum, in the temple of Concord, ordering stranglings without trial in the Mamertine prison a few yards away. No one else would write a panegyric about his feat: so he had written one himself: the clumsy rhyming line, *O fortunam natam me consule Romam*, congratulating the state for his great consulate, had brought him ridicule.

Cicero had then endured exile as well as lack of praise. He had lived in fear for prosecuting gangsters like Publius Clodius Pulcher, former husband of Fulvia, Antony's wife. He had endured his beloved daughter's marriage to Caesar's short, fat rabble-rouser, Dolabella. His son was a student drunk. All were trials of life with which philosophy had dealt and could deal again. A poet would propel that life into the future and preserve it there.

* * *

Next morning the news came that Antony himself, to Cicero's alarm, had summoned the senate for the following day – to the temple of Tellus, south of the Forum, close by the Palatine. Twenty-four hours before he had been in hiding, forty-eight hours ago very much the junior consul. Now, while Dolabella was still unconfirmed, he was the sole consul, able to summon meetings and magistrates as best suited his ambitions.

Dolabella, still with the assassins, had motives to stand in Antony's way but not much means. Without Caesar's support he might not even become consul. Though charming when he cared to be, he was widely hated. He had caused the death of hundreds in riots for and against his campaigns to cancel private debt, most urgently his own. Cicero, whose son-in-law he had briefly and expensively been, especially hated him. Backing Dolabella had come at no small cost even to a dictator. He was a plausible addition to the assassins' cause but hardly a reliable one.

A few months later, when Gaius Trebonius was being interrogated under Dolabella's torture in the Asian city of Smyrna, it was clear that the fat worm had turned and turned again. But two days after the murder it had not turned again yet. Dolabella was still concentrating on the consulship that had been Caesar's final gift – and he was not alone in hoping to combine denigration of the dictator with acceptance of his will.

Antony was thinking on a broader and grander scale. Trebonius had done him a favour by keeping him in street conversation while his colleagues were butchering inside. It would have been difficult for anyone to defend Caesar from so many daggers and equally dangerous both to have done nothing and to have attempted and failed. As a result he was both lucky to be alive and looking firmly forward now that Caesar was dead. Perhaps Trebonius remembering their shared exasperations on Caesar's campaigns, tipped him off. Perhaps someone else had already tipped him off. Antony wanted the maximum support for himself. He was better placed than anyone once the deed was done.

Parmensis, if he were to stay in the story, could only wait. Against Cicero's advice the assassins had given Antony valuable time to marshal allies and a plan. Gaius Cassius and Marcus Brutus, their rivalry unresolved by their shared success, had also to wait to see which of them, by wanting to kill the consul or spare him, had better predicted their futures.

5

A LIST OF MANY NAMES

View of the Forum and Palatine Hill, Giambattista Piranesi (1756)

The temple of Tellus stood among the grand houses of the Carinae district, the old Latin name for the keels of ships, squashed in among homes that jostled as in a crowded harbour. The most fashionable hills of Rome, different in history and character, were all inhabited by families who knew they could never live anywhere else, who were rivals but neighbours, sharing religious observance, disputes about temple maintenance, footpath repair and water supplies. Politics on the Carinae, like the rest of life there, occasionally required maximum violence but preferred maximum cooperation thereafter. The assassination of Julius Caesar in the Field of Mars, and the compromises being planned at the temple of Tellus, constituted a grand example of this rule. The thereafter was not, however, far ahead, the question of what to do next as urgent as if the state were itself a man stabbed and bleeding.

Cassius Parmensis knew the temple. The Cassii were among the earliest owners of the land where it stood. More than 400 years before, from this western spur of the Esquiline hill, his notorious ancestor, Spurius Cassius, had been sent to death by his peers for pandering to popular demands and attempting, it was feared, to make himself king. Yet Antony was making no political point by summoning the senate there; it was most of all convenient for his own house which he had purchased, at too high a price, he often complained, from the confiscated estate of Pompey. Cicero was a householder here too, a vigorous complainer about the temple's cost of upkeep.

Tellus was the goddess of the land. While the latest temple building was about the same age as Pompey's theatre it was plainer, more purely Roman, a home for a goddess who was as old as the Lupercalia. At its heart was an ancient sacred stone, the *magmentarium*. Displayed on its wall was a large map of Italy, *tota Italia*, a representation of the whole land that was deemed to be Tellus's domain.

This map was a decoration designed for the minds of the Roman people. Cicero wrote often and fondly of a single country under Roman rule but this was a very recent truth and in some parts of *tota Italia* hardly a truth at all. The lands of Tellus were a patchwork of places where men spoke different languages, recognised different gods and different histories.

Latin was spreading fast across Italy because it was the language of the uniters, of the very recent conquerors. But in baths and bedrooms, away from political business, men and women spoke Greek, Oscan, Umbrian, the Picene languages of the Pompey family lands which no outsider knew. Those Picenes who worked the soil for the assassin, Minucius Basilus, had risen against Rome only fifty years before. The temple itself was dedicated to a victory against them. Its walls told other stories than that of one city's escape from Tarquin kings.

Caesar had accelerated the integration of Tellus's Italy, just as he had reformed the street plan of Rome itself, writing rules, rewarding his supporters and soldiers, granting citizenship, punishing protest. But this had been a process too slow for the more ambitious provincials, too fast for the ancient families of the Carinae. There were senators from Cisalpine Gaul, from Parma and Mutina. There were senators in the temple from almost every area but not many, not yet.

* * *

The meeting could not begin till Antony arrived. He could be forgiven delay in the light of what had happened to the last man in sole command to enter the senate. It was the day of the festival of Bacchus and there were duties to be done. The mood was of mild murmurings against the assassins but no assassins were there. There was expectation of advancement and advantage by some, by Dolabella most of all, but no immediate unrest.

A few stones were thrown when the praetor Cinna approached the temple entrance wearing the toga that had been awarded to him by Caesar, the one that he had theatrically discarded on the Ides of March. Lepidus's soldiers had to stop this first protest going further. Antony and Cicero were said to be in useful negotiation. The waiting went on.

Meanwhile the map showed truths just as important for the future as anything that Antony was preparing to say. It showed borders only of mountains and sea, rough spaces, not many individual places in an outline the shape of a soldier's boot, main roads, more about how an army might leave Italy than how a government might run it. For both military and political reasons Romans preferred to fight their civil wars abroad.

Parma was somewhere at the highest point of pink plaster

beneath the brown swathes of the Alps. From there an army might reach Greece northwards and eastwards by land when summer cleared the mountain passes. This would never be an ideal way to leave Italy.

Ariminum was Parma's exit to the northern Greek province of Macedonia, Antony's for the following year if the decisions of Caesar survived the debate. But Brundisium, further down the eastern coast, was much the better port. From there Caesar had led his ships to hunt down Pompey at Pharsalus.

On the west was Italy's magic side, the places of Homer which people knew even if they had never seen them. In the waters of Sicily, an essential route for Rome's corn, was the island where Odysseus, struggling home from Troy, had been cursed for blinding the Sea God's son, the Cyclops, the beach where Odysseus's sailors had killed the cattle of the Sun, redoubling the curse upon them. Sicily, the ball for the Italian boot to kick, was still an island of Greeks.

Behind the Bay of Naples was an entrance to the underworld. From a dead, blind prophet Odysseus had learnt there how to appease the great god of the sea. Between Sicily and Italy were the straits guarded in myth by the monsters, Scylla and Charybdis, and in fact in 44 BC by unpredictable pirate bands allied to Sextus Pompeius, son of Pompey, who controlled the routes to Spain.

Water was the essence of Italy as well as its land. Nowhere on the plaster map was more than 70 miles from the plaster sea. Water made its boundaries, even tiny streams like the Rubicon. To prevent an invasion of Italy by sea required control of only two ports, both clearly marked, Brundisium and Tarentum still further to the south. Roman generals might with difficulty take armies to Greece to fight against each other; neither could ever bring their armies back if Italy was hostile in the other's hands. That was maybe the map's most important lesson.

Parmensis had his roots in the lands drained by the Po where an army could invade and often had. He was to find his future on the triremes, double-enders, beaked rammers and broad carriers, waxed and painted in purples, reds and yellows brighter than on the Tellus map but less familiar to the natives of the city. When men spoke to the crowds in the Forum they stood behind the *rostra*, the rams of ships captured three centuries before in battle at Antium, the port founded by a son of Odysseus. But their minds were much more on the land, legionaries more numerous among their listeners, or past or future legionaries. Sailors were at sea, their ports far away. The riverside dockyards of the Field of Mars had long decayed. Successful sailors called themselves soldiers on their tombstones, *milites* not *nautae*. Parmensis was a poet born into Homer's *Iliad*; his life was in the *Odyssey*.

All those sympathetic to the assassins could ask where were the land armies that might support them. The answer was not encouraging. They were in the provinces still controlled for the rest of 44 BC by Caesar's allies, men who had not been consulted about the killing and had not heard any philosophical arguments about their prior duty to Rome.

No help could be expected from Africa. Gaius Asinius Pollio, who commanded as a praetor in Spain, had crossed the Rubicon with Caesar and been a loyal follower since then. Pollio was a wealthy poet, orator, playwright and historian of his time, possibly open to change but aloof and cautious. He hated Cicero, as so many did, and would be reluctant to share with him any cause; he also needed his legions to face Sextus Pompeius.

Sextus had seven legions of dubious loyalty except to Sextus himself. Lucius Munatius Plancus, less distinguished and reliable to no one, held the more distant parts of Gaul.

In Cisalpine Gaul, in Asia and in Bithynia beside the Black Sea the next governors, if Caesar had been alive, would have been Decimus, Trebonius and Tillius Cimber. But these provinces held only two legions in all and Antony might try to stop the three assassins taking even those. None of Rome's foreign encampments was on the wall of the temple. All were high in the minds of those assembled before the consul arrived and the balancing of the forces of the state began.

There were the usual items for procedure, auguries and intro-
ductions, bickerings about precedence. Cicero set out what he and
Antony had agreed. He explained to his fellow senators that there
was a problem of formal logic as well as traditional power. If Caesar
were judged to have been a tyrant, the assassins ought to be praised
and his deeds undone. If Caesar had been acting lawfully and right-
fully, merely doing the jobs he had been given, the assassins ought
to be themselves killed, humiliated, their supporters hunted and
crushed. But middle ways, he added, did not need to be excluded.
He had a suggestion, with some of his usual examples from history,
to back it up.

At the end of the debate the compromise made in the temple of
Tellus seemed a piece of masterful politics. The assassins were denied
a vote of thanks but granted an amnesty. All Caesar's appointments
and decisions, his *acta*, were to be maintained for two years, including those favourable to the assassins.

Decimus would be a consul in 42 BC; there would be a good
chance of helping Brutus and Cassius to the same position for the
following year. Men who had removed their togas of office in solidarity with the assassins could freely, with minor embarrassment,
put them on again.

Dolabella kept his consulship for the rest of the year. The rabble-rousing aristocrat who wanted an end to all debts, who had
shared Antony's first wife, who had married and abandoned Cicero's
daughter, whom Caesar had rescued as little more than an enforcer,
was the man jointly in charge of everything in Rome. He proposed
that the Ides of March be declared Rome's new birthday.

Cicero still had deep suspicions. He thought that Antony was
inventing some of Caesar's *acta*, his decisions from both before and
beyond the grave. He doubted, for example, that the dead dictator had really intended to give full citizen rights to the Sicilians.
Cicero had a long interest in Sicily but only Antony had the wax
tablets which would prove Caesar's extension of *tota Italia*, or maybe would. That argument, and others, could wait.

It seemed to be a morning to forgive, forget and to hang on to what one had. To the mass of the anxious the deal of March 17, only two days after the Ides, between Antony for the spirit of Caesar and Cicero for the absent assassins, offered the fastest possible return to the peace and order that most in the neighbourhood of the Temple desired.

For the people of Rome, in seventy-two hours, there would be Caesar's funeral. They would hear the terms of Caesar's will. Antony would give them the good news of generous cash gifts to every citizen. He would also be able to say anything else that he thought to be to his own advantage. Even from the temple of Tellus he was listening closely to reports on the mood outside. Wearing a breastplate under his tunic, he had left the chamber while Dolabella was endlessly speaking, in order to hear and see for himself.

In the assassins' camp on the Capitol there was also anxiety about the people's mood. Decimus wrote a letter revealing his own worst fears for himself and the assassins' future. Their most experienced fighter, famed for bold innovations, the tearing down of enemy sails with long hooked poles, showed a lack of fight and imagination that was close to helplessness. The man who had for Caesar razed Gallic towns, raised fleets, forced the civil war surrender of Massilia and won positions of enormous power, seemed hopeless when Antony, his senior in Caesar's service, was against him.

Decimus's highest anxiety was to take his Cisalpine province, first to get permission to leave Rome as an ambassador-at-large, even to emigrate to Rhodes or to Sextus in Spain and, if he had to stay, to employ a bodyguard at public expense. He was not the inspiration that his admirers had expected.

Cassius, too, saw cold realities ahead. He had been opposed to permitting Antony to give a funeral speech. Brutus had overruled him. Cassius would be right in his hope but wrong to think that his hope could have affected the outcome. The assassins could not have stopped Antony from speaking. Any attempt to have done so by force would have failed.

The assassins had no plan of their own. Support for them, such as it was, rested on the fear of Caesar that they had already removed;

it stopped at the senate doors. Lepidus's legions and the masses on the streets were equivocal at best, probably hostile if put to the test.

Brutus made a speech in the Forum which failed to move the mood. He tried to be practical. He offered guarantees to the soldiers of the land promised for their past services; but not all were entitled to land and for those that were, the question was whether the guarantee was worth more than air. Nor was personal advantage the sum of their desires.

The death of Caesar had left a void into which confusion flowed. A theatre crowd had cheered the assassins, or had seemed to, but had confused Gaius Cassius with his brother Lucius who was opposed to Caesar's killers. It was hard to be sure whose side anyone was on. The people were restless, fickle and only slowly coming to terms with a new world.

War might come. Or business as usual might be done into the far future. If there was to be war the assassins' hopes lay in their provinces in the east. Those provinces were their prizes of peace too. Immediate anxieties stemmed from whether the vote in the temple was strong enough for its decisions to stand. Antony had personal control of Caesar's will and the papers under which Caesar's further will might be expressed – or maybe imagined. Decimus, the only assassin to be a named heir, prepared gloomily to leave Rome to protect his province by force, as best he might, if force were the better way.

That night there were two meetings for dinner, Cassius, in the senior role he could claim at last, with Antony, Brutus with Lepidus. The assassins were given Antony's young son as a guarantor of his father's good behaviour. Cassius took a knife with him to the dinner nonetheless, promising to use it if he saw signs of a second Caesar. Antony kept his chain-mail beneath his tunic.

* * *

The Forum on funeral day, even before any mourner had spoken, was not safe for the assassins. Cassius saw that clearly; he was enraged. Brutus was more relaxed, enraging Cassius further. Cicero had defended the Tellus compromise with learned precedent from the history of Athens more than three hundred years before; amnesty for the guilty few was necessary to save the mass of the innocent. Maybe this was a good argument but many of the people who would decide if the compromise held were unfamiliar with it.

The date was the twentieth of March. The assassins were no longer a united band. Some were still on the Capitoline hill. Many blooded daggers and tunics were hidden away in homes along with the men themselves. Cassius Parmensis could have reasonably left for his family home in the north, retracing his familiar route along the *Via Flaminia* and the *Via Aemilia*, through the highlands and marshlands to Parma. He could have prepared the way for Decimus Brutus to follow, judging rightly that the sooner a single killer of Caesar controlled men under arms the safer that all of them would be. Instead he stayed.

Down at the foot of the Capitoline, the scene in the Forum was of a riot about to happen, a swirling crowd anxious that, however and wherever Caesar's body was to burn, it was to be on terms dictated by his loyal voters not by his family, friends or murderers. The assassins had clear sight of the *tabularium*, the national record office that stood immediately below. Beyond it the house of the *Pontifex Maximus*, which Caesar had long used as his home, came in and out of view behind damp clouds of cooking smoke.

The plan was first for speeches and then a procession from the Forum to the Field of Mars where a funeral pyre was ready. Caesar's ashes were to fall on the site of the unbuilt theatre that should have held the trophies from his triumphs over Gaul, Egypt, Africa and the Black Sea. To all those looking from the Capitol it seemed already that this second manoeuvre might be as hard as outshining the achievements of Pompey would have been.

The centre of the celebration was hard to discern from above. Clearly visible was a model of a temple, a copy of one of Caesar's grandest statues, the dictator's chair beside his blood-stained toga. Somewhere there was the diminished corpse. There was mournful music and chanting, lists of great deeds and countries conquered.

Deeper within the crowd was what looked much more like Caesar's body, commanding attention and so vivid that it could only be a model, an effigy in wax which turned on a spit so that each of the twenty-three wounds could be seen by those who had delivered them. From beneath this eerie machine boomed another list, the names of the killers, slowly, individually, murder charge by murder charge, verdict of guilt by guilt. The voice was of an actor, hired by mourners or fired by passion of his own, the part that of the dead dictator: Marcus Brutus, Gaius Cassius, Decimus Brutus, Gaius Trebonius, Tillius Cimber, Pacuvius Labeo, Pontius Aquila, Quintus Ligarius, Servius Sulpicius Galba, Lucius Minucius Basilus, Cassius Parmensis, Rubrius Ruga, Sextius Naso, Caecilius, Bucolianus, Marcus Spurius, Decimus Turullius and onwards until the list began again.

Gaius Cassius, Cassius Parmensis, Decimus Brutus, Marcus Brutus: those who could hear heard their own name above the rising hum of hysteria; more heard from the heightened repetition by friends. Antony began to speak. It was harder to hear what he said than to hear the response and the roll-call: Gaius Trebonius, Tillius Cimber, Pacuvius Labeo, Quintus Ligarius, Lucius Minucius Basilus, Cassius Parmensis.

The consul did not, it seemed, incite the mourners against the men hiding in their homes or on the Capitol. He did praise Caesar for his victories and the wealth he had brought to Rome, mightily as was reasonable in a funeral address but terrifyingly too. Antony, like Caesar, like Cassius Parmensis and his cousin, was a literary man when he chose to be. He spoke in an old-fashioned flamboyant style. Within the show were speeches from popular plays, about Electra, the avenger of her father Agamemnon, son of Atreus, nephew of Thyestes – and of the heroic fighter, Ajax, victim of Odysseus's tricks at Troy.

Not everyone in the crowd knew of Marcus Pacuvius, the ancient playwright from Brundisium, although many knew his line for Ajax, 'O that I should have saved these men so that they could murder me!' It did not matter whether the hearers recognised the source or not. One cry for vengeance followed another.

The wax model Caesar was raised and lowered, turned and turned again, dripping red as though the daggers had barely left it. Antony read selectively from the will, eliding the section in which the dictator adopted his sister's young grandson, Octavius, as his primary heir, shaming his secondary heir, Decimus Brutus with words that hardly needed saying, lingering instead over Caesar's gifts to the Roman people, the use of his personal parks across the river in perpetuity, the cash donations to all that came, in truth, from the state treasury: Caesar had made little distinction between public money and his own.

Few would have recognised the name of Octavius even if they had heard it. Antony knew his name, his place in the extended family of Caesar and his somewhat decorative service in Spain. In no respect did he see the teenager as a threat. Nor did the assassins much note the heir who would avenge his adopted father's death with a ruthlessness incomprehensible until it happened.

The ceremony lurched from one unplanned moment to another. Not everyone was hostile to the assassins. Not everyone was even who he seemed to be. Lucius Cassius, an obscure supporter of Caesar, was cheered. Some of those cheering seemed to think he was Gaius Cassius. The poet Helvius Cinna was murdered by mistake. His killers wanted Cornelius Cinna, the praetor once seen as sympathetic to the assassins. Lepidus's soldiers were less effective at protecting the poet than the politician. The wrong Cinna's head was carried off on a spike.

Caesar's body, made smaller still by the theatrical show around it, had to be burnt where it lay. The pyre piled on the Field of Mars remained merely wood. The mob threw everything it could find in the Forum to create a new pyre. Men broke chairs. Women tore away jewellery and clothing. Bands dispersed with burning torches. The assassins noted nervously the routes that the fires took through the narrow streets.

6
ENTRY OF A YOUNG HUNTER

Tereus Confronted with the Head of his Son, Itylus,
Peter Paul Rubens (1636–8)

To the surprise of almost everyone, both on the Capitoline hill and down below in the Forum, Caesar's will included an heir to his personal name and fortune who was not one of his confidants, not even a prominent supporter, rather a slim, frail boy, recently seriously ill, who was only eighteen. This Gaius Octavius Thurinus had been about to take the seemingly impressive rank of Master of Caesar's Horse: but that was a courtesy title. The will was barely six months old. No one knew how he might have changed it had he stayed alive. Octavius had been its big beneficiary and may not even have known.

The new Caesar was the son of a minor politician who died young, who was rich enough to have a house on the Palatine but renowned only for suppressing a slave revolt in Thurii thirty years before, on the coast between Italy's heel and toe, during the wars against Spartacus. Octavius was the grandson of the dead Caesar's sister, one of two who were both called Julia. He had been a very junior member of the dictator's staff for the wars in Spain. Beyond those facts lay mainly conjecture, mostly idle it was thought, since a scrawny youth currently studying poetry and rhetoric on the other side of the Adriatic, seemed hardly likely to impose himself between Antony, the senior consul, and the even more distinguished assassins.

Octavius's mother and stepfather disapproved of the inheritance. Caesar's name was a dangerous ornament. It might easily have gone to the son of Caesar's other sister Julia, whose name was Quintus Pedius and had served, without excess distinction, in both Gaul and the army that crossed the Rubicon. This was a rare Roman moment for a parent to prize indistinction, the absence of fame, to note the warnings of the wise Epicurus on the risk to inner peace from public life. Death by twenty-three cuts from colleagues and friends was a powerful stimulant to that thought.

The heir himself, however, disagreed. He was soon on his way to Italy, by boat to a safe harbour south of Brundisium. He was due early in April. Early rumours suggested that he would want confirmation of the will and some of Caesar's money, maybe no more than that. Payment was reasonable enough in everyone's view although Antony might be reluctant to pay.

Regardless of Octavius's parents' views and status (and at Rome it was hard wholly to disregard them), Caesar's assassins and mourners asked what kind of heir he was himself. Imagination was ready to replace ignorance. Ancestry was ever the easiest evidence. Idler gossip, carelessly collected by Cassius Parmensis for future wit, suggested that his origins lay in banking and bread-making, the screwing of loans and the kneading of women's flesh as though it were dough; that his great-grandfather was an African perfume seller, his short-lived father an extorting governor of Macedonia as well as a usurer. Antony, political heir and consul, would surely do a deal with such a boy and that other bigger deal, the hard forged Tellus compromise, would extend into the future until the assassination, like the execution of Pompey in Egypt, was a mere dramatic incident.

Meanwhile Gaius Cassius and Marcus Brutus pondered their next move; so too did others at the lower levels of the assassins' command. They did not need to stay together. There were arguments both for staying and for leaving Rome. By staying they might maintain the compromise with the senate. By leaving they might be derided as runaways but live to find armies and fight their cause from their provinces. Brutus did not want to leave his wife, her health still frail after her attempted proof of fearlessness under torture. Porcia wanted the assassins to be vindicated at Rome, to join them on the right side of history.

Brutus, still the praetor in charge of justice for the city, had also the official duty to sponsor a day of games, gladiatorial and theatrical, in the weeks ahead, a show that might usefully measure the popularity of his cause and perhaps, with imagination, increase it. Currently the new popular spectacle in the Forum was a rapidly rising altar to Caesar, constructed from wood by a curer of horse diseases claiming to be an avenger from the family past.

The assassins, keenly hunted to be victims for this sinister shrine, more than ever needed Antony for their personal protection. Brutus had begun to find his seniority over his cousin a hindrance rather than the advantage once noted on the Palatine hill. As urban praetor he needed senate approval to be away for any time longer than ten days. Whether or not that was granted would depend on whether Antony judged it to be in his own interest. Cassius was more free to come and go as he chose.

When Octavius arrived in Brundisium it was to a warm welcome from Caesar's supporters and veterans. He made sacrifices to the memory of his new father and, in the accepted Roman way, took a new name, Gaius Julius Caesar Octavianus. A growing crowd greeted Octavian as he travelled slowly into Italy, meeting citizens who had the right to vote at Rome but rarely a good enough reason to visit. While Antony and the assassins were vying for the Roman votes, Octavian was testing his popularity elsewhere on the Tellus map.

Antony quickly recognised the threat. He did not counter in haste. He did not attack Octavian. He tried to join him in devotion to Caesar. He increased his indirect attacks on the assassins, celebrating the dead dictator as *parens patriae*, father of the nation. The killers could afterwards be seen as murderers of their father, parricides, the kind of criminal for which the worst ancient punishments were reserved. In the middle of April Brutus was allowed to leave the capital, a move which suited both Antony, who did not wish Octavian to exploit his tolerance, and the assassin himself who could organise his games at a safer distance from the riotous celebrants of Caesar's cult.

Seen from the Capitoline hill, these devotees in their temporary temple, their numbers growing every day, began to take on a perilous permanence. Caesar was rapidly entering the pantheon of Rome, a newcomer of rare flamboyance, like an Isis from Egypt or a Dionysus from Thrace.

And then, just as suddenly, they were gone. The wooden columns were gone. The curer of horses was gone too, killed by the troops of Lepidus who were still watching every exit and entrance. Dolabella took the credit as consul. It was not clear whether, in removing the shrine, Caesar's former allies were primarily protecting his assassins or proving to his heir that there were limits to devotion to a father. Antony probably approved both aims.

A new conflict was coming. Until Octavian transformed the political terms Antony had been a saviour to the assassins. Without him they might not have survived the first few days. With Octavian's arrival vengeance became competitive. It seemed that the amnesty might be guaranteed only for assassins who left Rome. By the middle of April all of them had gone.

Amid the uncertainty Trebonius took the road to Asia, though carefully and not by the main roads. Tillius Cimber left for Bithynia. Cassius's movements were unknown, Cassius Parmensis's too. It was hardly a set of triumphs for Caesar's killers but, with Decimus and three legions in Cisalpine Gaul, new legions awaiting them across the Adriatic and Antony still conciliatory at home, there was still good hope.

One of the first to sense the new and very different threat from Octavian was Cicero who had also retreated from Rome and was enjoying some seaside relaxation in Cumae, one of the old Greek towns on the bay of Naples. The 'young man', as Cicero liked to see Caesar's heir, was on a tour to meet influential politicians and assess his prospects. The old man, in his first report of the visit, was both flattered and impressed, describing Octavian as 'totally devoted to me'. The following day he changed his mind, alarmed by the threats from Octavian's entourage that death was the assassins' rightful due and that Antony's balance of forces was no balance at all, not one that justice could accept.

Decimus too saw the change in the political cast. The first of the assassins to command legions in their defence, was already protecting himself around Parma and Mutina. New ditches through the swollen land were becoming new streams beneath reinforced palisades. Already he saw how the new instability at Rome might affect his governorship of Parmensis's family home and the rest of Cisalpine Gaul. Antony, marked for Macedonia by Caesar's living wish, was rumoured to want the nearer province instead now that Caesar was dead and a new Caesar was in Rome.

Any new law to legitimise this claim to Parma and beyond, would not only strengthen Antony's position against Octavian; it would remove what was then the assassins' only armed base. Decimus was an anxious realist. He saw a firm triangle of old forces, Antony's, the senate's and the assassins'; he saw Octavian forcing the triangle into a less stable square. The weights and shapes were shifting. His place was being squeezed.

The veterans of Parma were on sale, it seemed, to the first or highest bidder. Lepidus was hiring the Thunderbolt legionaries. It was unclear for whom or how he might use them, or for whom or how they might be ready to be used. It was like the board game that the soldiers played, gambling their pay in an imitation of the battles in which they had earnt it. The board was becoming bigger all the time. Decimus was writing home letters both self-serving and desperate for reassurance, promoting small successes like a man who hoped the whole game could be smaller again.

In Rome, a first business meeting between Antony, the consul, and Octavian, the heir, had been brief and cool. Antony's brother, Lucius, had helped by using his power as a people's tribune to permit Octavian directly to address the people. That was the high point of their cooperation. Octavian wanted money, Caesar's or Rome's whatever the difference might be. Antony argued that the formalities of adoption were still incomplete. His immediate concern was that the four legions based in Macedonia, an asset for the wars planned by Caesar in Parthia, should be transferred, along with his governorship, to Cisalpine Gaul. The rumour of his ambition was a reality.

In June the law to enforce Antony's change of plan was put to the people. The senate, which might have denied approval, was bypassed by bribery. Antony paid for the manoeuvre. The new law duly passed. He gained a legal title to Parma and Mutina, Bononia and the banks of the Po, the gateway to Italy from the north, but would have to seize them first.

In the same month Brutus met his mother, Servilia, her daughter, Tertulla, who was married to Cassius, his own wife Porcia, all the most intimate in the assassins' cause, at the family's house in the Roman port of Antium. Cicero joined them from his house nearby. Favonius, an opponent of the assassination before it happened but afterwards a supporter, was also there.

The mood was grim. Cassius was for moving east and maintaining the fight, Brutus, for attempting, as long as he could, to stay at home. Cicero criticised Brutus. Servilia was outraged at his tone. Everyone complained about the absent Decimus. Servilia had plans to fix the senate. It was like a family row. Cicero described a ship of a failing state that was 'falling apart'.

* * *

Marooned in Mutina, Decimus was depressed and fearful before even hearing of the talk from Servilia's house party. He was not yet fighting but, whatever the view of him among his friends, he was the sole bulwark of the assassins against Antony, also the hope of many other senators opposed to Antony.

This was a bigger burden than Decimus desired. He still had his province and Caesar's former legions but his title to them depended only on possession. Apart from the bribery of the people's tribunes, which was not unusual, there was nothing illegal in what had been done by the people on Antony's behalf. Due process had been followed. He was rightly insecure.

Decimus's position rested on the moral authority of the senate and the moral force of the compromise agreed after the Ides of March. Against him were both the new law and a growing worry whether his legions would fight against Antony when the order came. It was hard to be sure. Caesar's former troops might prefer a united front against Caesar's killers, whatever the vagaries of opinion in the Campus Martius or the salons of Antium.

Alone and trapped within the new geometry of power, Decimus was nervous and ignorant of its latest shifts, assassins vs Antony, Antony vs Octavian, the senate divided within itself. Marcus Brutus and Gaius Cassius were merely at the edges. Decimus was the man digging defences for imminent battle. His fellow killers of Caesar were watching from Servilia's couches, content, it seemed, that Brutus's mother should use her influence, much of it gained in Caesar's bed, to keep them safe.

Whatever might loom ahead, Decimus had immediately to face the ambition of Antony, whose new desire for vengeance was exaggerated to please the troops, and Octavian's all too real desire for vengeance. Lepidus's loyalty, though nominally to the senate, could not be guaranteed to an assassin fighting with the senate's support. Nothing in Decimus's career with Caesar had prepared him for the aftermath of Caesar's murder. He had too much time to ponder that truth.

It was as though the dictator had never died. Reports spread out along the roads to the countryside of Octavian's largesse to the people and loyalty to his father, the young heir's popularity, of a kiss and handshake between the younger would-be Caesar and the older, a celebration reclaiming the Capitoline hill from its recent history of occupation by assassins. The little that was clear was disturbing.

Marcus Brutus, unable to attend his own praetor's games, was still in Italy but almost in hiding, reduced to arguing about dates and times on the programme and which play by one of Rome's few tragic playwrights might best suit his bill. Lucius Accius was a favourite. He had been a great figure. Cicero, when he was very young, had once met him. But choosing plays, for all their propaganda possibilities, was arguably not how any of the Antium party should be spending so much time.

Accius's versions of the legacy of Thyestes were attractive but perhaps too pointed for the present troubles. His *Atreus* and *Clytemnestra* were both about the killing of kings and Pompey had already used *Clytemnestra* to open his own theatre. Other episodes ranged from the eating of children to the sacrifice of a daughter, the killing of a father by his son and the son's pursuit by furies. All might be misunderstood by Octavian.

The safer choice was between his play about Marcus Junius Brutus, the Tarquin-slaying ancestor whose legacy was supreme for the assassin of Caesar, and his one about Tereus, a mythical rapist whose family became a flock of birds. Antony would probably reject a play that promoted Brutus's family. That left the birds. Roman revenge-tragedy had long been about politics; politics in 44 BC was soon to be a long, unfolding tragedy of Roman revenge.

Cassius and Brutus were both left to sail the coastal waters with a prospect of low-level assignments, only possibly to be amended by Servilia, humiliating enough to encourage further departure. Porcia stayed at Rome. Antony's brother, Gaius, got the credit for the lions, ballet-dancers and bears – as well as for the *Tereus*, the play about the swallow and nightingale. Brutus got the massive bill. Porcia, whose family history had left her huge wealth, was able to help him pay it.

Decimus had occasional cause for encouragement. In July gladiatorial games were held in Caesar's honour and a comet fell through the sky, an ill omen which Octavian announced as a sign of his father's journey to the gods. He could not, however, reinterpret all the bad news. Sextus reported that Caesar's death had been rapturously greeted in both Spain and Africa. Pompey's son had seen the joy himself, while campaigning near Carthage, 'an explosion of rejoicing and a revolution in the people's minds'; the assassins' cause was helping his own and the two causes were intertwined.

Sextus seemed decisively to have rejected an offer from Antony to return as his ally to Rome. The master of Spain and Sicily would not be considering Antony's offer, he said, until all armies were demobbed and his family house by the Tellus temple was restored to him. The first was a fantasy, the second hardly less so since Antony was living in it.

Only one truth was clear. As a result of Octavian's arrival Decimus would soon be the last of Caesar's leading killers on the Italian peninsula. In August Marcus Brutus published an assassins' testament, proudly parading their love of the old constitution, their reluctance for civil war and the unbreakable connection between Rome and themselves. He then, quietly like a summer holiday maker, set off for the sea.

Porcia wished him a fond farewell on Italy's magic coast south of Naples, comparing herself to Hector's wife saying goodbye to her husband at Troy. With mythic history as ever in his ears, Brutus sailed away from Italy, crossing the Adriatic ahead of Cassius, each to their different destinations and different supporters in the eastern provinces.

The remaining assassins followed. Only Pontius Aquila, still without his lands donated by Caesar to Servilia, took the road back to Parma. Decimus, despite his command of three inherited legions and several others he had raised himself in Cisalpine Gaul as Caesar had done, was even more cut off from anyone he could trust.

Cicero disapproved of the assassins' departure so far from Rome just as Brutus disapproved of Cicero's dealings with Octavian. The febrile mood of the Antium party remained. It did not, however, stop social courtesies, Brutus's agreeing to become a Latin teacher in Athens to Cicero's young son, Marcus Tullius Cicero Minor, or praising him to his father for republican spirit.

Civilities were easier abroad. When Cassius arrived in Athens he added lessons in oratory for the young Cicero. Both he and Brutus were awarded bronze statues of themselves close to those of the ancient Athenian tyrant-slayers. Brutus could not have asked for more. In Athens an assassin could carry his morality with him and be appreciated for it. An exile could study peace while recruiting for war. The east was hospitable as the west was not. Egyptians and Syrians demonstrated on the clear side of Caesar's killers. The only cloud in the eastern sky was the prospect of Dolabella, with a promise of one of the Macedonian legions from Antony, leaving to claim the governorship of Syria for himself.

* * *

In Rome, with the assassins out of the country, politics was a daily struggle of feints and deception between Antony and Octavian, two potential tyrants who each needed to pretend to his soldiers that they were on the same side, Caesar's side. In September, in order to counter some of Octavian's support in the streets, Antony proposed that Caesar's name be added to the annual list of days in honour of individual gods. He also supported a new statue in the Forum to Caesar as father of the nation. Octavian, celebrating his nineteenth birthday and confident of his unshakable supremacy over Caesar's troops and voters, sought to undermine what remained of Antony's support in the senate.

These events received Cicero's analysis but did not much help the assassins' cause. Not for the first time he had retired into literature. He had begun a dramatic dialogue about the arguments leading to the Ides of March. He also had a new essay entitled *De Gloria* on the false glory for which Caesar had been aiming. The author was uncharacteristically nervous about giving it publicity.

What Cicero needed most was an open rift in Italy between Octavian and Antony. Together – or even seeming to be together – they could defeat Decimus and stop the assassins coming together in the east. Cicero could not command troops but had every skill to sow the discord he required. When Caesar's father-in-law, the Epicurean grandee, Lucius Calpurnius Piso, made a vigorous attack on Antony, Cicero, no friend to Piso, decided that the time was approaching for his own more substantial assault. The question was merely that of the precise moment.

At the end of November Antony left Rome to take command of the four legions of veterans that had landed at Brundisium from Macedonia: his brother, Gaius, was to take over for him in his former province. Immediately two of the best of these legions chose to abandon the consul for the heir. Antony, admiringly observed by Fulvia, his wife, imposed a form of antique punishment, forcing the leaders of the mutiny to draw lots for bludgeoning their fellow victims to death. It was a grisly scene that failed to change minds and only damaged Antony's cause.

At the same time Octavian too found obstacles against his progress. He wanted to march back with his new legions to Rome. His troops refused. They were happy to fight Caesar's assassins but still reluctant to fight a man who claimed the mantle of Caesar. Antony saw his chance and denounced Octavian to the senate, relying again on the constitutional legality of his action against the treasonous illegality of his rival. The legions, he argued, were rightly his.

To Cicero's satisfaction the two would-be heirs to Caesar's power were behaving like jealous dogs. Octavian had just passed his nineteenth birthday. Antony, twice his age, seemed on top but mainly in bluster and noise. When he left for Ariminum and his new Cisalpine province Cicero hammered the split further open by beginning a sustained attack on Antony in speeches that were abusive, even by the standards of the age, and obsessive even by his own standards. Cicero asked Brutus if he might fairly call them *Philippics*, the name of the greatest Greek speeches against a threat to liberty, Demosthenes against Philip of Macedon, father of Alexander the Great, three hundred years before. He waited anxiously for a reply.

The answer came first in more practical than literary form. On the first day of the new year, when Antony and Dolabella were no longer consuls, their veteran successors, Aulus Hirtius, an early supporter of Octavian, and Gaius Vibius Pansa, showed the strength that the consulship could still exert. By April, after anxious vacillations, they had declared Antony a public enemy, allowing Caesar's heir to place his own forces alongside those of the senate and Decimus. Even Sextus, it seemed, might join the official party. The triangle of power had flattened into a straight arrow aimed at Antony's head.

Hirtius, better known in his old age as a gourmet and a writer, prepared for war along the *Via Aemilia* in Decimus's support. He sent forces ahead; he would himself leave for Parma as soon as his health allowed. The roads to Cisalpine Gaul were once more crowded with troops.

Antony had loyal support in the senate, one of Caesar's former generals Quintus Fufius Calenus in the forefront, but he was quickly in deep danger. His advantage, as so often, was only that every part of the group opposed to him was suspicious of the other. Cicero had a host of enemies. Hirtius's greater passion was still for completing the reports of Caesar's own wars, left unfinished at his death, than for returning to the Rubicon himself. He was a 'continuator' of another man's biography, not a continuer of conflict, and he distrusted Pansa.

Sextus held the new title *praefectus classis et orae maritimae*, prefect of fleet and coast, but was only shakily reconciled with the senate; he had just built a new base for his own troops and ships in the western Mediterranean port of Massilia. Decimus, pinned for the winter behind Mutina's walls, was an assassin and might or might not be helped by troops previously loyal to Caesar. Octavian's troops, angered by Antony's executions at Brundisium, were reliably loyal only to Octavian. Cicero and Octavian were becoming closer but were hardly yet allied.

Cicero was both expectant and exultant nonetheless. The old might yet defeat the new, the constitution conquer those who defied it. Brutus would tell him just how brilliant his speeches were. Antony, for all the divisions within his opponents, would fall first. Decimus would triumph. Octavian would see sense. Rhetoric had hardened to reality in the orator's mind.

TREBONIUS UNDER TORTURE

The Gulf of Smyrna (c1870)

Whether by land or sea from Mutina there were a thousand rough miles to the port of Smyrna. In January, 43 BC, Gaius Trebonius, there at the gateway to his new province on the eastern shore of the Aegean Sea, knew almost nothing of what was happening in Cisalpine Gaul. Decimus Brutus, his fellow assassin, knew even less about events in Asia.

Both men were facing vengeance for their part in Caesar's death but their rival avengers were distracted by each other. Octavian was, tactically and with some embarrassment, on Decimus's side against Antony on Italy's northern border. Antony would have happily hunted Trebonius to death but had bigger problems on the road to

Cisalpine Gaul than anything yet apparent in Smyrna.

Of the two assassins Trebonius seemed to have the better place. He was settled in a seaside town between Lesbos and Ephesus where the streets were named for its temples; terraced gardens hung like necklaces on its hills. Once one of the sites of mass slaughter of Romans which Pompey had avenged, Smyrna had become better famed for contemplation, commerce, pleasure and the arts of forgetting.

For Decimus, already depressed, there was nothing equivalently contemplative or pleasurable about Mutina, the marshland military colony, with Parma to the north and Ariminum to the south, that still bore the scars from the brutality of Pompey. But both assassins were in towns where the future was about to echo the past, indistinctly, inexactly, without doubt, with horror. How the one connected to the other would only slowly be understood.

Trebonius was a man whose training for Smyrna prized alertness above almost any other virtue. He had fought in Gaul and Britain where sudden danger stood behind every wall and tree. He was not naïve. His weapons were equally words and steel. He understood the means to motivate his men. On campaigns with Caesar wages and promises of more were often not enough.

He could inspire with speech. He was respected. The humiliation of the last day of his consulship, the colleague who had joined his name on the lists for less than a day, Caesar's joke, one of Caesar's last jokes: all that was behind him. It was rumoured that Marcus Brutus himself, less a general than Cassius, might join his staff. Trebonius too had been city praetor. He understood money and the law. He had survived to the age of fifty in harsh times. But he was not ready for Dolabella when Dolabella came.

Rome's Asian province stretched for six hundred miles from the Aegean to the eastern end of the Mediterranean. It was the former land of Lydia, once ruled by Croesus the gold king; it held Sardis, whose mines and mints set the standard of purity for all precious metals; its capital was Pergamum whose last king had chosen the Roman people as his heir and bequeathed to them every part of his

domain, every brick of sand and silver, mud and gold, every weapon, every slave.

Asia looked west to Greece, whose ancient towns studded its
coastline, and east for hundreds of miles to the Parthians who, with
the most reason to thank the assassins for Caesar's death, remained
an unconquered, still threatening power. Smyrna, beautiful not just
by its citizens' own accounts, was one of its prettiest ports. Sailors
praised its twin harbours, its waters deep to the edge of its walls, its
town plan like a chequerboard, created like the map of Alexandria
by the mathematical Greeks. Its main street was called the Golden.
One of its goddesses was Rome itself.

It was by Caesar's gift, confirmed by the senate after the Ides of
March, that Trebonius held Asia, its wealth and, he hoped, its loyalty. His job was to secure its taxes and recruits for Rome; that meant
legally for whichever cause the senate decided was Roman, but in
practice at this point for Caesar's killers. Gaius Cassius was doing
the same to the south of him, Marcus Brutus maybe to the north.

Dolabella's arrival in Smyrna was a surprise. It was nine months
since Trebonius had welcomed him to Capitoline hill on the night
of the Ides, lightly mocking his dress for the consulship he had
not yet won, hoping then that one ambitious aristocrat, notoriously available to the highest bidder, might be followed into the
assassins' camp by more. But Dolabella, not for the first time, had
disappointed.

In January 43 BC he was on the side of Antony, flattered by a
promise of a future military command against Parthia, Caesar's true
inheritance. He had advanced from taking over Caesar's consulship
to being a former consul, much more lucrative than holding the job
itself, a senator for the rest of his life, no longer aiming to cancel his
debts by revolutionary law but, more traditionally, to tax his way
fast out of bankruptcy through the extortion of an eastern province.

Trebonius had no reason to expect a visit from a hopeful governor whose destination was Syria, a treacherous six hundred miles
away by mountain land, much closer and more easily reached by
sea, via Miletus, Rhodes and Cyprus, almost a pleasure cruise at

almost any time. Trebonius's deputy in Asia, Publius Cornelius Lentulus, was a member of Dolabella's extended aristocratic clan. Perhaps Dolabella had a higher than usual Roman fear of January storms – or was planning a family reunion.

The visitor told his suspicious host that he would not be with him long. He would be taking his troops to Ephesus, a short distance down the coast. While Trebonius agreed to give all the help that a legitimate Roman governor would expect, he barred Dolabella from admission to Smyrna. Dolabella and his legion would have to march, camp by camp, like an army of reoccupation. Although his name derived from the word *dolabra*, a spade for raising walls and digging ditches, this was not a recent tool in Dolabella's armoury.

The two men spoke carefully. Trebonius, away from Rome the longer, had the more news to learn. Dolabella seemed firmly to be Antony's man still, his past career as Antony's enemy and cuckolder slipping ever further away. But Antony himself was not the same man. As had become clearer to all the assassins, the compromiser of the Ides of March and the deal-maker of the temple of Tellus had since become an anxious rival of Caesar's vengeful heir. He need-ed to follow the wind of that revenge or fail. In order to bring old soldiers behind him, he needed to show himself even more deter-mined to kill Caesar's killers than was Octavian himself.

Trebonius and Dolabella began by arguing about money. There was reasonable discussion to be had about which Romans had the right to whatever tax revenues from Asia were due to Rome after Caesar's death. Mark Antony, by imaginative use of Caesar's private papers, had already diverted funds to new supporters, Dolabella not the least of them, counting out public gold in Fulvia's kitchen bas-kets. The unwelcome visitor to Smyrna shouted for more cash, the most consistent cry of his life.

The two men, the short, angry aristocrat and the calmer, tall-er general argued briefly about some missing cavalry that had somehow been diverted northwards to the army of Brutus. They had interests in news of the same people. Aside from his abuse of Antony how was Cicero himself? Dolabella, the orator's former son-in-law, was still in dispute about a dowry. Trebonius, Cicero's admiring anthologist, was probably better informed.

How was Gaius Cassius? News there was scarce. Cassius was the assassin who caused the greatest concern to Dolabella; he was the candidate of some in the senate for the Syrian command that Dolabella was travelling to claim for himself. How were the others from that first night on the Capitoline? The Cascas? Probably with Brutus. Turullius and Cassius Parmensis? Commanders in Cassius's fleet which, as the sailors of Smyrna reported, was rapidly making the Aegean the assassins' sea.

After their talking Trebonius retreated behind the walls of Smyrna. He was a careful man, a master of siege and counter-siege as he had proved for Caesar by breaking the resistance of Massilia on the Mediterranean coast of Gaul, only six years before, when Caesar was about to cross the Rubicon. Dolabella was then with Pompey. Decimus Brutus, last heard of besieged by Antony in Mutina, was in charge of Caesar's fleet that same summer – for all of them a world of time away.

Outside the walls of Smyrna Dolabella returned to his legion. Trebonius, whose plans to recruit a legion had barely begun, returned to his governor's house. Late at night Dolabella returned too. In Cassius Pamensis's words: *Nocte intempesta nostrum devenit domum*. He had seen how to enter the city and in the darkness he brought trusted soldiers and a man he called the Samarian, a maker of weapons from the Greek island of Samos, birthplace of Epicurus but hardly itself a haunt of Epicureans.

A soldier found Trebonius first, asleep in his room and casually, with a joke, said he had come for his head. Trebonius demanded to see Dolabella. The soldier said that if he insisted he would have to leave his body behind first. Dolabella arrived. There was no known struggle. No one else awoke.

Any comedy was over. The Samarian was not just an armourer. As was common enough in his trade, he was a torturer too. He knew about heating knives, sharpening whips and hauling a human body on the rack of wood and iron that the Romans called a horse.

He knew how to challenge deniers of the fear of death.

He had his machine. It was easy to move. He knew the numbers of the holes through which to pass the ropes, the positions for sharpest pain, for the fastest and the slowest death, for no death at all. He could improvise. His usual business was the torture of slaves whose evidence, in the event of legal disputes, was deemed untruthful among the Romans unless supported by terror. To tear apart a former consul, commanded to the rack by a fellow former consul was a novelty but, as a practical matter for the Samarian, no more than that.

For the victim and his victor this night scene in a house in Smyrna was a horror for the first that would soon be famed as a horror for both. Dolabella resumed his interrogation while the Samarian twisted his very versatile ropes, his tools designed for sharpening stakes and swords, his whips meant for cavalry men, the armoury of a Roman army on the move. The torture lasted for two days.

Dolabella did not care about the conspiracy to murder Caesar, the men or their motives. It was only about money. Except for Dolabella's hopes of hidden pay for his troops, the questioning did not even matter. It was about the lesson that would be left behind when it was over.

This would be a lesson from Antony's man, to Caesar's legions that Caesar's memory was safe in Antony's hands. Romans did not torture fellow citizens. That was the law. But law came from the past. The present was another country. Just as Caesar himself had been different from ordinary men, so must his avengers be They had to be like the Furies of tragedy, hounding down the guilty until the last stain was cleansed. Gaius Trebonius, commander for Caesar, publisher for Cicero, plotter on the Ides of March, was the first assassin to die.

It was a slow death, the kind that even the most dedicated Epicureans found it hard not to fear. If a pupil conquered the fear of death did it matter if the fear of slow and painful dying remained? Epicurus said it should not remain. Even a slow death was short by the standards of life and the emptiness thereafter. Epicurus himself had died slowly and painfully and kept his principles. But he had a kidney stone not a killer with rope and blades. And he was the master and maybe not to be matched.

The soldiers got Trebonius's head. They placed it on his ornate chair where on a normal day he would have judged traders' disputes. At the close of business they kicked it along the pavements in sport, abandoning it beneath a statue of Caesar, tipping the rest of his mangled remains over the city walls into the deep sea. Beheading was their theatre. They had their jokes in the end.

On the next day Dolabella ordered his own business as usual, striking his camp, preparing his next camp and leaving behind his cousin, Cornelius Lentulus, to keep control. His destination was first Ephesus, where a part of his force would leave for Syria by sea, and then to Syria himself overland, camp by camp in the way that every soldier knew.

There needed to be nothing else out of order. The rare had to be followed by the routine, as quickly as was possible. As on the Palatine, so in a distant province: the aspiration was the same.

For every Roman soldier the camp was the world. Routine made a place Rome. The three same blasts on a bronze horn ordered the morning movement whether a legion was in Asia or Gaul, the eastern Mediterranean or the wet lands of Parma. The first was for the packing of tents, the loosening of ropes, the lowering of poles, the rolling of a thousand sheets of soft leather. The second was for the loading of the baggage of war onto animals, the third the order to march, local allies to the fore, the legionaries behind, cavalry to left and right.

Before every nightfall, officers rode ahead to choose the site for the next camp, marking out the bounds between Rome and the rest, streets with coloured flags, the Cardo running north to south, the Decumanus east to west, each night the same streets, measured by the *metatores*. When the main mass of men arrived, the boundary became a ditch and a fence of stakes, not impassable, only a yard deep and across, but enough to mark what was Rome and what was not.

Dolabella would have had his own tent, around it the tents of his staff, within them trenches not as deep, filled with dry grass and reeds for a bed. Outside would be a platform, for the making of a speech, if that were necessary, and for the watching of birds to find good auguries, necessary always, whether the sky was full of desert vultures or the herons of the marsh.

As far as possible away, at the bad end of the rows of rising tents, were the shithouses and the bread ovens. Every soldier knew his allotted place, the same letters and numbers every right, the same roof of leather from which next morning, at the sound of the horn, he would emerge again like a moth from a chrysalis.

If a man's tent was number twelve in line A by the River Po of Gaul it was the same by the River Hermus of Asia: first left, second right, the Decumanus dividing the tenth cohort from the ninth, the Cardo, the north-south hinge. There was never a reason for a man to be lost. On the road from Smyrna there were changes of place but no change of address.

8

DECIMUS BESIEGED

Augustus as a young general (early 1st century AD)

In February 43 BC Parma was not the place that Cassius Parmensis knew before the assassination of Caesar. Antony held it by his purchased mandate from the people of Rome, with Gaius and Lucius his loyal brothers and four legions to whom nothing could be denied. Parma provided no protection itself to make an occupier feel secure, little bar some sharpened stakes in its sluggish river. Precious cavalry, trained to fight foreign enemies, were harrying savagely for food through the winter water.

Decimus Brutus, the assassin and governor whom Antony needed to supplant, was besieged in Mutina twenty miles away with two veteran legions and one of new recruits. The *Via Aemilia*, crossed by seven rivers between the two towns, was more mud than stone. The local veterans who had not joined one side or the other had fled. The surrounding farms were empty of the cattle, sheep and corn that had filled their barns just a year before, most of it already behind the walls of Mutina, enough, Decimus hoped, for some twenty thousand men to last until Hirtius, Pansa or Octavian arrived on behalf of the senate.

While he waited, Decimus's hopes were mixed with the fears of a realist. Neither of the consuls had a record that matched Antony's in the field: Hirtius was sick and Pansa was puffed up with grand moderation, proud of his new appointment as an augur prophesying with birds. Perhaps Octavian would be willing to relieve his father's assassin from Antony's siege, just as the senate, relishing its restored powers of political management, had ordered. But that was only an optimist's possibility.

Caesar's heir, it was said, was keen to show his preparedness to put the constitutional above the personal. His soldiers, however, were in a simmering mood to disagree and disobey. Legality and propriety could not be taken too far when Decimus was deemed the most treacherous of all the assassins. Even Octavian himself could not yet be certain how his troops would decide.

Perhaps there would be help for Decimus from others keen to support the senate against Antony, especially if they thought that the senate would win. Pompey's son, Sextus, far away in southern Gaul, was receiving rare praise from Cicero for his 'modesty, responsibility, fairness and honesty' which, in other words, meant his being everything that Antony was not. But Sextus's reply from Massilia was merely supportive. He was moving down to Sicily from where he could turn on or off the corn supply to Rome. He would not do more. He would not send troops.

Decimus had no choice but to be patient. News was scarce. The siege was not total but half-knowing could be worse than no knowledge at all. Military reports for Mutina did arrive from the countryside, but slowly and unreliably, mainly in small boats through the shifting streams of the Scultenna river, sealed letters alongside sacks of millet, fresh meat and salt for preserving the meat he had in store.

The invalid Hirtius had already made a valiant start up the *Via Flaminia* and *Via Aemilia*, abandoning his bed and Caesar's unfinished memoirs, and taking from Antony the town of Claterna, beyond Bononia, some fifty miles away. That much Decimus knew. He may also have known the senate's strong support for Marcus Brutus in Macedonia, its more guarded approval for Cassius in Syria.

On a good day for Decimus the assassins' prospects must have seemed promising even if his own mood was often bleak. When spring came he intended to break out of Mutina and drive Antony back towards the relief forces arriving on his behalf from Rome. His enemy, currently the public enemy, would be trapped. To the north-west the legions of Gaul and Spain would hear the news and, whatever the duplicity of their commanders (he knew them all too well from their shared days with Caesar), they would repel Antony too.

On a bad day Decimus could not be certain how his forces would fare against Antony and where his old comrades, Lepidus, Pollio and Plancus, would put their support in a world where their old certainties had gone. The first of them an old aristocrat, the second a soldier historian, the third a diplomat in the best spirit of the Palatine, they would surely, he hoped, support his legal authority. Yet he was nervous that there could ever be good will for him from soldiers once commanded by Caesar. Octavian, driven by his very personal vengeance, could even less be relied upon.

Mutina made a man depressed. He could see too much bleak water. He knew too little of what lay in the near beyond. Whatever Pansa and his augurs might say, thick clouds of birds told nothing. Whatever he felt, he had to show confidence to his own men that the will of the senate would prevail, that the desire to restore old republican rule would be greater than the power of revenge, that Antony, crushed between the senate's various forces, however separate in aspirations they might be, would for the last time be gone. With Cicero wielding words for the assassins, Decimus could seize the credit for Antony's defeat and use it to plan his next military moves.

It was not clear what those moves might be. From the east the news remained scarce. Decimus did not know how successfully or not Brutus was using his new command, nor even where Cassius was, nor that Dolabella was marching deep into Asia. Decimus was closer to Rome than Brutus but often, it seemed, so much further away.

Brutus had the advantage of Cicero's greater closeness and confidence. In Macedonia he could receive regular letters and even copies of some of the orator's latest speeches against Antony to the senate and people, opportunities for the two men to joke about their noble name, *Philippics*, and whether the title was deserved. Was Antony as much a threat to Rome as Philip of Macedon had once been to Greece? Had Cicero outdone even the great Demosthenes in defending liberty?

Decimus would have wanted to answer yes to both those questions. Did it matter that Demosthenes, for all his rhetoric about keeping Athens free, had failed in his purpose? He hoped not.

Decimus may have had some of the same despatches as his cousin but he was not as much part of the conversation. Marcus Brutus benefited from news from all parties to his mother Servilia. Decimus's mother, Sempronia, loved parties too but not of such a useful kind. Neither assassin yet had the report that the ripped corpse of their friend, Trebonius, was already on an Asian beach, his head in Smyrna an object lesson beneath a statue of the man he had helped to kill.

As February came to an end, the shocking news of the first assassin's death came from Rome. As Decimus looked around him nothing much had changed. Mutina was still holding out against Antony; the consuls were still camped along the *Via Aemilia*. Once he had read Cicero's account of Trebonius's two days of torture, the ghastly details from the latest, the eleventh, of Cicero's ever more inflammatory *Philippics*, nothing was the same. However exaggerated the rhetoric might have seemed, the message was clear: in the new landscape of politics Dolabella, the torturer of Smyrna, and Antony, the besieger outside his walls, were as indistinguishable as crows in the crowded fields.

Dolabella was Antony's man but Cicero, for rhetorical purpose and by his own skill, had made the two into the same man. Just as Antony had invaded Cisalpine Gaul so had Dolabella invaded Asia. Both were monsters. Both aimed to destroy the good. Tolerance by the senate of one meant tolerance of the other, and the same destruction of liberty.

The orator had vividly summoned the scene in Smyrna, the rack, the whips, the foreign arms-maker firing his forge against a great man of Rome. Death was inevitable, a kindness sometimes and always owed to nature; torment and tortures were man-made, a fate owed only to the anger of the savage. Trebonius had been as serene as Dolabella had been sub-human, as accepting of pain as the great heroes of the past when they had endured the barbarian brutality of Carthage, as philosophical in his acceptance of terror as Dolabella had been a terrorist.

Decimus had no illusions about the limits of rhetoric. Cicero's words could move minds. At Mutina only legions and their willingness to fight would decide the outcome of the struggle. But the horror in the senate's response had been a clear help to the assassins. Even strong supporters of Antony had agreed that Dolabella was a public enemy and that his estate be forfeit to the state. This was powerful progress.

In the months under siege Decimus had greater grounds to appreciate Cicero than he had before the assassination. The *Philippics* were loud and long, outrageous in abuse, maybe excessive even to a man who had Antony trying to kill him every day. But they were potent poison. Every senator knew Demosthenes's desperate denunciations of Philip of Macedon; many had learnt, recited and imitated them in school. They had the force of a failed past against the perils of a failing present.

Decimus himself was not a literary man. Trebonius had been the man for Cicero's words; Cassius, Brutus and Cassius Parmensis too still were. If Trebonius were still alive he would have been the assassin most usefully employed in counting and cutting the *Philippics*. Trebonius the editor was instead, Decimus learnt, hardly now more than a rhetorical aid himself, a useful symbol, first for Antony of his newly found vengeance against Caesar's killers, secondly for Cicero of the fate faced by Rome if Antony, his vicious brothers and his thug Dolabella, were to win the war. No one needed to be literary to understand that.

The senate had been unusually outraged by the report from Smyrna. There was not just the affront to dignity in the torture and murder of one former consul by another. There was the fear that, in the continuing terms of business between themselves, a bad precedent had been set, the process of healing after violence set back. Dolabella himself had to be hunted down as he had hunted Trebonius. It had to be clear how far out of line the avenging of Caesar had brought him.

It was less clear how this was to happen and who was to hunt the hunter. New legions were needed to confront Antony in Cisalpine Gaul. Their soldiers had to be lured, encouraged and praised. After the story of the rack, the eleventh *Philippic* contained a wordy tribute to the patriotism of the new recruits to the senate's cause. It also displayed a pedantic defence of why Cassius should be the man appointed to punish Dolabella, to lead the southern theatre of the east just as Brutus did the north.

Cicero's argument on behalf of Cassius was as critical for Decimus Brutus as the raising of new legions. An alternative course for the senate would be to switch either Hirtius or Pansa from Cisalpine Gaul to Asia. If that route were taken, it would leave Mutina disastrously more dependent on Caesar's heir and the legions of Lepidus, Pollio and Plancus. These were men who while nominally loyal to the senate, had a proven loyalty only to a dead dictator whose wishes could be interpreted in many ways. Decimus either needed Cassius to get the command against Dolabella or the pursuit to be postponed.

Postponement won. Cicero's case for Cassius was weaker than even so confident a rhetorician required. Decimus's rule was, at least, legitimate. He had Caesar's and the senate's authority to hold Cisalpine Gaul. He could rely on the compromise in the temple of Tellus even if the people's assembly, its tribunes bribed and corrupted, had declared otherwise. Cassius, by contrast, lacked any legitimate basis to be in the east. Cicero preferred to avoid that inconvenient truth.

By advancing the case for Cassius, Cicero also alarmed the senate about the assassins' growing strength. At a time of perilous extremes, Rome's elders were always seeking middle ground where they could find it. The consul, Pansa, led the moderate opposition, as he liked to do, and Cicero's pleadings failed.

Decimus's interests remained protected. But it took several weeks of anxiety before the good news reached him that the hunt for Dolabella was to wait until the consuls had raised the siege of Mutina. Then and only then could they take on their next task. Decimus Brutus was as happy with that as he was increasingly nervous of nearer events along the *Via Aemilia*.

* * *

When Cicero wrote to Cassius in February he began with a wish that he too had been an assassin: if he had been 'invited to the banquet on the Ides of March there would have been no leavings', he boasted and Antony would be dead. Instead and in fact, Cicero had been merely a sympathiser, and remained so still, while Antony was alive, camped outside Mutina and set to claim the road that led to the Rubicon. Cicero's moan about his missing invitation was satisfying only to himself.

By the middle of March Hirtius and Octavian were closer to Antony but still reluctant to strike. They claimed to be awaiting Pansa's four legions of new recruits from Rome. Cicero was meanwhile still bidding to persuade Sextus to the senate's and the assassins' cause, praising him as he had once praised his father, Pompey the Great, speaking out against the injustice of Antony occupying the house of the Pompeys, all to no avail.

Around Mutina, Antony grew angrier and more aggressive. His enemies did not attack but were enemies nonetheless. The bigger battles were elsewhere. He was frustrated by the blighted countryside. The food that his forces needed had gone. The young men were gone. Every living thing was as grey and sullen as the sky.

The citizens of Parma paid the price of his dissatisfaction. He allowed his brother, Lucius, free rein upon the women and children of the town. If the Boii had returned south from their new home in Bohemia they could hardly have taken greater vengeance. The legionaries burnt, raped and enslaved; their victims received none of the rights of Romans that Caesar had granted. Cicero luxuriated in denouncing the lust of Lucius's men and the cruelty of Lucius himself. Decimus wrote a letter to Cicero of two surviving words, *Parmenses miserrimos.*

The twin towns, united at their birth one hundred and forty years before, varyingly tested by Caesar and Pompey, became like lumps of bloody meat on a skewer. On the Roman road that ran through them, through the rivers that ran by, warring Roman armies made camps, held different sections, pushed slowly one way and another. Antony used his cavalry to taunt and provoke. His divided opponents preferred to wait. There was no high point in Mutina from which Decimus could watch. He had to rely on the river boat reports.

Antony began moving his forces against the approach of Pansa, hoping to defeat the fresh reinforcements before facing battle with the veterans of Octavian and Hirtius. Pansa's troops had experience of neither battle nor the marshlands where Antony was preparing to fight. They were spirited and patriotic, just as Cicero had claimed to the senate, but that was all.

On both sides of the *Via Aemilia* as it left Bononia, amid tall reeds and hidden islands, Antony's men waited for the recruits to pass the tiny town of Forum Gallorum, barely more than a staging post. It was a day of hail. The sky clouded the water. By the time that Pansa's scouts had spotted the first metal among the swaying leaves and insects of early spring, it was too late. Antony's trap was set.

Cries for help quickly reached Hirtius and Octavian who sent reinforcements to their untried reinforcers. Within a few hundred yards there were soon three separate battles, the first on the narrow raised road, the second and third in the marshes either side. Antony gained the first advantage. Visible on the solid ground he fought at the head of his own troops. Invisible in the mud his men fought viciously, sword to sword and shield to shield. Even Antony's cavalry, an unlikely advantage in a swamp, was able to make misery for Pansa's recruits, his tiny African horses able to twist and turn like the midge clouds around their heads. Pansa himself was wounded though not, it seemed at first, too seriously.

Antony was the winner. The trap had been a triumph. But his first thought had to be for the siege back at Mutina. Retreating as a victor, he met Hirtius's veterans advancing towards him. This time the advantage was with the fresh, closely formed legions of the senate. Caesar's famed *Legio Martia* scattered Antony's troops through the same icy marshes where they had successfully hidden. Only with great difficulty did the survivors return to their main besieging camp.

Antony seemed at this point to be defeated. Good news travelled fast – to Mutina and to Rome. Hirtius wrote to the senate. Galba, Decimus's fellow assassin, wrote a plain man's account of events to Cicero who, in turn, delivered a final triumphant *Philippic*. The senate handed prizes to its generals. Octavian was hailed as *imperator*, the title of his dead father, for doing little more than watching the small force that Antony had left behind. Cicero reported Pansa's wound as bravery not a loss.

Decimus was less excited. In Mutina he needed food more than praise. He was all too dependent on Octavian, his formal friend and most vindictive enemy. He then heard that Pansa had unexpectedly died. If any force were to destroy Antony as the senate had demanded, he and Octavian, Caesar's secondary and primary heir, his killer and his would-be successor would have to fight closely together. Decimus expected little and doubted everything.

His doubt was soon justified. Octavian, with Hirtius beside him on the senate's behalf, would have no better opportunity than this to relieve Mutina. He did nothing. He waited. Antony saw the hesitation as an opportunity and struck first, ordering his weary survivors, some ten thousand men, back against the senatorial camp. Mud rose around the rivers. Fields were swamps of slime. Lead shots, shaped like acorns, sharpened with inscriptions of abuse, flew from both sides' slings.

Decimus watched from Mutina's walls. The sight of Caesar's veterans willing to kill each other in new causes, Antony's against Octavian's, was good for an assassin to see. He joined the battle himself. The killing, conducted in a terrible silence, was as close and intense as any could remember from their shared days under Caesar, giving sword or taking sword, tasting mud, sweat and blood.

His fellow assassin, Pontius Aquila, Decimus's banker and the man who would not stand for Caesar's triumph, fell somewhere around the leaking brick ponds where sheep were once dipped and soldiers hid. His family estates around Naples stayed with Servilia. He became the second assassin to die.

Galba survived. So, for a while, did his vivid reports. Various self-serving accounts of advantage and valour were carried to those who wanted them. The confusion of Decimus himself was the closest to anything certain. Hirtius, till recently Caesar's invalid ghost-writer, was said to have been killed in combat close to Antony's own command tent. Octavian was credited with leading the rescue of his body, a story that hugely helped his reputation: hitherto and afterwards Caesar's heir had few such stories.

The senate forces, despite the loss of both their consuls, seemed again close to victory until again Antony surprised his enemies. He chose suddenly to end the battle of Mutina and retreat. He feared losing the loyalty of his legionaries when Octavian, with the name of Caesar, was so near. He saw bigger battles in the future and his place in them too much at risk.

Fearing also that Pansa's forces would regroup without their commander, and that he too might be encircled and besieged, Antony looked about him and took the long view. His officers objected. He overruled them, abandoned the broken walls and withdrew north along the *Via Aemilia*, battered by his enemies' assaults but still in the bigger fight.

Gradually the fighting ceased. Slowly the river waters took back hold of the ground. Both Antony's and Decimus's forces were left badly weakened, Antony's by defections from Caesar's former legions to Caesar's victorious heir, Decimus's by starvation and disease during the siege. Octavian alone had an army whose strength was growing.

Decimus still wanted victory over Antony, although fearfully, pleadingly in a letter to Cicero at the end of April, and with little confidence of the support to make it secure. Antony's aim was only to escape, his hopes dependent on help from the approaching legions of Lepidus, Pollio and Plancus, other players nominally directed by the senate but with a large personal stake in the aftermath of the Ides of March.

Decimus's last chance to complete his duty for senate and assassins alike was to defeat Antony decisively before he could appeal to these potential allies, killing, if he could, the man whom he should have helped to kill a year before. He saw the chance and took it. His spirits rose. He briefly occupied the ruins of Parma before setting off in pursuit.

Ahead of him he anticipated the first firm success since his arrival in Cisalpine Gaul. Behind him was the added encouragement of good news from Rome, that he was the new hero of the city, that Caesar's secondary heir on the Ides of March, had the ever more ingratiating support of Cicero and the senate. He had the command of all forces opposing Antony. He was promised a triumph through the streets when he returned.

Nor were his fellow assassins forgotten. The sons of the fallen hero Pontius Aquila were rewarded with a public statue of their father and a repayment of the money he had spent on the senate's behalf. Decimus, often so easily prone to depression, did not stop to think whether his optimism was too high, too soon, the praise of himself perilously great.

He did not stay thoughtless for long. While he was chasing Antony and contemplating his triumph, Octavian, by what was soon clear as careless contrast, learnt that his own reward from the senate was nothing more than accusations that he had acted only for himself. There were even rumours that he had organised personally the deaths of both Pansa and Hirtius in order to gain one of their vacant consulships. Cicero, it was said, would be his perfect colleague.

Octavian's soldiers were outraged. Octavian himself hardly needed to be. While the declining forces of Decimus and Antony moved north and west, the one in tired pursuit of the other, the expanding army of their rival, roused by the slights to Caesar's heir and the better prospects they perceived for their own pay, moved south to Rome. Octavian no longer even pretended to help Decimus.

'Parmenses miserrimos' were Decimus's only words to survive from the shattered home town of his fellow assassin. As he wrote in a letter to Cicero from Dertona, a week later and a hundred miles west, Octavian was neither taking orders from him nor giving orders to his own troops. This almost autonomous army, which contained all the legions originally raised by Caesar and one of the new legions raised by Pansa, knew what it wanted.

The son of Caesar, emulating and avenging his father, crossed the Rubicon, marched down the *Via Flaminia* and entered Rome. The praetor in charge of the city greeted him by committing suicide. Three legions, formally at the disposal of the senate, immediately defected to him. The consulship was the minimum that these soldiers would demand for Octavian. Hirtius and Pansa could have grand tombs in the Field of Mars; the undertakers of Rome charged no fee out of respect for such heroes.

At the other end of the road from Cisalpine Gaul, Decimus found his glory fading fast. Lepidus, Caesar's Master of Horse and guardian of the Forum at his death, had already joined Antony. His troops had given him no choice. Mutina had not left Caesar's former forces wanting more of each other's blood. Plancus, ever the diplomat, toyed with Decimus for a few further months before Pollio arrived from Spain and preferred his troops' view over the senate's too. Any enemy of Cicero was liable to be Pollio's friend. Antony was safe.

Decimus tried to counter with diplomatic rhetoric of his own. He attacked Antony for enlisting convicts and snatching soldiers randomly from the streets, He gained no advantage. His troops peeled away. Unlike the gladiators he had brought to the party on the Ides of March the legionaries were free men. They could seek any commander who claimed a legal title – and there were many from which to choose.

Decimus still wanted very much to be the hero, to be loved and respected in some small part of the way that Caesar had been. Gradually his aspirations fell. He looked in on himself. He was without money. He was in debt. He feared for his family. His mother, Sempronia, was as vulnerable as she had been when falling into the Catiline conspiracy twenty years before – still glamorous but with less love of politics. Decimus wanted repayment of his personal expenditure at Mutina most of all.

The dinner companion who had flattered Caesar to go to his death, who had first seen the threat to the assassins from Antony, was falling from conqueror to fugitive, albeit one backed by awards of the senate and the words of Cicero. He headed eastwards, with such of his forces as remained true to the assassins' cause, hoping to reach Marcus Brutus and Gaius Cassius in Macedonia or wherever they might be.

He protested his fearlessness in letters home but the tone was of a man terrified. He had the promise of his triumph, his procession through winding streets, his chariot ride up the Capitoline hill from the Forum, but he could not claim it. He could hardly dream of matching Pompey's triumph or the heroic marble statue where Caesar died (no one ever did) but he faced a long march on which to think of his lesser honours and how his enemies were trying to take from him even those.

Antony, demanding more from his men and new allies, put out the word that Decimus Brutus be killed. The death of another assassin would rally further the troops. Its manner would depend on who had the opportunity to deliver it, quick or slow, maybe a better death from a Gaul sympathetic to a slayer of Caesar, a worse from one vengeful against a man who had helped Caesar slay so many tens of thousands of Gauls.

Decimus was the first assassin to know that he was hunted. Trebonius did not know until Dolabella and the Samarian came. Pontius Aquila might possibly have been a prize target for Antony's men at Mutina but in the tight press of battle a specific prize was a luxury; a legionary killed the man ahead or might more easily be killed himself. Decimus was a man marked out for vengeance.

He was no Epicurean. He had all the old Roman reasons to fear death, the dark unknown where exceptional crime (and assassination might well be seen as such) might be exceptionally punished. Ghosts and gods awaited him. He had the time to fear death, to look back at his life, to await the knock on the door at morning or night, the swift blow if he was lucky. Plancus protected him for a while. An Alpine chief called Camelus heard Antony's order. He saw his interest in killing Decimus as the soldiers of Egypt had seen the death of Pompey. Nothing more was reported. Decimus Brutus was the third assassin to die.

9

PARMENSIS AT SEA

The Young Cicero Reading, Vincenzo Foppa (c1464)

Cassius Parmensis knew how to flatter a fellow poet: read, praise, quote and praise again. In the summer after the death of Decimus, in June 43 BC, he wrote Cicero a letter recalling congratulatory lines that the philosopher, politician (and would be poet) had written once about his own defeat of the Roman rebel, Catiline. Cicero had then shamelessly (and crudely) congratulated the state for his own great consulate, calling for soldiers' arms to give way to the civilian toga, military laurels to the language of debate: *cedant arma togae, concedat laurea linguae.* The defeat of Antony, wrote the man from Parma, was yet another Ciceronian triumph, fit to match his suppression of that power-grabbing, debt-cancelling Catiline conspiracy twenty years before. In Rome's new 'darkest hour', he declared,

Cicero's civilian words had proved themselves again more potent than everyone else's arms, bringing freedom to the city that was so tightly fused with Cicero's very life.

When he wrote this letter Parmensis was in Cyprus, on a remote promontory of its northern coast called Onion Point, his mind somewhat detached from events in Italy in his absence. One advantage of such literary flattery was that it was, by its very nature, unreal. To students of oratory it was advice called *captatio benevolentiae*, the winning of favour before business began, much recommended before judges and juries. Cicero deemed it an essential tool of the advocate's art, which did not mean that he any the less appreciated its direction towards himself.

Cyprus was a small and faraway place. Parmensis was hardly honoured to be there. To a sailor from Italy it was the last island before the wealthy province of Syria. To Roman governors it was a very modest prize, only recently and uncertainly a part of their empire, brought to them first by Fulvia's first husband, Clodius, in a row about his capture by pirates, taxed hard by Porcia's father, Cato, handed over by Caesar to the Ptolemies of Egypt but of no consistent significance to any but perfume-makers harvesting sweet marjoram around the birthplace claimed for Venus.

To a lover of Homer it was maybe the *Odyssey's* most eastern island, the land of Circe's magical transformation of his men into pigs and her strict instruction to him not to kill any cows belonging to the Sun God if he wanted to reach home. Probably not even Odysseus, not in anyone's imagination, had reached Onion Point, a scrubland peninsula that pointed up to Asia like an insulting finger. All around bobbed the warships that Parmensis was commanding on behalf of Gaius Cassius, a mixed fleet built, extorted and stolen from the richer islands and towns of the surrounding coasts.

Parmensis's praise of Cicero from his Cypriot base was harmless, and maybe even essential, but his analysis lacked the latest news. His mind was not where a well-informed man's would have been, on the resurgence of Antony, whom he presumed to be defeated and in flight. It was fixed on Dolabella who was less dangerous but much closer, the main threat to Syria, maybe to Italy too, some said.

Parmensis was confident that Dolabella was doomed. Four assassins, Cassius, Tillius Cimber, Turullius and he himself had all been in pursuit of Trebonius's torturer. Success would soon be theirs. His own mind was on the future – beyond any fears of his own and out into the sunshine of the old republic where power would once again be spread and a man from Parma might have his share.

After quoting Cicero's poetry as though it were a masterpiece and promoting himself for advancement in Cicero's Rome, Parmensis set out over fat columns of prose his personal achievements in the assassins' cause. Star-struck, proud to play a part, he hoped that 'the greatest of former consuls' would be even more impressed with him than he had been on the Ides of March.

As an assassin, in the service of his fellow assassins, he went on to explain himself – with rather more pedantry than poetry. He had launched all the ships that he could find. Finding was as much an admiral's art as building. The eastern Mediterranean was full of former warships that might be future warships, wooden hulls that were flotsam like any other wood since only trade ships, full of pottery, stone and iron, ended in the sand and rock of the sea bed.

He had pressed gangs of rowers into service despite the obstinacy of the local communities, particularly that of Tarsus, a nuisance one hundred and fifty miles to the north-east, close enough for him to threaten again if he chose. He had paid these crews: Romans did not use slaves to row. He had handed over to Cimber the task of persuading Dolabella's captains to change sides – and had come to Cyprus before setting off to join Cassius's already large fleet in blockading Dolabella himself in Laodicea, the closest town on what the Greeks called Syria's 'white coast'.

There would, he predicted, be no need for a battle. Lines of well-drilled triremes, well supplied, their rowers well rotated, their captains keeping close formation, would keep cargo ships away. Grand houses and tombs, once glories above ground, had been made rock for an impassable underwater wall. Gaius Cassius himself controlled the approaches by land. Laodicea was laid out with many fine streets and squares, libraries and baths but, without food through its fabulous gates, Dolabella would be starved into submission.

This was a very satisfactory letter for Cicero to read. In fear of too much success for the assassins the senate had rejected his plan to put Cassius in full charge of the Asian and Syrian campaign, preferring to wait till the consuls had liberated Decimus at Mutina. With the consuls dead and Decimus gone, Gaius Cassius had taken over the hunt without instruction. The senate had accepted reality and given Cassius the job. That was very satisfactory too.

Power's balance was shifting. While the western front had crumbled, the eastern was looking strong for the killers of Caesar. Brutus had captured Antony's brother, Gaius, in Macedonia and had him as a hostage. At the same time as the Senate had elevated Cassius it had recognised reality over rhetoric and given Sextus an official naval command. Dolabella would not have long left in his dissolute life.

The number of assassins was increasing, not just the number of their supporters. In Asia the mood was approaching that of the evening of the Ides of March itself. Dolabella's man, Cornelius Lentulus, still in charge of the province, was just one of those pretending to have wielded a dagger when they had not. It was a mark of rising honour to have heard one's name resound from Caesar's waxen image on its turning spit in the Forum – or to say one heard it.

Lentulus saw pretence as the best way to keep his job. He too wrote to Cicero, reminding him how, after Trebonius's terrible death, he had raised men and money for Cassius and had formed his own fleet to curb Dolabella's ability to combine with Antony in Italy. He had endured the obstruction of the great naval masters of Rhodes, putting Rome's interests before his family, quoting from Euripides to intensify his point.

He had spent his own money, he pleaded, minting his own coins without which Cassius would have been unable to do his glorious duty. Lentulus claimed no ambition for himself (enthusiasm for liberty had been nothing but a trial to him, he added) but, with Cicero being so influential in Rome, he would like an extended time in office to recoup his considerable outgoings. This seemed not much to ask.

Meanwhile in elegant Laodicea, Dolabella had no such eyes for the future. Blockaded by the assassins on land and at sea, his walls battered, his guards bribed, he could see barely beyond the end of each day. He had to be hoping that Cassius had neither a vicious mind like his own nor his own Samarian. Unprepared to take the risk, or maybe seeing no one left to lie to, Trebonius's torturer decided on suicide as the best available death, stretching out his neck for the sword of his guard.

10

BASILUS MEETS HIS SLAVES

The Massacres of the Triumvirate, Antoine Caron (1566)

Cicero's failure to be invited to 'the dinner on the Ides of March' meant that he was still safe in Italy, only an honorary assassin, able to hope that Octavian would destroy Antony as Cassius had so successfully destroyed Dolabella. While Antony and his creature were, for all important political purposes, the same 'foul traitor' to the Roman state, Octavian, by contrast, could be humoured, he thought, contained and educated by an older, wiser man.

The assassins who had wielded daggers increasingly saw the futility of this conceit. Cicero wanted to be above the stage pulling strings and balancing his puppets' power, still joking that 'the young boy Octavian should be honoured, lifted up and lifted off', arguing more practically that Brutus should come back to Italy since the threat to their shared interests was greater there.

Brutus was tempted. Bad news from Rome added to his desire to return. Porcia, after months of stinking summer sickness, had died. The fever from the Tiber had taken her. The willingness of Cato's daughter to suffer torture to keep a secret had never been tested. Suddenly she was a mere part of her family history, her support for him only in the past.

Devastated for his own family (though his mother may not have been too distressed), Brutus still knew better than to enter the Italian trap. Cicero urged him to use his wife's death to steel himself to be even more a servant of the people. Brutus knew that, while Caesar's heir was still alive, this service had to be abroad. Octavian was ever more clearly an avenger. Revenge had brought him both pleasure and power. He had an instinct for risk. He was growing tired of jokes about his youth, from Cicero and anyone else, particularly unamused that 'lifted up and off' had a double meaning of both his elevation and his murder.

Even if Brutus had dared to return, the assassins were in no way organised to meet him. They were scattered, Basilus hidden deep in Picenum in a household notorious for his brutality to his slaves, Parmensis at sea, few knowing each other's whereabouts, none with control of troops. Cicero still sought to deal with the dictator's heir by charm and deceit.

Cicero even hoped that, when Octavian was elevated to be consul, his own old age might fit him not just to be a tutor but also to have the free second consul's place. Perhaps he was buying time but his hopes lasted longer than the facts should have allowed. Only at the end of July did he write to Brutus admitting that, like Decimus before him, he had lost control of Octavian. This was by then a statement of the extremely obvious. It was Cicero's last letter to Brutus.

Octavian had by then begun his march on Rome. Mutina and Parma lay behind him. Antony was behind him too, but not as a threat, barely more than a supplicant. Caesar's heir had a cold eye on the next slice of his inheritance. He crossed the empty rivers and fields, through relics of marsh warfare in mud cracked and dry, his progress rapid. In his final miles along the *Via Flaminia* he was supported by two more legions newly arrived from Africa.

He met no opposition. His army camped on the Field of Mars where, only a decade before he had exercised horses as child. In the middle of August, with the only force in the city and the power to demand the consulship from the senate, he took Rome's highest office, aged 19. It was not Cicero but Quintus Pedius, the still safely obscure son of his great aunt Julia, who became his colleague – and immediately put his name to a law that made vengeance against the assassins the duty of every Roman.

Octavian ensured that Antony knew of the change that was coming. A much bigger change between them was ahead. Letters, mediators and informants travelled the road faster than soldiers. Signals shone in the nights. The *Lex Pedia* ended the amnesty that Antony and Cicero had passed through the senate in the Temple of Tellus. Those who had killed Caesar were criminals. A court was summoned to establish exactly who they were, to make a legal list from the names that had resounded from the dripping waxwork at the funeral.

This time no holder of those names was on the Capitoline to note his new distinction: Marcus Brutus, Gaius Cassius, Tillius Cimber, Pacuvius Labeo, Lucius Minucius Basilus, Cassius Parmensis, Rubrius Ruga, Sextius Naso, Servius Sulpicius Galba, Marcus Spurius, Decimus Turullius. Names appeared of sympathisers too: Gnaeus Domitius Ahenobarbus, another pardoned devotee of Pompey, was on the list that he had failed to reach on the funeral day. Few knew whether he had held a dagger or not.

The charge was the thing. Every magistrate of the wider Roman world was required to discover and arrest those listed to face the new justice. Antony and Octavian, hostile to each other still, had been forced together as one in that command. From this point on, Dolabella became a noble executioner of Trebonius. The Alpine killer of Decimus Brutus may not have known of the *Lex Pedia* before despatching his victim but Camelus, whatever means of death he had chosen, had acted within the law.

With the speed of bad news every assassin learnt he was a hunted man. He might be tried and found guilty whether he was in Rome,

in the empire or beyond. There was no defence in law or philosophy. Some found new confidence in the rightness of their action.
Others shrunk away.

Some found shelter in their own minds. Those, like Gaius Cassius
and Cassius Parmensis, who were Epicureans had conquered the
fear of death or said they had. They claimed both a better life as
a result and greater strength of mind to help when their country
needed them. The test of their belief was becoming harder.

Caesar himself had not feared death. His hunted killers would
quickly discover whether or not they feared it, how much and maybe even why. All assassins, whatever the certainty of their beliefs,
had to avoid their hunters for as long as the *Lex Pedia* stood if they
were to stay alive.

Households and friends were at risk too. Parmensis had maybe already brought down the brutal reprisals upon the town of his
family. He could not know how much his name had been the cause
of Lucius Antonius's license to rape and murder in Parma. Feeling
guilty or not, he would in future have to become more cautious
when seeking ships and cash among the Rhodians and the Tarsians;
Decimus Turullius too. There was a price on their heads that any
betrayer might claim, punishment for any who concealed them.

The safest place for the assassins was with the eastern armies of
Brutus and Cassius but the open sea had also become the haven of
those opposed to monarchy. That was the proud message on the
silver coins which Sextus was producing for his campaign to control the waters around Sicily. Parmensis was in the same element.
In every place on the Tellus map, except for those with the most
devoted slaves and friends, there was no safety.

In Rome itself, Octavian was the assassins' judge, jury and
relentless pursuer. He held the initiative and set the agenda. Antony,
resilient in the foothills of the Alps and reinforced by Lepidus and
former soldiers of Caesar, was ready to become his ally until he had
a better plan. Decimus was legally dead and Antony had the credit
for that. Octavian could afford to be generous.

Brutus and Cassius were tried and convicted in their very

visible absence. Two of Octavian's rising young supporters, Marcus Agrippa and Lucius Cornificius, had the honour of prosecuting empty chairs. Galba, the vivid reporter of Mutina, his wife more appreciated by Caesar than his bid to be consul had been, was executed. He was the fourth assassin to die.

Otherwise, the war had to come first. Basilus, Cimber, the Cascas, Cassius Parmensis and the rest could wait.

Cicero's non-attendance at the assassins' dinner, his jokes temporarily forgotten, was rewarded with permission from Octavian to leave Rome for the south. Brutus wrote a letter reflecting on Cicero's folly, love of flattery and fearfulness of death. Cicero wrote a grateful letter to the new consul thanking him for his forgiveness and protection.

* * *

Octavian did not stay still. The new consul, backed by some 50,000 men, took the mountain road, the smooth sections and the rough, back again north, back through the familiar towns on the *Via Flaminia*, Nequinum, Fulginiae, Cales, a massive display of intimidation, a marching proof of his own equality with Antony who had so long treated him as a boy. The bears and eagles were the same as those that the travellers from Parma saw before the assassination; the people were hungrier and more fearful.

Only the legionaries were richer, each with a personal reward of ten years' pay and the promise of another ten and land on which to spend it. In the fields before Ariminum the veterans of war saw where their gains could be settled in peace. They turned up into Cisalpine Gaul, west along the *Via Aemilia* as it stretched out over fields of grain. Faventia, Claterna, the signs of the assassins' war ever clearer as Bononia, Forum Gallorum, Mutina and the massacre site of Parma approached.

It was October. Some men had fresh memories of this road in April, the cold wind in the reeds, the bodies in the mud of the marsh. The summer's end and the harvests in the barns were signs of the wealth that would soon be theirs from the land they had earnt.

Octavian's army crossed the twin branches of the Idex river, the low flat land between the streams, and reached Bononia, the old Gallic town last held by the doomed troops of Pansa. A few miles further on they halted. They camped, the same camps that all legions made in all places. There was no safe ground. That was the assumption always safest to make. Ahead and approaching was an army of legions almost equally as strong as their own. Antony and Lepidus were leading their men down into what was soon to be the greatest concentration of forces loyal to Julius Caesar since the dictator's death.

Mediators had gone ahead but much was unsettled. The result might still have been war. If Lepidus and Antony had wanted to confront Octavian, this was their time. Instead all prepared to do a deal. A low-lying island in the River Rhenus, accessible by three bridges, had been identified in advance as a place where the three could talk without fear of one being assassinated by another, or one by two or two by one.

Their men occupied the banks. The will of all those watching the island was clear. They did not want to fight fellow soldiers of Caesar. They did want to destroy the killers of Caesar. They had their promised pay. Civil war had gone on too long. They wanted the farms that had been promised for their retirement. The men on the island were the ones who would make good that promise.

All three had their own loyalists. But of the three Octavian was the most credibly committed to those wants. Ruthless vengeance and high pay for enforcing it was what Octavian brought to the negotiating table. Not only his own men saw the value of that.

The wills and wants of the men about to negotiate were more divided than those of their soldiers, their trust in each other lower. Lepidus, the most emollient of the three, approached the first bridge with three hundred men, left them to protect his back and crossed over to the island first. He organised a search and waved his red commander's cloak as a sign for Octavian and Antony to follow. Each left his own force of three hundred men to guarantee a swift exit if the talking failed, if the negotiators needed protection from outsiders or each other.

In the middle of the island, in plain sight from the bridges and banks, the three sat together in council, Octavian in the centre because he was consul, an immediate cause of objection from Antony. The conference lasted from morning till night over two days.

They divided jobs and provinces between them out, for all the momentous illegality, those were, in many ways, the least important decisions that they took. To Octavian came Sicily, Sardinia and Corsica, most of which were under the sway of Sextus and not theirs to give, and that part of North Africa which was Roman, quite a small part. Sextus himself was condemned in his absence to appear before the court for Caesar's killers, another piece of wishful thinking; he became another honorary assassin, subject to the full penalties of his new status. Antony was to keep most of Gaul; Lepidus took Spain. Division of the east was delayed until the destruction of the armies of the assassins, the prime purpose of what became the Pact of Bononia.

The three men needed new legal titles to their authority, not dictatorship, not even a shared dictatorship, the word which, of all Caesar's legacies, was liked the least. Octavian contentedly gave up the consulship for which he had fought so hard. His cousin, Quintus Pedius did not need to be removed from office after attaching his name to Octavian's law, he was sick and dying. So was the consulate itself which would never again be what it had been in the past. The highest honour of Rome, the highest office so fiercely contested since Junius Brutus expelled the Tarquins, was awarded in advance for years ahead, on an island in the River Rhenus, by the decisions of three men who did not want it for themselves.

They instead decided to be *tresviri rei publicae constituendae*, a triumvirate for the regulation of the state, a shared responsibility with the single aim that Octavian had set since hearing Caesar's will, remorseless revenge against the assassins of his father, against anyone who had supported them and against anyone with the money to finance his vengeance. This was an oligarchy of the very fewest. No other title mattered than that of triumvir. No agenda counted more than that of Octavian. Nothing mattered more for life or death than whether a man was on the list of the 'proscribed', those condemned without recourse to law at Bononia.

The troops on both banks applauded – and prepared to march back again down the *Via Aemilia* and *Via Flaminia* to Rome. The rich lands of Ariminum, on the hinge of the journey, were the first among those already allotted as rewards for their rivalry. With their booty behind them they retraced the ever more familiar road, watched by the men, women and children whose lives were about to be destroyed.

Also allotted at Bononia were the first responsibilities to pay the triumvirs' bills. The first names on the proscription lists were carried ahead of the troops so that the extortion and killing could begin before the victims could escape. For every death there was a promised reward. When the senators of the Carinae and the Palatine first sensed the truth, hearing rumours, seeing signs of blood and absence, none could be certain that he and his family would not be next.

Any pattern was hidden at first. Soldiers invaded houses at night and seemed to select at random, seeking heads that they could exchange for bounty, slashing men as they ate and leaving only bodies on the couches. The scale of the assault was just as unknown. Hurried advice from Pedius that next morning there would be an official list of only seventeen names to be killed for cash did little except hasten the death, through shame, it was said, of the reluctant consul himself.

The massed people of Rome began to know what had happened only when, on separate days in November, each of the triumvirs led his bodyguard and a single legion into the city. There was official celebration before open slaughter. Pedius had either concealed or not known his masters' next move. One hundred and thirty more names were listed for executions that would be legal wherever and by whomever they were conducted.

The senate sent for Etruscan prophets. The oldest of them said that the Tarquins were coming back and that all Romans would be slaves except the senior seer himself. He then closed his mouth and held his breath till he was dead, the unlikeliness of this last act removing nothing from its power.

At the end of November the people's assembly passed a new law under the name of one of its tribunes, Publius Titius. The *Lex Titia* put the Pact of Bononia into law, the titles of the triumvirs, the allocations of their provinces and legions and the proscription of those they wanted dead. Unlike under the *Lex Pedia*, there were to be no courts, no fixed crimes. Nothing mattered but the name on the lists of the proscribed, the cash reward for every head delivered, every name ticked off. It was legal cover for vengeance on a massive scale.

The triumvirs published a decree, a call for the hunting of the innocent and the guilty without distinction. It was a terror. The pursuit of named public enemies was deemed of necessity to be in the public good, for the clear benefit of those whose names were not on the list. With war looming against the assassins abroad it was vital to have no traitors at home. People were asked to understand that the list was not a hostile act; it protected the innocent against agents of the state who might otherwise exceed their orders; it made the public safe.

To no one's surprise, least of all his own, Cicero, wealthy and preeminent among the honorary assassins, was among the names highest on the proscription list. Antony had every personal reason to hate him: hardly any politician in history had been so abused in speech and Cicero had also ordered the strangulation of Antony's mother's husband during the conspiracy of Catiline twenty years before. The triumvirs made their choices: and it was central to the pact between them that they did not veto each other's damned. Lepidus's own brother, Lucius Aemilius Paullus, found his name on the white wooden boards throughout the city, as did Antony's uncle, Lucius Julius Caesar, both names visible proof that loyalty to the newly defined good of Rome outweighed family ties.

This was one of the limits on Octavian's power, he could not save those whose names were proscribed at Bononia. Cicero had wanted to be one of the assassins; Octavian let him have his wish. Escape might still have been possible. Cicero could probably have sailed to join Brutus and Cassius, the Caecilii and the Cascas, Tillius Cimber, Turullius and Parmensis. He considered and prepared for flight but, depressed beyond action or even words, stayed in Italy.

A minor politician, with a soldier to assist him, sought the money, honour and favour of bringing this much desired head to Antony. Popilius Laenas, whom Cicero had once defended in court, had news that his sometime lawyer was travelling near Naples. He set off down the *Via Appia* in pursuit.

The task was not hard, the route well travelled, the prey well known. First Popilius found the young son of Cicero's brother, Quintus, who had gone back to their villa to get extra cash. Betrayed and tortured, the boy did not betray his father but Quintus, a soldier for Caesar and sometime enthusiast for Lucretius, quickly surrendered. Philosophy, more than his skill in a fight, was his friend in the end. The nervous bounty seekers agreed that father and son be executed simultaneously. Cicero's own son, away studying in Athens, missed the horror.

A former family slave revealed the route of Cicero himself. His hunters found him in a closed litter on a nearby sea shore path, exhausted but acting just as though he were on a holiday. In his hand he held a Greek tragedy, Euripides's *Medea*, an appropriate text on the subject of raging vengeance and slow and painful death. He stretched out his neck and asked for quickness, hoping that Popilius and his man were already well practised, seeing their hesitation, jibing how much worse it would have been for everyone if they had come to him first, if they had had no experience at all. It took both men and three sawing sword strokes before the hacked head was ready to be exchanged for reward. They took at least one hand too.

The Vengeance of Fulvia, Francisco Maura y Montaner (1888)

News of the new avenging spread down the *Via Appia* to the south and to the camps of Cassius and Brutus across the sea. Antony, more than doubling the usual reward to killers of the proscribed, nailed Cicero's head and hands on the ships' prows in the Forum from where he had delivered so many of the words he called his Thunderbolts. The target of the *Philippics* would take down from time to time the face that had delivered them and look at it while he ate. Popilius hoped to advance his career with a commemorative statue of himself. Most killers preferred to claim their cash anonymously as the law allowed.

Antony's wife, Fulvia, continued her path to the extremes of notoriety by avenging both her first husband, Clodius, whom Cicero had violently abused in court, and Antony, her third. Her life lay as much in insurgency against the state as did Porcia's in sacrifice for Brutus and the values of the old. She commanded the pricking with a hairpin of the dead orator's tongue and that the disloyal former slave who betrayed him should eat his own roasted flesh. Later famed for having 'nothing female but her sex', she coveted another neighbour's house and had the man's head hung above his door.

These reports came first as shocks. Not all were believed. Soon there were so many that only a numbing horror remained. Rome became a city of disembodied heads. A corpse with all its extremities connected was the rare body of a man killed by mistake, wasted work for the bounty-hunters whose skills were becoming as honed as even Cicero might have wished.

Pretenders died with the guilty and the guiltless. Trebonius's deputy, Lentulus Cornelius, one of those who claimed ambitiously to have wielded a dagger, was put on the list and killed. Caesennius, a rich man who claimed not to be proscribed, was forced to read his name aloud from the soldier's list; he lost his head on a busy street by the Forum while his mouth was still moving.

Caesar's assailant, Quintus Ligarius, so sick at the time of the assassination, was still available to die. Cicero's well-remembered success in gaining clemency for Ligarius from Julius Caesar remained a permanent reproach to Octavian's spirit of vendetta. The new Caesar was not going to cry for him as the old Caesar had done; if he was anxious about his burial, he should ask the crows to be kind.

Flight was the safest option. Escapers could live to fight on another day, and maybe hope to return when the madness was over. Some fled directly to Brutus and Cassius. Sextus too received newcomers warmly, paying those who brought proscribed men to him twice what they would have received in the abattoir of the Forum. This added to his status as the most distinguished honorary assassin, almost the third man on the side opposed to the pact of Bononia.

In Italy, vengeance was a virus everywhere throughout the Tellus map – from the Sicilian tip to the Parman approaches, from the end of the *Via Appia* to the beginning of the *Aemilia*. Death by beheading came to those guilty by association and to the wholly innocent. It came up and down Rome's rigid hierarchies, to slaves betraying their masters, slaves themselves betrayed. Wives ridded themselves of husbands. Soldiers searched marshes, sewers and cesspits, prodding randomly with spears, keeping their hands clean for the money that came from even the filthiest head on the list of the proscribed.

A man named Plotius was given away by the perfume with which he had made his hiding place more tolerable or attempted to mask his fear.

Another man, Icelius, had been one of the judges in the trial of Brutus and Cassius under the *Lex Pedia*. When every other judge cast a secret ballot to condemn, Icelius had voted publicly to acquit. In clear danger, his escape plan was to evade the guards at every city gate by joining the corpse-bearers under a dead body being carried to burial. He almost succeeded. The guards noticed that the number of bearers was greater than usual by one man but searched only the coffin to make sure that it was not somebody counterfeiting a corpse. The bearers themselves exposed Icelius as not being a member of their trade. Only then did the bounty-hunters claim his head.

Terror became ruthless business both for the triumvirs who had forty-three legions to pay and for the killers who profited from that need. There was a commerce of murder. Lenders of money feared their debtors, parents their heirs, farmers those who wanted their fields. Men might be scared to death, their spirits deemed to escape their bodies through their noses or other holes in their heads. Dolabella received a pardon, though too late for his debts to be relieved or anyone to benefit by this *post mortem* shift in his status.

The very rich might sometimes escape – by massive payments in lieu of their heads, by buying the loyalty of protectors or by loyalty long earnt before. It was not too much trouble for Antony and Fulvia to find names to replace those who had bought their erasure from the lists. The eloquent and wealthy, Messalla Corvinus, recommended to Brutus by Cicero, was proscribed, possibly by mistake but did not wait to check if that were so. Favonius, the wild philosopher before the Ides of March, escaped to join Brutus and Cassius in an assassins' war he had once so vehemently opposed.

The citizens of Cales on the *Via Flaminia*, sufferers from so much military movement since the Ides of March, fortified their walls and successfully protected a generous patron of their town. Sittius's life and freedom came at the small cost of exile in his home. Lucilius Hirrus, despite a reputation for vanity and stupidity, at least in the view of Cicero, succeeded in forming a small army of tenants and slaves and escaping to the coast.

Nocte intempesta nostrum devenit domum, late in the night he came down to our house: the line of Cassius Parmensis that so fitted the fears of the time, survived for history within a collection by Pompey's antiquarian and anthologist, Marcus Terentius Varro whom Caesar had twice pardoned and then appointed to be master of Rome's public library. Antony, despite the objections of many of his own friends, ordered that Varro be proscribed and his personal library sold.

Varro stayed in Italy but went into hiding. The scholar who first described the Latin language, the geography of Italy and the year-by-year chronology of Roman history survived one of Rome's most desperate years. A man with a similar name was terrified into pinning up a public declaration that he was not the Varro on the proscription lists: he had learnt the lesson of Cinna the poet and did not mind the jokes at his anxiety.

It was the proscribed Varro who preserved Parmensis's line on night, in two sections of his *De Lingua Latina* about quiet times when normally nothing happened. Neither his own slaves, who copied his words and maps, nor those of his host betrayed him as he added to his more than seventy works, this, despite the danger of their being decapitated themselves and the promise of freedom if they complied with the law of Titius the tribune.

While some slaves protected their masters, those of Lucius Minucius Basilus did not. The assassin from Picenum who received Cicero's first joyful congratulations on the Ides of March liked to mutilate members of his household for offences to domestic order, a lopped ear or nose to encourage good behaviour. In past years any retaliation by a slave would have come at spectacular cost, a hundred dead for the courage of one. Under the rule of the triumvirs it was a legal duty to take revenge on Basilus – or it may have been an accident. Law had ceased to matter. *Lex Pedia* or *Lex Titia* or no law? So many distinctions had disappeared. His slaves killed him.

Quintus Ligarius and Lucius Basilus were the fifth and sixth assassins to die. The armies of the Triumvirs in Cisalpine Gaul and northern Italy got their pay.

* * *

Not until Julius Caesar's descendants were terrorising Rome in the next century did a writer find a way far enough into the human mind to comprehend what Octavian had bequeathed. Lucius Annaeus Seneca, politician, philosopher and playwright, survived, and sometimes prospered, in times of vicious tyranny, negotiating the reigns of Caligula and Claudius, living through exile, promoting the imperial power of Nero and writing plays which probed obsessive madness as none had ever done before. Among his finest works, probably the only one from the reign of Nero, was a *Thyestes*, the struggle of two mythical brothers for the throne of Mycenae, their curses, cruelties and boundless immoderation. This was a story that Parmensis and many others had used before, a tragedy of rampant revenge, reason overwhelmed, two men bound by sexual betrayals, incompatible passions to rule, dynastic ambition and by the capacity of one of them for vengeance vastly beyond that of anyone else on the stage.

There were already many ways to make this drama. Greek writers had sometimes started at the beginning of the story, the seduction by Thyestes of his brother Atreus's wife, her help to steal the golden ram that gave the keys to the kingdom of Mycenae. Or they might put Atreus's angry return to power in Act One, the exile of Thyestes in rags (Euripides loved a hero in rags: it was one of his signatures) and the victor's unextinguished dissatisfaction with any ordinary revenge.

The core was always the same. To Atreus the death was not enough. Death meant the 'end of suffering', an inadequate punishment for the brother whom he wanted to suffer. Killing was only for 'weak kings': Atreus wanted a man in fear to beg him for death. Regular horrors were for common experience. Atrocity had to escape from cliché. Thyestes had to be the unknowing eater of the flesh of his sons, his heirs, unknowing until Atreus produced the proof of their severed hands and heads. That would be the beginning of the terror. That had to be the centre of any *Thyestes*.

Great swathes of tragedy, every *Agamemnon, Iphigeneia, Electra, Orestes* by so many writers, all stemmed from the plot. Any *Thyestes* was the big beginning. Atreus was a cold killer, consumed by the application of power, who regretted only not pouring hot blood into his brother's mouth. Thyestes was a brutal sensualist, an avid consumer of power's fruits. Any gods were as absent as any Epicurean could imagine or desire.

Seneca set his play in the shadows of an imperial palace like the one which Octavian, when he made himself the Emperor Augustus, came to build on the Palatine hill. He stared into the minds of the two rivals in ways that no dramatist would equal before Shakespeare. He drew inspiration from artists of the past in Greek and in Latin. His face of Atreus dripped with blood, his face of Thyestes with oil from his hair. Seneca became master of the mind's most secret processes, of myth made real, of black claustrophobia and sickening slow motion.

Cassius Parmensis wrote his *Thyestes* a century before Seneca did. Octavian as implacable Atreus, Antony as the man of more ordinary flaws: that was one way but not the only way. There was never an only way. Parmensis's play did not survive. Some said it was stolen from him.

THRACE

Dyrrachium   Via Egnatia

MACEDONIA   ■Philippi

Brundisium   ● Apollonia

THASOS   Melas Gulf

GREECE   ● Troy

CORCYRA   Pergamum

AEGEAN SEA   LESBOS

● Actium

LEUCAS   Smyrna

CEPHALLENIA   Ephesus

ATHENS   SAMOS

Corinth ●

IONIAN SEA   COS

CRETE

EID·MAR

MEDITERRANEAN SEA

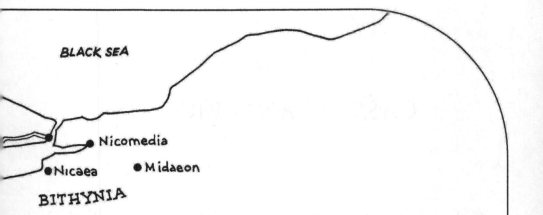

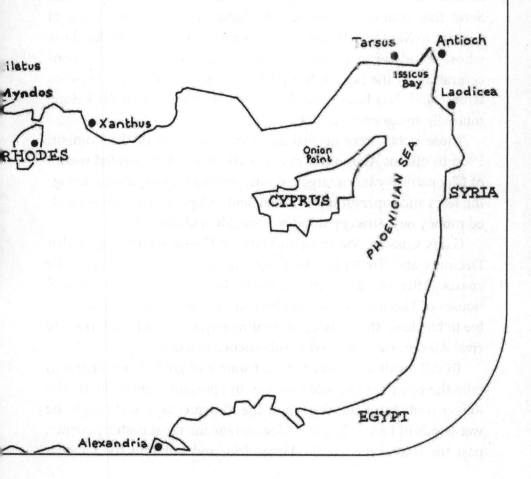

11

CASSIUS AND BRUTUS

In the autumn of 43 BC Parmensis was out at sea. A war that had begun with a cry of liberty, or so the assassins liked to remember, was now a war for money to prevent vengeance against themselves.

The theatre of this war was the water of the north-eastern Mediterranean, the arc along the coasts of Macedonia, Asia and Syria that connected Laodicea to Tarsus to the Onion Point of Cyprus, to Xanthus, Rhodes, Ephesus and Smyrna, to Troy for those whose minds were on deep antiquity, to Philippi for those concentrating on the nearest future. Their places on this line between Greece and Asia had made these cities Roman battlefields before, mutually antagonist and rich.

Those riches were needed again in a new war of the Romans. Even in distant Alexandria to the south, the well-protected wealth of Cleopatra became a target. Winter storms loomed ahead, bringing fears and superstitions to all ancient sailors. The assassins needed money fast. Strategy stood side by side with enrichment.

Gaius Cassius, the most military of Caesar's killers now that Decimus and Trebonius were both dead, led the looting of the coasts. After the death of Dolabella, he raided the temples and houses of Laodicea, those that he had not already broken for rubble to blockade the harbour. A wealthy city, once with ambitions to rival Alexandria, collapsed to subsistence in a day.

To sail north to Tarsus, the next source of gold, it was fastest to take the open sea but safest to stay in constant sight of land. The longer route ran from the top of the Phoenician Sea, through the wet winds of Issicus Bay, the Mediterranean's most easterly corner, past the town called Little Alexandria, and out into the Cilician channel where men traded wine, goats and clothes of coarse cloth. There was no money on the way but the quick rough route was an unnecessary peril for extorters; they faced enough human enemies without challenging nature too.

The people of Tarsus were as unreliable as the weather around them. Parmensis, writing to Cicero from Onion Point, six months before, had complained bitterly of the Tarsians, 'our very worst allies'. One faction there had supported the assassins; the other had chosen Dolabella. After the humiliation of Laodicea, every citizen of Tarsus had to pay the price of the assassins' need for cash. When the bill arrived their magistrates sold into slavery first their girls and boys, then their useless old and finally the young men needed for their defence. Still the bill was not fully paid.

Admirers and detractors asked how the assassins justified their thefts and enslavements in the cause of liberty, anti-tyranny or any other philosophical code of the Palatine. The answers lay in order and priority. A sailor who followed Epicurus saw no inconsistency in winning, seeking, stealing wealth as long as wealth was not the prime object that a man sought. Cassius's preferred objective was the peace of mind that could come only when tyranny was destroyed. Only as a secondary ambition did he need cash. Cassius minted his own coins but did not print on them his own image.

Brutus did display himself on his coins to mark the Ides of March, a determined, truculent profile, with twin daggers and EID. MAR on the reverse. He was a man of money and symbols. It was less clear how much he was a man of modern war. He was struggling to decide the fate of Antony's brother, Gaius, who was still a hostage in Apollonia, arguably a too short sailing distance from Italy, and not behaving as an honourable and grateful prisoner should.

Gaius claimed the courtesies of an old world at a time of the new. He demanded time and attention. Plotters in the pay of Antony were continually attempting rescues and he had to be moved in secret from place to place, a distraction from the main task of money-taking even when he was not a political danger to the assassins.

Any rich town was a target. Cities could be proscribed as well as people. The eastern coast was soon no less full of vengeance's victims than the western mainland. Parmensis was the head of a pack of ships, hunting the Mediterranean for money in the cause of defeating the triumvirs and returning Rome to its constitutional past. He was one of many different packs at different places and times. Coordination was complex.

The war at sea was not just about looting. Transport and supply were vital. Small ships would decide the war of massive armies on land. If the sea wars were won, an enemy's armies would be smaller, hungrier, less equipped; the advantage for the triumvirs of being Caesar's armies would be curtailed. That was the persistent argument of the naval captains pleading for more of the resources they had won.

Parmensis was playing his biggest part since the assassination, probably an even bigger part than on that day. His were the battles behind the battles. Every ship supplied the pumping heart of war. Tellers of war stories liked to follow an expedition's advance, to find the front line. There was always much less said about the back end, maintenance and supply, the wooden bridges bringing men, horses, bread and oil, breastplates and swords, pigs and wine. The job was to ensure that the legions remained fed, reinforced and informed of enemy failure. An army that had to forage was needlessly vulnerable. Romans, when battle loomed, wanted the least reliance on local supply. Caesar and Pompey had taught them that, along with almost every other lesson that a commander had to know.

Brutus had learnt those lessons, even though he preferred the lessons of the philosophers, but he was tiring of the war at sea. He wanted all war to be as soon as possible won – or lost. He believed that they had already raided enough. He was impatient for a battle for the history books.

Meanwhile, as Cicero had argued in so extraordinary a way, the Antonii were a virulent rash writ large on the body of Rome. Gaius Antonius was an ever more subversive force, even from his close confinement attempting to turn the minds of his guards against a killer of Caesar. Brutus was under pressure to execute him in his cell and, while nobly resisting, he had to endure the abuse of sceptics and cynics among his friends. The stubborn philosopher, Favonius, had argued before the Ides of March that the cost of a civil war was too high to capture his support. That cost seemed higher now.

In December 43 Brutus and Cassius met for a conference at Smyrna, the place of execution for Trebonius, the first assassin, the town which Romans remembered most for the meticulously planned massacre of their citizens, maybe a hundred thousand, by their enemy, Mithradates, in a single day in 88 BC. It took Pompey the Great, still then a friend of Caesar, to oversee the death of the king of Pontus, far away beside the Black Sea, and seize his magnificent treasure. So much of Italy's history was written in the waters of the east. In Smyrna Rome was everywhere.

Cassius was not pleased to be called to the assassins' conference. His preference was to stay at sea and raise yet more money by threatening Cleopatra in Egypt, a long, difficult but doubtless, he hoped, highly profitable journey. He would not need to fight, merely to negotiate a blackmail. The mother of Caesar's child would pay her due to any Roman power.

He sailed to Smyrna nonetheless. Cassius and Brutus had not met since they had left Italy at the end of the assassination year. War at sea required communication in order to cooperate as well as cash. There were new issues. The role of Sextus Pompeius had to be reconsidered in the town whose deadliest day his father had avenged.

Sextus's name on the proscription lists added to the prospect of his joining forces with the assassins, not merely supporting from the side lines. There was much gain to be got from harrying the triumvirs before trying to destroy them. Sextus was a formidable harrier. The naval case of Cassius prevailed. Brutus slowed his pace towards battle on land. First there would be further extortion, destruction, attrition. Parmensis the poet would remain between his rowers and the mast.

The triumvirs too were skirmishing with each other before taking on their enemies. In January, 42 BC, Octavian and Antony wanted to send eight legions across the Adriatic as the first phase of the force that would confront Brutus and Cassius when the time for battle came. Antony was confident; Octavian was cautious. Sextus was high in the mind of Caesar's heir as well as that of his assassins, his fleet around Sicily an expanding threat.

To protect himself against Sextus Octavian needed time. He had to promise the people of Rhegium, custodians of Scylla on the Italian side of the Messina straits, that their land would not be offered as bounty to his troops. He needed to appear in person and to be believed.

Antony sought instead a rapid naval victory over Cassius's fleet. This had become big enough to blockade Brundisium, the ever vital port for every enterprise. Only by working at sea together could the two senior triumvirs gain sufficient ascendancy to get their troops to Greece.

At first they cooperated and succeeded. The eight legions left and safely arrived. Then two of the assassins' admirals, Lucius Domitius Ahenobarbus and Staius Murcus combined their forces too, closing Brundisium to future reinforcements or returns. As the manoeuvrings continued, none of the participants on either side had a full sense of what was important and what was not. Distant coasts were where historic events would happen but not yet.

Italy itself, under the command of the third triumvir, Lepidus, was almost irrelevant until victory was decided. Rome had a new temple to Caesar the God, a new name formally added to the pantheon of the city. But Caesar's spirit had left the country. His killers and defenders were all moving abroad. Octavian had dragged Antony into the wake of his revolutionary rage. The assassins found the same stream drawing them on too.

To the disappointment of some of his admirers Brutus ordered the death of Antony's brother, Gaius, a Roman citizen and aristocrat, but no longer a bargaining counter. Keeping him alive made his gaoler seem soft. There would be no bargaining with the triumvirs. There could be absolutely none with the man who legally called himself the son of Rome's latest deity.

Money was still what mattered most. After becoming rich enough to fight, the priority of the assassins was to ensure that no enemy, neither Gaius Antonius nor the leaders of hostile cities, survived behind them as they plundered. They divided their targets. Gaius Cassius, with Parmensis in his fleet, took on the island of Rhodes, the greatest naval power outside the assassins' own power.

* * *

The Roman captains were learning fast. Their commands were not temporary, not for a year at a time as, like Roman magistracies at home, they once had been. Parmensis and his fellow sailors of the assassins would be at sea for as long as the task took, sensing their command in the rhythmic pulse of oars, the shaking of decks, the peculiar sense of isolation and safety that meant more than usual in these years of revolutionary civil war.

There was much to learn at sea that was not part of an education at Parma or Rome, more than could be learnt in the lakes of Cisalpine Gaul or in the river dockyards of the Field of Mars. A fleet was not wholly unlike an army: it contained slow, heavy infantry ships that, close together, made a platform on which soldiers fought almost as on land; it contained smaller ships, fast and light like cavalry; it had its own seaborne towers, archers toppling from its sides as though at a siege, its own signallers sounding horns and flashing shields. But a fleet was also a wholly different thing, variable in ways unseen except by those who lived with it month after month, year after year.

Troops travelled from home to war by broad-bottomed ships under sail. For the captains of the triumvirs the art was to catch the wind in Italy at Brundisium and cross the Adriatic at its narrowest point to Apollonia or Dyrrachium, the start of the *Via Egnatia*, a thousand miles to the opening of Asia on the coast of Thrace. This sea route was almost as much a Roman highway as that through the mountains and lakes to Ariminum. Parmensis had to be one of its highwaymen, alert to any new sail on any horizon, chasing, harrying, crashing and crushing hulls.

Transport ships were escorted by triremes, slim, low, fast, vessels powered by oarsmen and armed with a ramming prow in the bow and whatever grappling irons the captains preferred. Tactics and weapons, archers, swordsmen and engineers, had to match the infinite variability of the sea itself. The arrangement of the oars, the numbers of rowers, the weight fore and aft, were matters for argument and art. The seamen of Rhodes, the largest island between Cyprus and Crete, were the acknowledged masters of both, famed since the days of Homer.

Cassius knew the power of Rhodes, once the site of the famed giant statue of the Sun God called the Colossus. Like many rich Roman young men, he had studied and learnt his philosophy there in the schools of Posidonius, the greatest polymath of his time, whose studies covered everything from ocean tides to racial differences, the history of Rome to the size of the moon. His rival, Hermagoras, perhaps the most influential teacher of oratory of all time, taught his pupils to divide any subject into essential questions, the Ws as they became later known: who, what, when, where, why, in what way, by what means? Together they gave as good an education as a Roman could have.

In the summer of 43 BC the Rhodians wanted to talk rather than fight. That was usually wise when war with Romans, rather than argument about the nature of history, loomed ahead. They sent to Cassius one of his former classroom teachers, Archelaos, who concentrated first on the 'when' of the argument and moved on to the 'whats'. The islanders would, as ever, be happy to help Rome, he said, but only when the senate had specifically told them who and what constituted Rome in this case and time.

Cassius was not impressed. He was already with his fleet at Myndos, a secure seventy miles along the coastal arc, carefully training his troops to be successful marines and his captains to counter the unique and uncanny Rhodian skill in dipping a ship's prow at the point of impact to hole an enemy below the waterline.

The crew of a Rhodian trireme would aim to burst through a

heavier Roman line, turn in the tightest circle and smash from the rear. Rowers on the Roman ship, crammed in the damp darkness, would feel the momentary pause in the wave before the ram pierced like a missile, smashing oars and limbs to a pulp of wood and blood and salt.

Knowledge of this tactic, like knowledge of a rhetorical technique, did not make it necessarily easier to counter, nor the fear of it disperse. Cassius was drilling his men hard when Archelaus arrived with his warning to the assassin and self-styled Liberator of how Rhodes had protected its own liberty in the past from better enemies than him.

Cassius listened as though in a classroom before orating against the 'freedom-loving' Rhodians' intolerable support of the slavemaster, Dolabella, the 'freedom-loving' Rhodians' pitiless response to the victims of the triumvirs' proscriptions, the 'freedom-loving' Rhodians' ridiculous respect for the acts and heirs of Julius Caesar. He was enjoying the game of goading his tutor.

He posed a paradox to Archelaos, as though he were eighteen and under instruction again. If the Rhodians did not see him as the representative of Rome, he was free to treat them as though no treaty with Rome existed. If they did see him as the legitimate Roman authority they should obey him or be destroyed.

The Rhodians responded with a show of strength visible from Myndos bay, accelerating and manoeuvring to taunt what they saw as Roman weakness on water. Cassius ordered out his more numerous and heavier ships against them, watching from a highpoint on the shore as they succeeded where so many had failed, surviving the darts and feints, capturing three triremes and crushing two. He transported troops onto Rhodes itself, drawing out again an attack from faster, lighter ships, again winning with weight at sea as though with an infantry force on land.

Cassius watched as the Rhodians began hurling missiles from their walls. He knew that the city could not withstand a siege. So did a faction of the islanders themselves who, signalling a willingness to talk more generously than before, were surprised to find Cassius himself suddenly inside and amongst them, guarded only by a small force of troops.

A magnanimous victor, as he thought, Cassius ordered clemency for all the Rhodians bar a roll call of fifty whom he sentenced to death. He ordered all the gold and silver in the city to be brought to him, threatening execution to any who concealed their wealth. The results, drawn from wells and tombs and temples, were even more substantial than he had hoped for. Just as satisfying – and disconcerting to the triumvirs when the news spread – Gaius Cassius had defeated at sea the acknowledged masters of the sea. Parmensis alone took away thirty Rhodian ships for the assassins' fast growing navy.

The next target was Xanthus across the rocky sea of Lycium: in the east the Mediterranean was made of many little seas with individual names, Pamphilian, Cilician, Phoenician, reminders of the birth of sailing when the west was mere endless, nameless water over mud. Brutus destroyed Xanthus in a siege ending in brutality and mass suicide. Punishment was extreme even by the exemplary standards of Julius Caesar in Gaul.

Fire raged, maybe an act of war or a mass suicide. One woman in Xanthus hanged herself with a dead child round her neck and a flaming torch in her hand. Only her attempt to burn her own house down had failed. Brutus heard the story, cried, ensured that his biographers knew that he had cried, and accepted the surrender of the nearby ports of Patara and Myra. Their treasure followed without a fight, their citizens parading as prisoners outside their walls.

News of these successes spread fast enough that the victors did not have to repeat them. 'Oderint dum metuant: Let them hate as long as they fear': a line written by Accius for Atreus, later borrowed by Octavian's heirs, neatly summed up the message of Brutus and Cassius who accepted ten years' tribute from Asia in advance.

The assassins called each other to a victory conference fifty miles inland from Smyrna at Sardis, a great capital of kings long before the empire of Rome. Their massed joint armies made a public statement to allies, and potential allies, that Croesus himself would have understood. In private there were rows about past and future, how and why Antony had been spared on the Ides of March, why his brother had survived so long, whether Octavian and Antony were genuine allies and whether they might be divided. It took Favonius the veteran sceptic to find reasoned answers, quoting Homer on the superior wisdom of the old.

The two leaders discovered that they had developed differently since the Ides of March. Cassius was more relaxed and confident, Brutus more anxious and angry. Cassius, for reasons of diplomacy and philanthropy, wanted to forgive a Roman ally accused in Sardis as an embezzler. Brutus wanted disgrace and the full force of the law. Cassius had the respect for his seniority that he had always deemed his due. Brutus was impatient, pouting, almost more a boy.

The troops gossiped and exchanged such facts as they knew. Their pay was guaranteed. The assassins were reconciled for every purpose that anyone else needed to know. With their new gold heavily guarded on trucks drawn by oxen, they could match and exceed the money that the triumvirs were offering to their own men. Behind them one Antonius brother was already safely dead. Another would surely follow.

Ahead of them was the Hellespont where, in another war between Romans, Cassius had once surrendered Pompey's triremes to Julius Caesar. Every road was Roman even if its surface was more fit for the pack animals of Asia. There would be a hard march through sand and scrub but their soldiers were more used to that than were the triumvirs' troops to their crowded, rocking ships.

Parmensis remained at sea, harrying, supplying and preparing. By the end of the summer, two confident commanders for the assassins, keen to erase past error, knowing that they had no options bar fighting for victory, were leading nineteen well-rewarded legions and allied mercenary battalions out of Asia into Europe.

12

THE CIMBER BROTHERS

Brutus, Ides of March silver denarius (42 BC)

Tillius Cimber was an assassin with high ambitions for himself when the victory was won. He had played one of the biggest parts on the Ides of March, distracting the dictator, then pinning back the arms that held the world. He was looking forward to the spoils.

He was well known as a boaster, a brawler and a drunk. Not everything he said about himself would be true. He liked to march with a piss-pot, a wine flagon and a few good slaves to service his needs. He had to be kept busy if he was to be of any use at all. But, like Antony at the other end of the road to war between Caesar's champions and his killers, he was a highly capable drunk.

Tillius despised time-servers on the greasy staircase of Roman honours. He had risen high and fallen far and risen again, some of the moves by his own choice, others forced upon him. He had begun a political life in the senate and given it up. He owed his last return to Caesar who appointed him to the praetorship in 45, alongside Pollio, Plancus, Decimus Brutus and Basilus, and to the governorship of Bithynia and Pontus, the former realms of King

Mithradates who had slaughtered so many thousands of Romans at Smyrna. Tillius owed everything to Caesar as even Cicero, somewhat acidly, had pointed out.

He had turned against Caesar, he said, because the dictator would not pardon his brother, Publius, a too determined supporter of Pompey and of Cato. Caesar had drawn somewhat arbitrary lines between the forgiven and the unforgiven. Tillius and Publius had fallen on different sides.

Tillius had earned himself sympathy for Caesar's offence to his family, one that any Roman could understand. The brothers lacked widespread connections like the Cassii. They were committed to the connections between each other. Tillius saw many opportunities in a future Rome where power might be more widely shared.

As the assassins' army marched towards the Bosphorus Tillius was one of those who knew the ground. The familiar oak forests of Bithynia were fading behind them. He had helped raise ships there for Cassius. He had helped Cassius against Dolabella. He could do so again. Turullius, his junior among the assassins, was his aide and ally. After the war was over, both might hope for something better than building for the navy.

It had taken extreme bravery on the Ides of March for Tillius to offer his fake petition and pull down Caesar's toga for the first blow. Of all those who risked torture and execution that day, his risk, if Caesar had wriggled from his assassin's grasp, had been the greatest. He did not mind reminding his colleagues of this.

Northern Greece drew nearer. The Roman road ran between the mountains and the sea, swinging north-west towards the plain where Philip of Macedon, father of Alexander the Great, had once mined so much of the gold that paid for conquest, draining the marshland, expanding the local town and calling it after himself. At Philippi an army marching along the Via Egnatia from the west would meet its enemy from the east. Both sides knew, long before they arrived, that this would be their battlefield.

Tillius and his companions marched on, their soldiers and their slaves ready for their different tasks ahead. It was common for officers on the march in civil wars to imagine themselves as priests and power-brokers in a new era. While their men marched for money and farms, the captains contested for status, glory and houses on the Palatine hill. Pompey's officers before the battle of Pharsalus had divided the whole Roman world in their dreams. There was nothing wrong with raw ambition. It was part of the very greatness of Rome.

* * *

The water in the Gulf of Melas was warm at the surface, icy below, so calm that the soldiers could see their reflection, so clear that they could see its landscape of shipwrecks and rocks. This was a deep gash into the land they called Thrace, the word the easterners also used for the whole of Europe. To the south were the sites and sights of the Trojan War. On the northern shore Cassius and Brutus marshalled their forces for the final phase of their march – to a battle no less epic in their own minds.

Cassius stood on a high wooden platform with all the senators and assassins who had followed him this far. Heralds and trumpeters called for silence from eighty thousand armed men, legions tested in Gaul, cavalry hired in Spain and Gaul, Persian archers for whom the road beside the Melas was the furthest west they had ever been.

This was the last occasion, if not quite the last moment, when words might make a difference. Cassius was the senior of the leaders as battle loomed, the seniority that he thought he should have had before the Ides of March. Who, what, when, where, why, to what end, by what means? Cassius had learnt the lessons in rhetoric that the Rhodians had taught him in his gentler youth.

Who? That was the easiest question. All his listeners knew his name and the names of those behind him, Caesar's killers, their supporters, the senators persecuted by the triumvirs whether they were killers, supporters or neither. Then there were the men of Gaul, born with a love of Caesar, betrayed by those who claimed his name at Parma and Mutina, the Black Sea princes, the mercenaries from Parthia on their ponies, all of them bound together as one by present opportunity and danger.

What? The rules for orators required the substance of an argument to be early and clear. Nuance and evasion could come later. Money was the answer. The assassins had paid in advance what they had agreed. They would pay much more after victory. They had secured their treasury on Thasos, the nearest island, only twenty miles to the south. The troops could be sure of their pay.

When? Within days their courage and commitment would be proved and the payments begin.

Where? On the plain of Philippi, only a hundred miles to the east. A vast stage stretched out for them there, hills to the right, marshland to the left, natural barriers that their scouts had seen, that their commanders had chosen, high ground from which they could fight, low ground that was impassable to their enemy. The triumvirs' men were already on their way through Italy and Greece but still far behind. They would be weary when they arrived.

Philippi: the name itself had the sound of history. Philip may have been a lesser man than Alexander, his son, but he had left his name for both the speeches, Cicero's Philippics, and for the battlefield that would define the future centuries after his death.

Why? Facts were fine but reasoning was the essence of a textbook argument. The assassins had the moral as well as the physical high ground. They were protecting the constitution and the law, the independent powers of the Roman people. They were the ones who had raised and served Caesar, admiring his courage as all his fellow soldiers did, until he had ceased to obey the law and been about to be crowned a king.

They had killed Caesar for the sake of Rome. The senate of Rome had agreed, promising an amnesty, provinces and armies, not proscription without trial, the parades of heads and hands in the Forum, excesses which not even the ancient Tarquin kings of Rome had matched. The assassins were acting for all Rome.

To what end? He, Gaius Cassius, did not want to be a dictator himself. Marcus Brutus did not want to be a dictator. None of the men on his platform was seeking supremacy, only a place in which to serve. After their victory, they wanted Rome to return to how it had been at its best.

By what means? By their own bravery and the foresight of their leaders. And, in case their enthusiasm needed further firing, there would be an extra cash payment, beyond what he and Brutus had promised before, to all men and their officers in due proportion.

Their armies were secure. They could move forward, camp by camp, the usual massive mobile town reassuring all that they were in a Roman army. Every street running north to south crossed another east to west, every *cardo* with a *decumanus*. Everyone had his place in one of the quarters of the square. There was unusually abundant food for all from the fertile fields of Asia. They had cut the *Via Egnatia* and nothing could get through to the triumvirs' armies in the barren zones of worked-out gold mines behind King Philip's town.

That was Cassius's public argument. He had studied the art of speaking as though it were a science. He expected results. He prized the predictable. But offering the extra money, even though his extortions from Rhodes and the Greek cities allowed it, suggested that he was not as confident as he hoped to sound.

There were many fears that he did not show to his men, under-currents of doubt as he stared at the entwined colours of the water around him. There could have been a quite a different speech in the Rhodian manner, one deliverable only to himself, only within his own mind as his enemy advanced. He did not know precisely where Octavian and Antony were, whether they were together or as separate as they so often seemed. He knew that they would not be far away for long.

Who? That first question was not as simple as he had made it appear. There was Brutus as well as himself. Brutus was maddened by what he had unleashed. The death of Porcia was deep in his mind. He saw the future more clearly than the present and was too impatient to reach it. He did not see that time was on their side. Their local allies would not mind waiting as long as they looked like winners.

Antony would be impatient too but he had more cause, more fear of hunger, also more success from his impatience, in Gaul and at Mutina, as a tactician worthy to be Caesar's successor. Cassius did not want a race to the start.

So when? Cassius aimed to wait as long as it took to starve the triumvirs into retreat, to force their armies to question their leaders, to fear and to defect. To Brutus that sounded sordid, unheroic. He wanted the quickest victory of right over wrong.

What were the Romans alongside him really fighting for? Did fear of the Tarquins' return worry anyone four centuries after their departure? For Brutus the founding of the republic was a family matter but the army on parade at Melas did not fear resurgent kings, or want an endless avenging of Lucretia. Their memory of mass slaughter was in the civil wars of their own lifetimes. They wanted killings of citizens by citizens as soon as possible to end.

Where? The wherewithal of money and food was good but the where was everything. Their position at Philippi would be advantageous but, more than that, vital for maintaining advantage. Closure of the *Via Egnatia*, control of food and water from Asia: nothing mattered more. The 'where' was their strongest asset in both versions of the speech.

Why? That was the worst of the Rhodian questions. Caesar was hovering like a ghost over the road to Philippi – and his was in every way a malign spirit. Octavian, he knew, summoned Caesar up in everything he did, every word he uttered. Brutus claimed to have seen a terrifying apparition: 'What of gods and men are you?' he had asked. The reply came: 'I am your evil genius, Brutus, and you will see me at Philippi'.

Cassius the Epicurean was certain of one thing. No ghost had, in fact, stood before Brutus. There had been only a mingling of pictures, thin skins floating from the bodies around him like butterfly wings, like the useless old coats of cicadas and snakes, combined and confused within the mind but as material as any other matter. That was what Epicurus taught.

There could be no fact about a ghost. But vengeance was a more dangerous spirit abroad than any imagined being. Brutus was afraid. Cassius was not a self-deceiver. Octavian was a magician in politics, motivating men by his name alone. His vengeance against the assassins was stronger than all of Cassius's vindications of himself and of the Cascas, the Caecilli, Tillius Cimber, Turullius, and of Cassius Parmensis, the poet who had an evil genius of his own.

* * *

In Italy the recruiters for the triumvirs were still reinforcing, struggling to bring to Greece the money of the proscribed and the men whom that money would buy. Their main force arrived only in September, late for a campaign on a distant battlefield with poor lines of supply for a northern winter. Their confidence in the power of Caesar's name and memory was knocked by the assassins' success in bringing so many eastern legions to their side.

Transport by sea was becoming everywhere more treacherous – for ships carrying both corn along Italy's western coast to Rome and men and supplies east across the Adriatic. It was as though the water were another country, a separate empire which Caesar had never ruled and his successors could not even pretend to own.

From Sicily to Brundisium, through the lowest arc at the foot of the map in the temple of Tellus, the most powerful man was still Sextus Pompeius, youngest son of Caesar's defeated enemy. He had been a renegade for many years after his father's death, sometimes barely more than a pirate king. Since the Ides of March he had been massively reinforced by sailors from Africa and Spain and the wealth of men fleeing the proscriptions.

Sextus had become the leading figure among the honorary assassins. Cicero was dead. Porcia was dead. Other sympathisers came to the fore and fell back into the background, seeking advancement, assuaging their fears; Sextus attracted support of his own and anxiety from all sides.

For many of those fleeing from Rome, those guilty only of wealth, Sextus offered a great advantage in not being an assassin himself.

His forces in the Sicilian and western seas were nearer than those of Cassius and Brutus. He was more attractive to the conservative landowners of the Italian towns for whom Pompey's name, for all the brutality and disruption that Pompey had brought in his early years, still meant the stability of traditional government.

The old and rich badly needed a champion. No one's land seemed safe from confiscation. Anyone's acres might be seized and handed to new owners at the whim of the triumvirs. Ariminum, the coastal hinge on the crooked route from Parma to Rome, was just one home to the anxious where Octavian and Antony had promised soldiers their rewards for victory. Sextus seemed their best available protector.

As a partner in war, however, Pompey's son was hard to pin down. While Cassius, Brutus and the Cimber brothers were closing in on Philippi, Parmensis and the navy were part of a sprawling struggle for the sea lanes. Sextus seemed sometimes to be with them and sometimes not. He was honorary as an ally as well as an assassin.

The narrow passage from Brundisium to Greece, the end of the *Via Appia* to the start of the *Via Egnatia*, was closely disputed by all. On days of favourable winds the loaded troop transports took the triumvirs' legions to Dyrrachium at speeds greater than the triremes of the assassins could match. Ships of food and weapons that left in worse weather were at high risk of interception, being broken, sunk or turned back, every lost cargo a problem for the armies of Octavian and Antony on the barren Greek side of what would soon be their battlefield.

By the beginning of October it seemed as though the triumvirs had transported at least the minimum that they needed. Their last ships were leaving Italy. The conflict of arms was coming closer. The story of one of the legions on board, Caesar's famed *Martia*, named for the god of war, came to stand for the madness of what was happening before a battle which, in retrospect, would be deemed to have clearly changed so much.

The *Martia*'s voyage began as just another journey in a war where it already played so many parts. It was a return trip, a retracing of the journey that it had made when summoned back from Macedonia after the Ides of March. Its men had been first meant to help Caesar win Parthia, then to help Antony to take Parma and Mutina from Decimus. It had defected to Octavian and fought against Antony's cavalry in the marshes beside the *Via Aemilia*. It had been heroic in the senatorial cause when Octavian was on the side of Decimus and the senate. When Octavian changed the *Martia* changed. At the end of the safe sailing season for 43 BC it was on its way back across the Adriatic to confront the assassins.

Some ten thousand of its men had crowded onto the transports, the first to leave Brundisium making rapid headway under sail, escorted by their triremes. Then the wind suddenly dropped. The mass of the fleet was still barely beyond sight of land. Broad-bottomed hulls drifted like flotsam in the deadest calm before they were spotted by one of the patrolling captains of Cassius's trireme fleet.

Gnaeus Domitius Ahenobarbus was a Roman aristocrat who traced the red beards of his family back to the last defeat of the Tarquins, like Brutus and probably with better cause. Sometimes or sometimes not described as an assassin himself, condemned with them under the *Lex Pedia* but reluctant to join their cause, he was the independent master of this water. Other allies joined the hunt. Parmensis led his ships. The result was decisive. The first clash of the Philippi campaign ended in the most desperate first defeat of men ready to fight for the memory of Julius Caesar.

Around Mutina the *Martia* had successfully faced the threat of cavalry on land; it was helpless against its equivalent at sea. The legionaries tried lashing the ships together to make a wooden line on which they could fight. They then immediately faced flaming arrows fired onto their sides and decks, a tactic developed in the east and wholly new to them.

Soldiers chose drowning over being burnt to death. Ships floated like funeral pyres. Survivors on broken planks drifted slowly down the coast before surrendering and changing sides again. Seventeen triremes were added to the assassins' navy.

* * *

On the same day at Philippi, Cassius knew nothing of this first success. He was preparing for a battle that he still preferred to delay. His army, however, was restless. Brutus, he knew, was even more impatient, buoyed by the final phase of their march, a triumph that victorious men might talk about for years.

They had forced a passage through high mountain paths, successfully evading the forces that Antony had sent to halt them. They were masters of their terrain. Tillius Cimber, as sober in a crisis as he was useless at other times, had shadowed by sea, planning safe sites for camps among temple ruins behind the lines. Momentum and security meant morale.

And yet to Cassius, precisely because of that security, the case for delay seemed the stronger. The momentum had to be slowed. He held a perfect position on the wide, flat summit of a gentle hill; to the left of him was a smaller hill which he had also fortified; to the left of that was a stinking swamp where birds pursued insects and wise men stayed away.

His sight was always weak but he approved what he could see. To the right there stretched the wooden wall with gates and towers which his engineers had built with speed worthy of Caesar himself. A shallow river ran beside it, a moat that was a gift from nature. At the far end of the wall, too far maybe but there was no other choice, was the first hill of the sharply rising mountain range, as impassable and pathless as the swamp. That was where Brutus had his camp.

The noise and stench were overwhelming, the more so whenever the growing army of Antony moved closer, taunting and crying out for battle. He had told his men that they should ignore their enemy, that these were the cries of the hungry: they should light their campfires and delight that the smoke of grilling meat would roll down the undulating slope. Facing the sneers of Antony's men was safer at this stage than facing their swords.

Battle was a matter of constantly adjusting odds. The odds for the assassins were improving by the day. The two commanders at the marshland end of the lines, each side's better man of war, were pitched almost as in a duel, one armed against the other. Antony had been anxious, almost desperate, to fight; Cassius did not need to be and had never been. Almost two miles away, Brutus would face Octavian who was rumoured not even to have arrived.

The scale of the forces on both sides was already unlike anything Cassius had seen. He had fought against Caesar at Pharsalus six years before; then he had shared his fellow officers' dreams of a better world. This latest array of Romans against Romans seemed in one way a lesser thing, with a fake son of Caesar and a son of Pompey faraway. But the front line was wider and the ranks twice as deep.

The two sides were massed in contradictions. There were legions with Cassius who had previously fought for Caesar; and there were those who had fought against him. There were horsemen with the triumvirs who had been ruthlessly subjected by Caesar, in Gaul, in Spain and on the Rhine.

With those claiming to be the heirs of Caesar was the Thunderbolt legion, the XII, with the same lightning shields that shone in the dark in Parma when Parmensis was young. There were legions that, like the *Martia* heroes of Mutina, had crossed and recrossed the Adriatic. There were legions that after Pharsalus had never gone home, wherever home was. There were Thracian forces on both sides, unwilling hosts who were hedging their bets on the outcome. There were local kings behind him who would disappear at the first scent of defeat.

The wider the view of the two sides the more they seemed like a single simmering mass. Even if Cicero had been alive his words would have struggled to divide them. It was hard to hear a single sentence, even one's own. Maybe that was of no account. A soldier with lightning in his shield was worth a thousand words from anyone.

Cicero's last great service as an honorary assassin had been his death, the slow severing of his neck, the same jagged death as Pompey, the skewering of his hands and tongue on the rostra. Cicero had been vacillating and vain, obsessive against Antony to the point of madness, but his fame ensured that fear of the triumvirs' revenge remained deep in the minds of many fighting against them. Those who had escaped the proscriptions told his story of a family's execution beside the sea, their own stories and more.

Few of them were simple stories. Back in Rome Lepidus was the triumvir left in charge. With the assassins at Philippi was Lepidus's brother, Paullus, Cicero's ally, proscribed in either a political feud, a family feud, a boast to show how much love had to be abandoned in the cause of vengeance, or all three. If Cassius were to take a man at random from the battle field he could not guarantee to know which side he was on.

Yet even the recent past was disappearing around him as battle loomed. From the Philippics to Philippi, those who cared about Cicero or about confiscations from the rich were fewer than he had imagined when he spoke at Melas. Those with a principled hostility to the dictatorship of the triumvirs were more dominant with Sextus and Cassius Parmensis at sea. Idealists in the cause of the old constitution were hugely outnumbered on the assassins' side by those for whom any cause would do if they could profitably make it their own.

Brutus had his small band of young artists, scholars, Horatius Flaccus and fellow poets from the schools of Athens. Their leader was Messalla Corvinus, another man who could trace his family line to the first year of Rome's republic, burdened by history but proscribed more likely for his wealth than his independent thought.

Messalla much admired the military acumen of Cassius. His status made him third in the line of command. Together they had spent many hours looking back to the fate of Pompey, how Caesar had thrown the dice as he crossed the Rubicon, how sixteen months later his rival, the sometime 'teenage butcher' and aspirant to be Alexander the Great, had been forced to wager his whole life's work on the outcome of a single day.

Brutus was ready to gamble too. In words aimed at the record of history he looked back almost longingly at the fate of Cato, regretting how in the past he had criticised Porcia's father for disembowelling himself after defeat. Brutus had changed his mind. Cato had been right. If the gods did not bring him victory, he too would seek an end to his life with due praise for Fortune.

Cassius did not agree. Epicureans had no time for a god called Fortune. But he was careful in disagreeing. He hid his deepest doubts. On one night of waiting and talking he had kissed his fellow assassin in what was possibly a suicide pact of victory or death, or possibly not. No one around them was sure.

Manoeuvrings began. Battles were dreary beside the dreams of their conclusions. Antony sent men to cut a path through the mud and reeds, hoping to follow with a full force to the rear. Cassius responded, a mutual effort of military engineering, walls and crosswalls that might have continued for weeks. The days of delay rolled on, the odds continually changing.

Cassius, worn down and wary, agreed to Brutus's date with chance. This was where their conspiracy to assassinate had led although it was less a battle about the assassins than they had imagined. The other survivors of the Ides were with them but somehow also not. They should have been talismans of the army but somehow few seemed to care. Only Octavian cared.

Of the names that had rung out over Caesar's funeral five were already dead: the rest, their names sounding again on the charge sheet of the *Lex Pedia*, were still somewhere in the fight, Tillius Cimber, his close ally Turullius, Pacuvius Labeo, the brothers Casca and Caecilii, Rubrius Ruga, Sextius Naso, Bucolianus, Marcus Spurius, Cassius Parmensis. It was not always clear where precisely they were. On the battlefield their history was itself hardly more than a ghost. All that mattered was whether a man moved forward or back, pressed on or was pressed.

Cassius's last reassurance to Brutus was again that, if they failed, they need have no fear of the victors. The suicide pact had maybe hardened. There was more talk of failure than success and that was the talk that memorialists would remember. There was more delay, then suddenly there was fighting. It was never clear exactly who made the first move, what and why it happened.

Roars ran along the lines of troops, echoing from the mountains into the marsh. From the high vantage point of his camp Cassius saw ladders and grappling irons against the main wall immediately in front of him, swarming men and a cloud of missiles hurled and returned. Antony held the marshland that no one should have held. He was using swamp warfare just as it had been used by and against him on the *Via Aemilia*. His legionaries charged in tight formation, demolished what was in their way and forced the defenders to the side into the soft mud and sharp reeds that they thought were their best defence.

The noise from nearby rose above that from the faraway mountain side. To the right the main lines of the armies locked their shields and swords in what, even after Pharsalus and Mutina, was still the chilling sight of Romans against Romans. To the left the threat from the swamp was already to Cassius's high camp. Only minutes later the threat was a fact. Cassius had to retreat to a higher hill, watch as best he could and consider his next move from there.

His eyes were strained. His view was obscured. Everyone's distant view was obscured by dust. For an Epicurean what was seen was the only reality but it was more important what his men saw directly above them from down below, their commander's camp occupied, its tallest tent torn down, wisps of smoke, this time of destruction not of plenty, rolling down and away. The near sight sapped their will. Their lines, brutally balanced, slowly broke. There was no rout, equally no doubt for Cassius that his personal wager at Philippi was lost.

The sight immediately below was as clear to him as the scene around him was clear to his soldiers. The noise of battle was impenetrable to all. He could not face Octavian if Octavian had won; he could not face Brutus if Brutus had won. He looked for a signal. He saw nothing to encourage him. He chose suicide. He was a very Roman follower of Epicurus; he did not fear death but he did fear the shame of a failed public life.

He said goodbye to Messalla in Greek. He ordered an aide called Pindarus to sever his head, never knowing that on Brutus's side of the front there had indeed been a victory, the destruction of three of the triumvirs' legions, the looting of Octavian's camp, the taking of many prisoners, a triumph over Octavian even though Octavian himself had not been there. Gaius Cassius was the seventh assassin to die.

13

HUNTED TENT BY TENT

Parmensis was unaware of the pacts that might or might not have been made before the first day at Philippi. Encouragement to suicide was a common charge against Epicureans. Their critics jibed that if life was about preparation for death without fear, one should surely die as soon as this happy state was achieved.

Students of Epicurus countered that their inner calm made anything possible, including the most active public life if that were necessary or desired. They noted correctly that those Romans most likely to take their own lives came from their philosophical critics. Cato Uticensis was no Epicurean.

Cassius had been an Epicurean. He had chosen death by his own will – for his life story and without fear it had to be hoped. He had not chosen death for philosophical effect. Anyone might choose to kill himself. Philosophy never explained more than a small part of the world. The most stubborn and purist Epicurean, Statilius, had rejected the conspiracy because the enlightened should not trouble themselves for those in the darkness of stupidity: Statilius came to Philippi and died there.

For several days Parmensis remained unaware of the suicide of Cassius and its aftermath. His previously allotted task had been to have a fleet ready which he could bring either to the victory party, or to the wake of the defeated, or to the next phase of the war. He had some of Rhodes's very fastest ships. He was ready. Cimber was somewhere on the battlefield and also had ships.

Three weeks later, still safely waiting in the Aegean sea, Parmensis met the survivors of the second fighting day at Philippi. Some had sailed to him from Thasos, the nearest island to the battlefield, a lonely base of forests and hot pools where the assassins had kept their food, their weapons and their extorted pay for the troops. Others were jammed on transports, directly from the narrow beaches beyond the marsh.

When Turullius arrived too, he came with more ships taken from Rhodes. Strays and stragglers soon made a fleet, a community of the reconsidering. They wondered whether any other assassins were alive, whether Cimber was still alive. He was the sort of man who would be. No one was sure.

They also wondered what exactly had happened. Sailors exchanged differing stories of how the assassins' life on land had ended, some of them destined for the history books, most forgotten. The overall result of the first day at Philippi had arguably been a draw, maybe a victory when the news arrived of Ahenobarbus's success on the Italian side of the Adriatic. After the disasters of the second day, that argument had gone.

Even the first day had been lost. That was the solidifying truth. Brutus had not believed the messenger from Brundisium and his story of the Martian legionaries destroyed by catapults of fire. He had not seemed to believe in his own prospects either, becoming peculiarly obsessed by portents, by bees and birds and the silent monster ghost that had pursued him before. For all his history and philosophy he shared the debilitating depression of those being hunted to death.

Once the fighting on the first day had begun he had failed to alert Cassius to his victory in time. Or Cassius had misinterpreted the signs before his eyes, an ironic end for an Epicurean who trusted only what he could see. When the fighting was over, Brutus, the man of ideals, had become by all accounts himself a monster, ranting at his officers, slaughtering prisoners, promising that all of his victorious troops would soon add to their fortunes by pillaging Greece from Thessalonika to Sparta.

Brutus promised that the former realms of Atreus and Thyestes, the remains of mythical Mycenae and the thriving countryside around, would be raped in revenge for the deaths of Cassius and some eight thousand men. Poetic justice would be powered by vendetta. The young Cicero would be in charge. Fortunate to have missed his family's execution, he would be fortunate again at what would be a scene of random revenge, of tragic fact.

On the following day there was greater peace. Brutus regained his spirits. Octavian, it was agreed, had lost twice as many men to him as Cassius had to Antony. In Thasos Brutus gave Cassius due burial, building as grand a tomb for 'the last of the Romans' as time allowed.

Returning to Philippi, he worked to rally Cassius's demoralised forces, paying out yet more from the mobile treasury to those who had lost money in the looting of their tents by Antony's men. He moved his own headquarters to the marsh side of the line, reorganising the army under his single command, repeating Cassius's rhetoric that righteousness, winter and hunger would win for them the war.

The assassins' cause at Philippi was still alive at that point. Cold rain fell, worse for their less well-supplied opponents, the worst of October weather a reminder of worse still to come. Brutus harried the triumvirs' men at night. He diverted the river that was his defensive moat into an offensive weapon, flooding his enemies' camps, laying mud upon ice. But, without Cassius himself, neither tactic nor rhetoric was the same.

There were the same walls and cross walls, the same game of tactics played by engineers. Then came the same uncertainty as to when to start the fighting and where. Brutus had wanted delay, as cautious as Cassius had once been. His officers no longer wanted caution. He had been ruthless in killing his prisoners and threatening the realm of Thyestes, much feebler in enforcing his will on his own men.

Brutus faced the taunts of Casca, the assassin whom he had kept closest at his side and celebrated alongside himself on the coins for the troops. For the first wielder of the dagger against Caesar, Brutus had become too weak. His men had seemed to agree. They faced taunts from the triumvirs' side of the lines that avenging Caesar was a nobler cause than dying for his assassins.

This was not a choice that Brutus wanted them to consider for long. They might answer the question with agreement. If Brutus's men were not going to defect to Caesar's avengers they wanted to fight them, to redress the damage of the first day before defeat became fate.

Centurions backed their soldiers. The usual forms of discipline were fading. Local allies were changing sides or going home. Thracians with blue eyes like the sea were as fickle as they were famed to be. Both lines were boiling, the triumvirs' because they were turning up the heat, Brutus's because he had lost control.

An Ethiopian, not a black phantom but a man of unlucky colour in the wrong place at the wrong time, was torn apart outside the assassins' gates. A pair of fighting eagles, seen as prophecy by men and commander alike, was enough for the troops to roll and tumble upon each other.

Octavian was still playing no part, hiding in the marshes, his body swollen by the bites of insects. Most reports agreed on the decisive moment when Antony rampaged again through the marsh. A much greater part of his army followed. This time it was easier. While Cassius had guarded every hill in the rear, Brutus had not.

The front lines clashed. The assassins' centre fell back as though before a heavier machine. There were individual fights, almost like duels, vengeance against those marked by name and a mass slaughter, all on a scale seen never before in Roman civil war.

Antony was determined that no leaders or potential leaders would escape. He wanted the captains and the lawyers. Most of all he wanted the assassins. He ordered killing tours of the battlefield's furthest edges. He hunted tent by tent.

He destroyed. He counted the famous dead. His pursuit was not personal but tactical, just as, since the death of Cicero, it had always been. Its fuel, as it had been ever since the decisions in Caesar's will, was the wilder anger of Octavian. Those who sought burial for corpses were directed to the crows in the sky.

The lesser men more easily escaped, Brutus's student idealists, the younger sons of useful families. Messalla, companion of Cassius's death, turned down command of the assassins' forces and himself over to Antony. His fellow student from Athens, Quintus Horatius Flaccus, would become the best-known escaper, a poet ruefully describing how his 'wings had been clipped', how he had run away abandoning his *parmula*, safer in future without his 'little shield', safer still when he became a laureate of the next age.

Horace had been a student colleague of Parmensis in Athens. He would soon matter much more to him – and to anyone else who loved Latin poetry – but he did not matter much when the news filtered first down to the fleet. More important were Casca, perhaps the only fatal killer from all the wielders of the daggers, his lesser brother, the brothers Caecilii, Rubrius Ruga, Sextius Naso, Marcus Spurius, Publius Lentulus Spinther. These were the eighth, ninth, tenth, eleventh, twelfth, thirteenth and fourteenth assassins to die.

To those who had merely fought on the wrong side the triumvirs might show mercy. Horace could hope to be forgiven; Parmensis could not. For Brutus, who spent the night after the battle high up on a mountain above Philippi, the choice of fighting on was gone. Those around him with a chance of changing sides thought that they should take it.

Brutus feared the mercy of Octavian, absent and unknowable, much more than the vengeance that he knew so well. He railed against the ideals that had guided him to death in a faraway field, declaiming against 'wretched virtue' that he had followed as a fact but was no more than a word.

Porcia's brother, Marcus, had also died on Philippi's second day of slaughter. By his coming suicide Brutus was seeking a place in the tradition of their great father, whose purpose, unlike that of Cassius, was not to be free of the fear of death during his life but to set aside the fear when his murderer came. Death in battle, or by suicide in face of failure, would be less heroic if it was not something to be feared.

Whatever their differences, Brutus chose the same means of death as Cassius, quoting a line from Euripides's revenge play *Medea* that Cicero had held at his own death: 'Zeus, do not forget who has

brought these troubles upon us'. With a curse upon Caesar's heir
he called out his fellow assassins' names individually, sighed at the
name Pacuvius Labeo, and became the fifteenth to die.

Labeo, the faithful lawyer on a field without law, returned to his
tent, dug a grave beside his bed, freed his own most faithful slave
and asked to be stabbed in the neck. Roman war dead were regularly left unburied on the field. Labeo was a lawyer not a soldier.
He found the death closest to the customs of home. He was the
sixteenth assassin to die.

The many on the assassins' side who wanted to surrender min-
gled with the fewer who had to escape. Fourteen thousand legionaries were captured. Those prepared to bear the triumvirs' chains
preferred those of Antony. Favonius, the angry sceptic of assassination and sharer of Servilia's family council at Antium, saluted
Antony as imperator; he abused Octavian to his face and was taken
to Ephesus for execution. Tillius Cimber disappeared along with
his high ambitions, probably the seventeenth assassin to die but no
one was sure. Octavian and Antony vowed to build a new temple to
Mars the Avenger when they had hunted down every last man on
the list that had resounded beneath the funeral spit.

Out on the Aegean Sea, Parmensis remained with his ships. He
greeted and waited. Flags flew. Messages flew. Sometimes information flew. Brutus and Cassius were gone but their cause did not need
to come to an end. Parmensis, still a hunted man, was already looking back from Philippi and out towards the seas to a new beginning.

14

SEXTUS, HONORARY ASSASSIN

Sextus Pompeius Seeking News of the Battle of Pharsalus.
John Hamilton Mortimer (1776)

Two years after Caesar's death, his killers asked what sort of a man his heir had become. This was a difficult question until decades later when he was the Emperor Augustus and had answered it himself, with help of poets and historians, and had made it easy.

The young Octavian was a revolutionary, calling upon the old to do something new. He wanted power. He was unafraid of power's momentum. He had the most minimal inhibitions about where and on whom power was to be exerted. That was clear enough.

At a time when few understood the elements that defined a risk, he had an instinct for the use of time to improve his odds, the power of delay as well as speed, of patience and surprise, of probing dark places where others did not see. The future was not for him an enemy or a mirror of the past. It was an opportunity, it almost seemed his friend.

Meanwhile he was a twenty-year-old heir to a dead dictator, unbound from the reasonable and from the conventions that an enemy might expect. The head of Brutus was severed from its body not like that of Decimus on the orders of an Alpine chief, nor like Pompey's by command of an Egyptian Pharaoh, nor even Trebonius's by a hoodlum aristocrat's torturers. The face of Brutus was demanded by Octavian to be despatched to Rome for display at the foot of his father's statue: only rough seas sent it to the sea bed instead.

Much more than the assassins wanted to kill Octavian, Octavian wanted to kill the assassins. Julius Caesar's adopted son was Caesar as he might have become. He did not lead as Caesar had led. He stayed far from the front line. He hardly fought. On the first day at Philippi he had not fought at all. He had hidden in the marsh. He let his name do the fighting. He saw how much that name might win, how it might let him define what winning meant.

* * *

The assassins, fresh from defeat, had also, and more urgently, to return to another name from the recent past, that of Sextus Pompeius, the last surviving son of Caesar's enemy Pompey, cloaked in blue, bearded in perpetual mourning for his father, different from all the other rivals for Roman power. Sextus stood outside and was prepared to stand alone. If he could be brought inside, he might change everything. If Octavian was to be stopped, if Antony's mind was to be changed, Sextus might make the difference.

Pompey's younger son had never been easy to suborn. Like Cassius he was a pupil of the universities of Rhodes. His young teacher was Posidonius's grandson Aristodemus but no one ever suggested that he was loyal to a philosophy or to any predictable school of thought. He was an honorary member of the assassins' club but had not directly helped their cause. He was not, like Cicero or Porcia, with them almost at the start. He stood indicted under the *Lex Pedia*, in the same class as those who had killed, but had never come close to being a killer of Caesar. He had welcomed to Sicily anyone caught by the *Lex Titia* but was not himself in that legal net.

Sextus was a survivor, both as a man of the sea and as a moral example. Both qualities were his strengths. Regardless of his own personality and experience, he represented values of an age before the triumvirs, exaggerated by hope but remembered in the reality of a living person, values whose passing was still regretted and whose last representative was still revered.

The name of Pompey the Great was attracting greater sentimental support than at any time since the death of Cato. Pompey would have become as much a dictator, had he lived, as Caesar became. Many made that argument. But Pompey did not live and did not become a dictator. His memory and his heir could be linked to the idea of a good that might have been. Many made that link. Parmensis was not alone.

Sextus had present power as well as his potent symbolism from the past. He had the largest navies, the greatest practical interest in Rhodian theories on currents, winds, maps and tides. He was a proven leader at sea. He had fought alongside his elder brother in Spain after Pharsalus and the suicide of Cato in Africa. His forces had failed to defeat Julius Caesar there but that was no disgrace. He had escaped and, as some said, survived as little more than a pirate; but that was mere abuse, mud that did not stick, and even piracy was not a power to be dismissed.

Sextus's own memories made him hostile to the heirs of Caesar, not as brutal as his father, the 'teenage butcher' before he became 'the Great', but maybe ruthless enough. As a young boy he had ridden in his father's spectacular triumph. He had watched the parade of Pompey's head of pearls, the moon of gold on its gambling table, the statues of gods led first to the Capitol and then to his own theatre, Rome's grandest memorial museum. As a teenager, he had watched with his step-mother, Cornelia Metella, as his father was stabbed in the bottom of a small boat. He had heard how the severed head bled into Egyptian sand – and how Caesar too had seen that trophy of his triumph.

Later he added *Magnus* and *Pius* to his name, the first his inheritance from his father, the second the sign of his reverence for him. The beard on his square face stood for the potency of family in his life. Although reason and revenge were concepts that did not need to be close, he had more reason for revenge than Octavian could claim.

Sextus was more casual than Pompey, a lesser version of Octavian, maybe a version in reverse, but still with the power of a name, able to recruit from his father's friends, the defeated and the proscribed, able to control the sea routes around Italy and beyond until he could be stopped. The difference between them was the scale of everything about Julius Caesar, a revolutionary whose ambitions, curtailed by daggers, seemed after death to be greater still.

* * *

Parmensis considered his past. He had not fought at Philippi himself. He had not seen, smelt and heard the horrors of others. He was free of the guilt that comes from comrades to the left and right falling to the sword. He would not move forward with that terrible, personal vengeance which destroys so much.

He had never met Sextus. He had been born in Caesar's country; he had then been persuaded, gently led (it was hard to remember what was so unclear at the time) into joining Caesar's assassins. That had not meant his becoming a Pompeian. A man from Parma would have resisted that title, as fiercely as he would have fought off an assault by Gauls.

He considered his future. Life was no longer so simple. Words changed meanings. A Pompeian might be a friend. Parmensis was possibly the last assassin alive but he could not be certain. Life was certainly much safer at sea than on the land. He had no immediate cause to move from the waters around Rhodes and Crete.

Winter was still a month away. He had choices. Joining Sextus was one of them. The triumvirs' navy was nowhere to be seen in the southern Aegean. Parmensis and his crews were wanted and hunted but hardly as a priority. Their pursuers had to look first to problems in the east and west before they would look for any last assassin.

That seemed more than a hope. It was a reasonable supposition. He and his friends from the losing side at Philippi could feel safe for a while. The winning troops, as everyone knew, were the triumvirs' prime anxiety. They had been promised money, which Antony would have to find in the east, and land in Italy which would require Octavian's revolutionary ruthlessness to steal and redistribute.

Armed soldiers could not be left dissatisfied. Both the traders of Smyrna, their treasuries liable to prising open by torture, and the farmers of Parma, their families on the road to be refugees, were in more danger from Octavian and Antony than was Cassius Parmensis.

Parmensis was not even afraid for his life; his death was nothing to him as he had long repeated to himself. But, while he was alive, there was a growing security at sea, not just safety but an absence of care. He liked that security, just as he liked the lack of fear.

Slowly cruising between west and east, the small band of survivors from Philippi was growing larger by the day. At its new core were thirty ships that Parmensis had taken from Rhodes before their owners were aware of who had won and who had lost. To prevent any revolt when they heard the news he had burnt every other Rhodian ship except the state trireme of their diplomats and priests.

The citizens of Rhodes were almost grateful. The coastal cities of Miletus, Ephesus and Xanthus to the north were equally little threat to Parmensis's ships. Their people might be hostile but their treasuries and spirit had been emptied by the depradations of Dolabella, Brutus and Cassius. If Antony were to extract more he would have to bring a whole school of torturers like the Samarian who had despatched Trebonius. That would take patience and time.

If Antony were to apply diplomatic charm instead, that too would distract him from hostile pursuit. News came of his obsession with a young queen from Cappadocia, Glaphyra, who was seeking support for her son. At Ephesus he was granting pardons like a god, in Lycia relief from taxes, at Rhodes new territory, at Xanthus his permission to rebuild.

Laodicea, where Dolabella had ended his life, and Tarsus, once so helpfully uncooperative with the assassins, were to be free of all tax to Rome. Athens gained advantage, as it often did, simply by being Athens, cultural beacon of the world. Antony sponsored competitions for poets there. These were major projects. To Tarsus, close to where Gaius Cassius had first planned the death of Caesar, Antony had summoned the queen of Egypt, Cleopatra, the mother of the boy recognised, if not readily by Octavian, as Julius Caesar's son.

There was every reason for Parmensis to pause, look back and think. The coded conversations on the Palatine before the assassination had not prepared him, or anyone else, to plan the right way forward two years later. Those who feared civil war had seen their worst fears fulfilled. Those who saw dictatorship as worse than war had not escaped it – and did not even know who the next dictator would be. The enlightened in their gardens were less certain that they should ignore the anxieties of those not yet converted and still in public life.

An Epicurean might still, however, seek a peaceful place. Time was on his side. Antony's next aim, it was said, was to go further east, backed by the treasury of Egypt, taking yet further away the legions that had triumphed at Philippi. Parmensis had lost all enthusiasm for the Fulminata XII and their thunderbolt shields so familiar in his distant home. The Parthians were due soon to feel the onslaught that Caesar's death had spared them. Such a campaign was unlikely to be short.

Only the onrush of small events made contemplation hard. New ships joined Parmensis and swelled his force. Turullius was an early arrival, a second assassin who was still alive, backed by another fleet captured from the Rhodians and cash that he had extorted in better times, some of it minted by himself. A survivor from Brutus's staff had visited Rhodes before Antony arrived, had found the city in incipient revolt and taken away with him the entire Roman garrison, some three thousand men who had to be managed and supplied.

Cicero's son, freed from the grim task that Brutus had given him to pillage Greece, arrived from Thasos with other young men, keen to continue the struggle in nobler ways. Never deemed more than dull and ordinary by his father, reputed as a heavy drinker, he carried his own talismanic name. From Crete came the no less famously named Lucius Aemilius Lepidus Paullus, proscribed brother of Lepidus the triumvir, fortunate escaper and yet another symbol of the ruthlessness of the pact on the Bononia island to punish and divide.

All of them wondered what should they do next, where they should go. This was the central question for the continuation of the assassins' cause, however that cause was defined and whatever its future purpose. Paullus had held Crete and its deep blue waters for Brutus but could not hold it for a dead man. They paused around Ithaka and Cephalonia, the home islands of Odysseus, magical for sailors as well as poets but bare and impractical for long. Back up the coast there was Troy, an empty barren plain, Lesbos, a looted island, Smyrna, still in mourning, Ephesus and Xanthus, newly seduced by Antony, Sparta, spared by Brutus's death but unlikely to welcome his former allies. There was Samos.

Parmensis knew all the possible places. Sextus knew even better the choices that Parmensis and his fellow captains had to make. They were the sites he had passed with his step-mother and defeated father as they fled the battlefield of Pharsalus, those that they rejected in favour of their family friends in Egypt who were not friendly to a loser.

To Parmensis the writer, these were the realms of Homer and Sappho, Agamemnon and his cursed family, the first poets, the first imagined characters. But Sextus had no known interest in art. Other places might be remembered or imagined but safe winter harbours for a fleet in flight were still few.

Sicily beckoned. It was further distant from Antony, its inlets and islands ideal for triremes to hide and harry the transports carrying corn. Rome could be starved from Sicily, as Octavian knew and feared. Sextus himself sent ever more welcoming messages.

There was much civil argument to be had about how to respond. Some of the naval commanders preferred independence. Ahenobarbus, the aristocratic naval victor of the first day at Philippi, still stood sentenced to death with the assassins of Caesar. He was distrustful of anyone who might trade favours with the triumvirs and abandon him to the fate of Cicero, Basilus and so many. With his own silver coinage, celebrating a triumph that he could claim wholly for himself, he decided to choose nowhere, to be a gentleman of the sea, beholden to none.

For every captain there was a choice of seas as well as ports. The Ionian, Aegean and Adriatic were all possible seas. For Parmensis, the flagships of the assassins' fleet must have begun to resemble the parties on the Palatine before the Ides of March. There was much talk of detail, shared hostilities to a Caesar but differing degrees of commitment to other leadership and other places.

Meanwhile the fleet swelled in power and possibility. Admirals might argue but, whoever from the senatorial classes was in charge, experienced captains did the work of sailing. Rowers volunteered. Soldiers manned the decks. Even sympathisers on shore, preferring older Roman government to the threat of the new, were ready to help the reborn cause without knowing precisely what it was.

Slowly the ships of the losers at Philippi sailed south of Greece, north of Crete, into the southern part of the Ionian Sea. With the Adriatic up above them, their paths divided. Ahenobarbus headed north with seventy ships and two legions to revisit his triumph at Brundisium and further up the coast. Parmensis saw greater safety for himself around Sicily, better prospects, even after Philippi, of bringing Octavian down and saving himself for the longer future. He took his ships into a fleet of more than a hundred, with two legions, archers and well-paid crews, all sailing together into the sea country of Sextus Pompeius.

15

ABUSE AT PERUSIA

Hundreds of the hunted had been in Sicily for a year before the battles of Philippi were fought and lost. It was the only place on the Tellus map where they might hide without a sword. Most of the proscribed had not wanted to fight alongside Brutus and Cassius. They had preferred not to fight at all. Even in Rome, where so much status stemmed from the army, many men had never been fighters and never wanted to be.

Sicily was safe because Sextus protected all three lines of its triangle coast. It was familiar even to those who had never been there, as the birthplace of the Roman navy in two wars against Carthage, as the city's first province. Sicily produced corn in vast fields, watered, fertile, worked by gangs of slaves until the land was worked out. It was vital to Rome but still a place apart.

Antony had granted the islanders full Roman citizenship almost immediately after Caesar's death. It was one of the policies which he claimed, from his sole access to the dead dictator's papers, had already been decided. Cicero, who had successfully prosecuted one of their most rapacious Roman governors three decades before, had disapproved. He thought that the islanders' gratitude for rights and freedom should be reserved to him alone.

This argument in Rome, like so many that came later, had little impact on Sicily itself. Sextus Pompeius took control of the island before the details of Caesar's citizenships and rights could be enacted – also before, when Antony became a public enemy at Mutina, they could be rescinded. It did not matter what Caesar had ever said. The only Roman who mattered in Sicily was Pompey's son, who welcomed fugitives from the triumvirs in ever greater numbers to a place from where an exile might one day return home.

Old Rome was moving down the Tellus map. Senators from the towns below the Rubicon found temporary asylum beyond the rock of Scylla and the whirlpool of Charybdis. A line of lesser aristocrats filled the lists of Sextus's officers, a Lentulus, an Arruntius, a Vetulinus, all potent names at the time. Parmensis, fused by tyrannicide into the highest rungs of society, was in easy company. Among other arrivals whose presence recalled the Ides of March was Lucius Cornelius Cinna, the praetor whose life was saved through his confusion with a poet.

With Brutus, Cassius and so many others dead, Sextus offered those fearful of Octavian an alternative name in what was a war of names. This was the time when the combined fleets of the new Caesar's enemies might have most successfully moved against him, preventing the export of Sicilian corn, blockading supplies from other sources, raiding ports, using hunger as a weapon, forcing battle with Octavian when he was much weaker than he seemed.

That would have been the policy most in Parmensis's interest. If it had succeeded he might have become a minor hero in Rome, maybe more than that, as one of the last assassins when Caesar's heir was as dead as Caesar himself. Both Sextus and Parmensis knew the dangers that Octavian faced in redistributing the land of Italy to his soldiers – and the even greater danger to him of his failing to do so.

Sextus was a prominent man of Rome even though he had spent so little time in the city, popular despite his power to make the people starve. He was in close communication with Lepidus and with Antony. He knew his opportunities. He let them pass.

Antony was far away, his motives and ambitions hard to discern even by his closest friends. Lepidus was cowed by Octavian. Sextus saw too little information and too many risks. He did not master risk as Octavian so effectively did. He let his advantage slip. He stayed in Sicily, welcoming political defectors, semi-professional pirates and the merely frightened.

* * *

At the other end of the map, Octavian's revolution was about to reach back to the banks of the Rubicon. His armies had to be rewarded. Farmers who had escaped the triumphs of Caesar feared brutal confiscation from his adopted son. Past beneficiaries of Caesar's rewards were no less anxious that their gains be safe.

The prosperous Italians of Ariminum knew well what it was to be a military town, a 'colony' of former soldiers, to have half their land and more handed out to newcomers as a pension. Their own wealth had begun in war and they wished to keep it in peace. The victors of Philippi, soon to arrive from Greece, were their foes even while they were still at sea, likely to be more vicious in grabbing for themselves even than they had been in killing fellow Romans.

To reinforce their fears the men and women of Ariminum needed to do no more than to look west up the *Via Aemilia* to Mutina and Parma, towns barely recovering from the depredations of legionary recruiters and the battles between Antony, Octavian, assassins and the senate. *Parmenses miserrimos*, Decimus had written to Cicero. The people of Parma were pitiable still. Parmensis would have been no hero in his home town had he been unwise enough to return.

Ariminum was the most north-western Italian port, the peak of a triangle of trade links with other towns of the Adriatic coast and beyond. To the north was the valley of the Po and the lakes called the Seven Seas. The inland towns of Mantua and Cremona were also on the lists for confiscations. To the south-west were gentle hills, fertile fields of sand and clay, the rising *Via Flaminia* to Rome, road of so much traffic since Julius Caesar's last winter.

The people of Ariminum had pride in their elegant town, in its history even of violent times. They lived in Italy, not in Gaul. That was important and, although there were rumours that all of Cisalpine Gaul, like Sicily in the south, was to be made part of Italy, that had not happened yet. The Roman general and historian, Gaius Pollio (Antony's ally, it was said), had nine legions of occupation there, making Parma as different from Ariminum as the Ariminians wanted to keep it.

Their main streets, their Cordo and Decumanus, their intersecting axes north–south and east–west, were the same as in anywhere built by Romans, fixed town or shifting camp. But they had Greek facades and some grandeur. In their marbled central square Caesar had declared the start of his civil war with Pompey. Let the die be cast, he said, quoting in Greek from a favourite comic playwright to a suitably appreciative crowd. With the Rubicon at his back the die was cast. No one, certainly not Caesar, knew then where it would fall. To the horror of the people of Ariminum, six years on, it was still falling.

Those fighting as Caesar's heirs had lost tens of thousands of men in two battles at Philippi (only propagandists ever even tried to count the numbers) but the most immediately troubling men to Octavian were those who did not die. Some had chosen to stay where they had fought, to farm and form a new colony. Others were with Antony, ready to retrace the steps they had taken with Brutus and Cassius, newly contemplating the completion of Caesar's ambitions in Parthia. But more than 40,000 men were coming home.

Octavian wanted them to be both content and concentrated where they might help him best in the future. His plan was to give his legionaries what they had earned and to give it fast. Delay might bring resentment from the recipients and resistance from the newly dispossessed. This part of his revolution could not wait.

Octavian's authority rested on Caesar's name which was his name too, and on the confidence of his troops. He had no funds to pay the price of farms in Ariminum. He had marked it among eighteen prosperous towns whose hinterlands were to be seized from their owners, divided into patches of around forty iugera, twenty-five acres, each patch to be handed to a veteran and his new farming family, each old family to join the landless of the roadsides and towns.

* * *

Parmensis and the sailors with Sextus were some of the first to know about the new uncertainties in Italy. News flowed faster over water. Octavian had landed at Brundisium without opposition. He had been invisible when his ships flowed into the harbour. He was sick, it was said, and playing as small a part as he had in the battles. His returning army was a massive unstable force, still a machine, sometimes more like a disease. It had an order that could be disordered at any time, the sooner the better as his enemies hoped and whispered.

But military discipline had held. Military gossip hardly mattered. No one needed to see Octavian as he peered out towards land, lines of sharp-pointed prows before and behind him, bulging transports beside them, rows of men ready to seize the beach in case Italy had become a foreign country. The captains were in command. There was a plan to get on shore, wave upon wave upon the waves. Needless instructions at this stage would do nothing but confuse.

Only when the sea was behind him did Octavian have the task that only he could fulfil, one that he could hardly have imagined, only two years before, when he first arrived there as a student from Apollonia, a surprised and sudden heir to the dictator Julius, the brother of Julia, his grandmother. He needed many new settlements of satisfied, committed supporters. He had the sole responsibility to turn his inextinguishable young man's revenge into something else that would last.

He had to deal with two consuls for the year, 41 BC, both appointed at Bononia, each linked to the triumvirs by birth and marriage but neither a reliable help. The first was Publius Servilius Vatia, son-in-law of Caesar's mistress, Servilia, husband of one of Brutus's sisters, a veteran conservative of Caesar's age but no admirer of his heir. The second was Lucius Antonius, Mark Antony's vicious youngest brother who, like Sextus Pompeius, had yearnings for the old republic but had also adopted the title *Pietas*, to show his family loyalty above any other.

Vatia's daughter, also named Servilia, was the woman to whom, before the Bononia pact, Octavian had been engaged to be married; the relationship had ended in order that the young Caesar might instead marry the daughter of Antony's wife, Fulvia. This was the kind of dynastic shuffle that the soldiers on the river bank had found reassuring while vengeance slowly fell upon each killer of Caesar. The rejected daughter was offered to the son of Lepidus instead. The consulate was Vatia's consolation prize for whatever degree of humiliation he had felt.

Lucius had once supported energetically the distribution of land to veterans. That was when he was asked to do so by Julius Caesar. When Octavian asked the same question, Lucius was less helpful: he wanted reassurance that soldiers in Antony's legions would be as generously treated as those of Octavian himself. He formed a close alliance with Fulvia who became quickly the senior partner, exploiting both her populist political connections and the links to gangland Rome that she had made through Cicero's enemy, Clodius, the first of her three husbands.

Octavian also faced resistance from within Ariminum itself and the other towns under threat. Even those whose farms were safe objected. To landowners with long established rights Octavian's forces were no more welcome as neighbours than as armed invaders. The difference between being a *miserrimus Parmensis* of the present and a *miserrimus Ariminensis* of the near future did not seem very great.

Deputations travelled down the *Via Flaminia* and up the *Via Appia* from the south, demanding not that the promises to the troops should be broken but that the burden of settling them be spread more fairly around the country. The people of Rome itself, not directly threatened, used the opportunity to protest at everything from proscriptions to the price of bread. The problem of dictatorship, even a triple dictatorship, was that everything could be laid at Octavian's door.

Antony was absent, initially in Cappadocia, enjoying, it was said, his royal mistress Glaphyra, and soon to be on his way to Caesar's sometime Egyptian partner, Cleopatra. The benefit to Octavian was

that Antony's missions in the east could increasingly be character-
ised and criticised in this way.

Lepidus was present but increasingly powerless and easy to
ignore. After missing the glory at Philippi, he stood accused by his
triumviral colleagues of conspiring with Sextus against them both.
Octavian had taken Lepidus's former provinces to compensate for
the embarrassment that much of his own share under the Bononia
Pact, Sicily, Sardinia and Corsica, was still under Sextus's rule.
Caesar's assassin, Parmensis, had freer access to the island coasts
than Caesar's heir had.

Octavian tried to appease the landowners with modest relax-
ations of his programme's rules. He succeeded only in angering
his soldiers. In Placentia, on the *Via Aemilia* beyond Parma there
was a mutiny. The farmers of Ariminum and Bononia were not any
the more reassured. Antony's soldiers demanded even more land
as insurance against the weakness of their champion. Even in the
towns that were not targeted for expropriation, there was fear that
they might be next. Rural Italy was simmering with resentment
towards Rome. The Roman mob sensed only weakness. Octavian
needed troops to ensure that he was safe even on the Capitoline.

In the north, Lucius and Fulvia saw an opportunity, deciding to
act on their own against Octavian, to do for their brother and husband what he would not do for himself. They offered warm words
both to the landowners and to the legionaries loyal to Antony, one
side fearful of life-changing losses, the other that they were not
gaining enough. Lucius gathered troops and treasure. Fulvia quietly
incited the mob that had once helped Clodius against Cicero – in
times that had once seemed so vicious.

Their supporters, coordinated or not, took several Italian towns.
Antony was, at most, controlling only at a distance. Octavian challenged his challengers. Losers in the battles against Octavian fled
to Sextus, further strengthening the army and navy in Sicily. Little
changed except the new sense of insecurity felt by all.

Lepidus was nominally responsible for the security of Rome.
Lucius forced him to flee. The triumvirate was in trouble, barely in

existence. Octavian recalled an army that he had sent to Spain and concentrated on the crisis in Italy. He retreated south to regather his forces and his thoughts.

Lucius retreated north along the ever more familiar *Via Flaminia*, aiming to meet the seven legions of Pollio, his brother's man in Cisalpine Gaul, and of Ventidius, Antony's master of military supply. In Parma, it was as though there were ever only one story, the marching of rival Roman armies through their streets.

In this winter of a looming new phase of civil war, Pollio, Ventidius and Lucius were still too far apart for the more powerful pair to help the weaker. All of the Antonians, if Antony could claim such a party, needed to come together as one. Lucius needed a place in which to wait, to play for time and hope.

At Fulginiae, at the lower edge of the Appenines, a peacetime traveller on the *Via Flaminia* might once have turned east to Hispellum, passed through its twin-towered Gate of Venus, and then north-east to Perusia near the upper reaches of the River Tiber. When Lucius entered Perusia, one of the most ancient and colourful towns of the Etruscans, it was as if he too were a temporary traveller. He waited for his reinforcements to arrive. That surely would not be long.

Lucius was confident of support from Pollio, a general closely allied to his brother who, in the tracks of Julius Caesar, was conscious of his reputation, wrote his own history and cared also for the historical verdicts of others. Ventidius had long experience in maintaining and supplying armies and seemed no less reliable in the family cause. What Antony himself wanted from his allies Lucius did not know, an ignorance that was maybe what Antony wanted most.

Perusia high above its fertile plain, was a place of confident display more than military might, theatrical temples protected by terraced walls dating from the time of the Tarquins. The Etruscan towns were reminders that Rome did not owe its art and architecture to Greece alone. Perusia's oldest roofs were swirls of painted terracotta, forests of leopards and panthers, herons, sphinxes and pomegranate trees. Its houses were built in circles, its streets deep cut, its places of worship peculiarly backless, sideless, marked out by massive tripods of bronze, all for air and show.

Winter was a dangerous time in the malarial marshes of the upper Tiber but Lucius did not expect much more than a tourist's stay, only until Pollio and Ventidius brought their forces to free him. Supplies were short but they had boats on the swollen rivers and the Perusians themselves would provide. Their pigs and cattle were of legendary size. Some of their herdsmen had already been displaced from their farmland by legionary veterans at Hispellum. All of them feared worse to come if Octavian's plans were not spread further afield or stopped.

Together, Lucius, his officers and hosts, prepared to look down on the fighting plains of Umbria and plan how Octavian would be defeated. Mark Antony in Egypt might not know precisely the intent but all Antonians, family and allies alike, would be beneficiaries. Sextus Pompeius would hear and respond by sea. Rome and the whole Roman world would be grateful to see the weakening – even the defeat – of Caesar's revolutionary son. The war at Perusia, like the town itself, became a sequence of extravagant scenes. It was a mystery even while it was being fought. No one intended it to be what it became, not Antony who was not even there, not his brother Lucius who was marking time, not Octavian who was testing his rivals, his soldiers and himself.

The first sign of Octavian's presence was an army of engineers, the men of war that Caesar had promoted to the front line of power, discovering in Gaul, as no one had before, how fast millions of tonnes of earth could be dug and raised to change the chances of victory. Octavian had learnt well his father's lesson. As usual when he was at war, it was not clear whether he was there or not himself. Trees fell. A wooden wall began to run across the cold mudded landscape, a deep ditch behind it, almost like a living thing, stretching to the Tiber on both sides of the town.

To harry the diggers and builders Lucius sent out cavalry. Octavian's supply base was captured and dispersed. News arrived that Fulvia, calling in favours from who knew where and when, had persuaded one of Antony's most cautious allies, Lucius Munatius Plancus, to march from Rome with reinforcements. Plancus had already scattered one of Octavian's legions that had been moving cautiously from the south. The Antonians were confident.

They were also an uncertain alliance. Fulvia, though a formidable woman, was no substitute for her latest husband. Plancus despised Ventidius as an upstart mechanic, mule-driver and pillager, all of these essential requirements for a man supplying an army but best kept away from the officers' club. Pollio, who had stood firm in a long losing war against Sextus in Spain, loathed the unprincipled Plancus. At this point they were in the ascendant nonetheless. If they stood together they had more forces. Caesar's heir might perhaps have been persuaded to retreat, losing some of his magic gambler's reputation in a place where all could see.

Instead Octavian ordered more of his legions into the region whose fields of grain and grapes he had promised to give away. He had a new commander in the field, Marcus Vipsanius Agrippa, a fellow student from Apollonia only a year older than himself, whom he had appointed to prosecute the assassins in the courts and learnt to trust. Even more importantly, Octavian's soldiers could look around from the hill tops and see what they were fighting for, acre by acre to the Tiber and beyond.

Inside Perusia Lucius lacked food for his troops. He had neither Ventidius himself nor Ventidius's skills. He also lacked a message. He could not seem to back the local landowners against the victors of Philippi. Not even Antony's most loyal advancing reinforcements would fight for that: every legionary wanted his bounty.

The alternative was to try saying that Antony would be fairer and more generous to every former soldier than Octavian would be. That was the path that Lucius chose. It was a difficult one. Antony's will was clouded by his absence. Octavian's revolutionary commitment to redistribute the land of Italy was present and clear.

The cost of war for that land was ever more visible too. The Romans had become used to fighting their civil wars abroad, to ravaging faraway places, Greece and Asia as they had before, Pharsalus and Philippi. Parma and Mutina were outside Italy in Gaul, only just in Gaul, but just was enough to make the difference. Although Pollio had not yet crossed the border, Ventidius was nearer and already occupying Ariminum. Agrippa had an opposing army at Ariminum's gates.

War south of the Rubicon would despoil what the soldiers on both sides were fighting and hoping for. Officers on both sides recognised this. They began to think and act together to ensure that neither of the triumvirs betrayed their promises. From the lower levels of the armies came an unusual political force for peace, united more by shared interest than the interests of their commanders.

On the road back to Rome lay the army of Plancus. Trade in the capital was depressed, food soaring in price, Octavian taking the blame and Sextus seen as a potential saviour. But in Perusia the hunger was harsh. Prosperity was the palest memory where Octavian was tightening his blockade. Lead slingshots carried printed taunts to the starving as well as sexual abuse of Fulvia, then safely caring for herself beside the Temple of Fortune in Praeneste, more than twenty miles the other side of Rome.

Octavian himself joined the jibes against Fulvia, writing that she wanted to fuck rather than fight him, her personal revenge for her husband's fucking Glaphyra in Cappadocia. He was not keen on this 'fuck or fight' message, he said, any more than he would have been keen on buggering a man who had asked him for the service.

The war at Perusia was like a propaganda play. These letters in lead, quickly buried when the battlefield returned to farmland, remained as rare reminders of how men roused themselves to fight a civil war.

'Hail Octavian, suck me off', wrote a shot-maker, carving carefully into the clay mould from which the missiles were cast. 'I'm going like lightning for Fulvia's *landicam*', wrote another, sending the rarely written word for clitoris from the legion whose shields had once flashed over Parma. 'To you who are going to starve', 'open your over-fucked arse', *esureis, culum pandite, laxe*: it took great skill and luck to kill a man with a sling, much less to harness his hatreds and hidden fears.

Within walls where he had never meant to stay for long Lucius forbade the feeding of slaves, or the freeing of them lest they escape and reveal the extremity of the famine. The mud of mass graves held those for whom there was no more grass to eat. Local leaders were in despair. Their streets were like stage sets where a theatre was closed by plague. Perusia was closed to more than just its normal business.

Thirteen legions loyal to Antony arrived finally at Fulginiae. The Perusians saw their camp fires and felt briefly confident of relief. Lucius, to show spirit to his rescuers, made a last assault on Octavian's wall. Then, just as suddenly, the firelight disappeared. Pollio, Ventidius and Plancus, briefly suppressing their mutual dislikes, had discussed tactics. Calenus, Antony's stronger ally, was still in Gaul. Plancus, beginning a long and successful career of caution, had argued that Perusia was not the priority.

These commanders had already let down Decimus at Mutina. Neither their soldiers nor officers were keen to fight unless there were a better reason for being loyal to Antony than what was presently before them. A brother and wife could not make the promises of Antony himself. Octavian made his own case. The armies dispersed.

Once again Octavian had shown his intimidating hold over Caesar's name and legions. Lucius and Fulvia were no match for Caesar's heir. Lucius surrendered to Octavian with a speech stressing republican ideals, personal beliefs of his own, not the property disputes of war. Octavian pardoned him.

Antony's veterans in Perusia were pardoned too, again by request of the soldiers in the victorious ranks. Octavian executed the local leaders, sparing only one man who was lucky enough, when in Rome, to have voted under the *Lex Pedia* for vengeance against the assassins. A less lucky colleague killed himself before he was killed.

Fulvia fled to Brundisium. The mother of the Antonii brothers fled to Sextus, suggesting what some in Sicily hoped might have been a pact planned for the future. The prospects of Turullius and Parmensis depended almost wholly on Antony and Sextus at some point combining to bring Octavian down.

The victor then freed his victorious men to pillage what remained in Perusia, a promise that he failed to keep only because fire from the suicide's funeral pyre did the destruction with more devastating speed. It was the spring of 40 BC. Winds were high. Stories spread of human sacrifices on the Ides of March on the steps of Caesar's temple. The beacon brought truth and untruth swiftly over the sea to Sicily.

16

PARMENSIS ALONE

Ariminum to Brundisium (40 BC)

Around Ariminum the measurers began their work. The skill of the military *metatores*, essential every night for making camp and needed too for every new town, was deployed to divide land south of the Rubicon into farms for the victors of Philippi. Just as the Boii had once been forced from Bononia, Mutina and Parma, former Roman owners were removed by force or offered servitude where once they had been masters. Homeless, indebted, without the land that defined them as citizens, they filled the streets of Ariminum itself or fled to luckier places along the *Via Flaminia*.

Results were mixed. Some legionaries were born to be farmers and knew the life. Some knew that nature was deceptive, that tempting flat fields might need ten times more from the plough than a steeply sloping farm on a mountainside. Others knew nothing and preferred practising their old trades, extending their shares by force rather than by herding flocks of goats. Often there was more to be gained by fights over whether fifteen acres on a sandy hill was the same as twenty on the plain, or by gambling acre for any acre as they had always done with their pay while on the march. Food production fell.

Only poetry was the great gainer. The farmers of Mantua and Cremona, tending livestock beside the crater lakes, belonged to the life and memory of Virgil, Publius Vergilius Maro, the most potent artist of his time. Mantua was an Etruscan town taken over by Gauls two centuries before. Cremona had itself been born as a Roman military colony. Both suffered the arrival of men entitled by Philippi. Virgil's countryside poems, his *Eclogues*, evoked the sadness of helpless shepherds in a fantasy landscape of ancient Sicily and modern Gaul, despair when even a modest plot of marsh, reeds and stones is stolen: *miles habebit barbarus*, the barbarian soldier will possess.

Among the landowners around Perusia was the father of Sextus Propertius, a very different poet, a rich young man of Rome and Latin pioneer of the pains of love. Readers of Propertius's first book, a sequence about his misery-bringing mistress as the be-all-and-end-all of life, had suddenly, and at the very end, to confront something both shocking and seemingly outside what had come before.

The subject was an exhausted soldier, his eyes swollen with terror, escaping through Octavian's battle lines, and before him the almost dead body of his brother, fallen not in the siege itself but in its random aftermath. 'Save yourself for our parents' sake,' says the dying man, 'but tell only part of my story, only how I escaped, not how I died; our sister can bury me but any handful of earth from these Etruscan mountains can be my remains.' The speaker is a *miser* not as a wretched lover but as one of the *miserrimos Parmenses*, a victim of confiscation, reaction and revenge.

Much of what later became known as Augustan poetry, so defined to praise the patronage of Caesar's heir, was the poetry of the triumvirs' war. In his *Eclogues* Virgil used ruthless occupiers and the newly landless to define the time; Propertius took the dripping graveyards of Perusia.

* * *

Lucius Antonius's humiliation had not ruined his family's cause. Antony's allies felt a compensating need to show that they were still on his side. Pollio, the new consul for 40 BC as decided in the Bononia pact, persuaded Ahenobarbus, still patrolling between Italy and Greece, to abandon his gentlemanly independence and bring his seventy ships into Antony's service. Around Sicily, even Sextus the honorary assassin, ever sensitive to changing winds, seemed finally about to intervene: Parmensis might soon be with him back in Italy.

Fulvia, who had reached the coast with a squad of cavalry, immediately sailed out of Brundisium under Ahenobarbus's protection. Plancus was her escort. Her aim was a meeting with her absent husband in Athens, partly to explain events at Perusia, partly to hear his own explanations about Cleopatra.

Each had heard reports, Antony's probably more reliable than his wife's, but in person in Athens there might be greater frankness. The news from burnt Perusia, the wild stories of human sacrifice as well as the brutal weapon of starvation, had brought unexpected contempt for Octavian, an opportunity in the war for popularity which Antony, his supporters argued, ought not to miss.

Many details of the story of Perusia were new to Antony when Fulvia and Plancus arrived. They were able to show their actions in the best possible light, as doubtless was he. Glaphyra was in the past. Cleopatra, the latest in the long line of Ptolemies who had ruled Egypt since the death of Alexander the Great, could be a powerful ally and financier of their cause, a necessity that sentiment should not hide. If he had plans to return to Cleopatra's bed, he had no need to share them, nor Fulvia to care too much.

For Parmensis, at sea with Sextus, Antony was already much the lesser danger of the two triumvirs. His brother, Lucius, the devastator of Parma as well as loser at Perusia, seemed keen to redeem his reputation, speaking nostalgically of the world before Caesar, and beginning to sound almost like an assassin on the Ides of March. His mother, Julia, Caesar's cousin, had sought protection from Sextus and joined an embassy which he sent to Athens.

Uncertain prospects suddenly looked good. Parmensis could look forward to success beyond and despite the fate of Perusia. Fleets hostile to Octavian might soon control both eastern and western coasts. Sextus and Antony together would have some five hundred ships of various kinds.

The alternative alignment of allies, a pact between Sextus and the vengeful Octavian, would be catastrophic for Parmensis. It seemed unlikely. There were rumours that Octavian had offered to marry into the Pompeian family if that would help his cause. That seemed unlikely too.

In Athens Fulvia persuaded Antony that he could safely use his new domination at sea to return to Italy, ideally as soon as possible. At minimum he needed to maintain his equal status with Octavian. To do that he could no longer ignore the claims of the legions for land. He had to outdo his rival in generosity, not be seen on the wrong side where his wife and brother, through lack of competence rather than ill intent, had left him. He needed to be seen by his own people, the crowd who only four years before had cheered him purple-cloaked in the Forum, chain-mailed at Caesar's right hand, half-naked at the ritual of the *Lupercalia*, all when Octavian was a mere student abroad.

Antony may not have needed much persuading. He had enjoyed as little success as Octavian since the triumph at Philippi. He had not progressed against the Parthians, whose leading general, to the embarrassment of all, was Quintus Labienus, self-styled *Parthicus Imperator*, Great Parthian Commander, and the son of a former senior officer for Pompey and Caesar. Nowhere, it seemed, was it possible to escape Rome's civil wars. Labienus had occupied cities as important to Rome as Lydia and Miletus.

There had been little money left in the towns of Asia; Antony's satisfactions in Cappadocia and Egypt had been of a mainly personal kind. His mother and many of his sympathisers were under the protection of Sextus, still formally his enemy. Friend and foe were changing roles at speeds hard to monitor from a distance. He had lost the allegiance of eleven legions in Gaul when Calenus, his loyal commander, unexpectedly died. He quite readily agreed to re-join the battle at home.

Antony and Plancus left Greece for Brundisium. The voyage was smooth but entry to the port was denied. Antony blockaded the port himself and raided neighbouring towns from the sea as far north as Sipontum at the peninsula of Garganus, the heel-spur to those who saw the Tellus map as a boot and Sicily as the ball at its toe.

Sextus, reassured of support by Antony, decided that this was his time. He sailed north and took Sardinia from a cowed ally of Octavian, also the two legions that were garrisoned there. He threatened the deep eastern harbours of Corsica. He returned south and laid siege to Thurii, the city between the toe and heel of Italy whose name had been part of Octavian's own name. He welcomed fresh reinforcements of cavalry men who had ridden to him rather than support Antony's cautious ally, Plancus.

On the western coast of Italy he ordered an attack on the old Greek fortress of Consentia, landing cavalry from transport ships. Parmensis, fighting at the other end of Italy from his home, was on the offensive. The tighter the links between Sextus and Antony, the better was his chance of forcing Octavian into error, rescuing hope, some hope at least, from the memories of Caesar's assassination.

Octavian attempted his first direct confrontation with Antony by sending Agrippa to reoccupy Sipontum and other lost parts of the east coast below the Garganus pensinsula. This was not a success. His local veterans were happy to re-enlist in his cause when they thought that Sextus and the assassins' party were their target; they went home rather than fight against their ally from Philippi. Octavian was left with a huge army outside Brundisium but no certainty that it would agree to fight Antony for the main exit route to Greece.

Antony led a cavalry charge, riding with spear and sword, against reinforcements for Octavian's army at Hyria on the northern side of the Garganus. Memories of Antony's reputation for bravery, and Octavian's for mere strategy, were enhanced. Equality between the two triumvirs had been restored but with it, just as after Mutina, came grounds for pause and reconciliation.

The triangle shifted. The triumvirs put their old joint interests above their simmering distrust. Antony did not need Sextus as much as he had thought. Sextus, not Octavian, was left as the one alone. Parmensis was even more alone.

In this fragile peace Fulvia played the last role of her political life. She suddenly died, of unreported causes near Corinth in the heart of Greece, a convenient death at a characteristically useful moment. The widowed Antony was suddenly free to marry Octavian's widowed sister, Octavia and, with reduced risk of contradiction, the blame for every recent misunderstanding could be laid at Fulvia's many doors.

The messier the conflict appeared, the more people were needed to blame. Fulvia, absent victim of the lead shots of Perusia, was even more abused when her absence was permanent. A path for diplomacy opened. Pollio negotiated for Antony; Octavian's man was Gaius Maecenas, a courtier of growing power who set the pattern for many future imperial successors, acting solely for Octavian, never taking a position in the senate or anywhere independent of his master. Together they set the rest of the terms for what in October, 40 BC, became the Treaty of Brundisium. As seen in Sicily, for Parmensis and his cause, this was a looming disaster.

Brundisium itself was a central part of what became a wide and comprehensive deal. At the vital port which Ahenobarbus had come to control, the man so independent after Philippi received both his reward and his marching orders, the governorship of distant Bithynia where the assassin, Tillius Cimber, forgotten and presumed dead, was unable to challenge him for his once promised post.

Lucius Antonius, forgiven for the short remainder of his life, became governor of Spain. Lepidus, who was not present, was allowed Africa. Gaul remained with Octavian. Italy was to be common ground. The two signatories divided the rest of the Roman world between them, more neatly than in the aftermath of Philippi and much more perilously for the last assassins.

Death for the killers of Julius Caesar was less important for Antony than Octavian but it was an issue on which Antony and Octavian had easily agreed before. It had become sometimes the sole issue. The only two senators who had defended Caesar from the daggers on the Ides of March, Gaius Calvisius Sabinus and Lucius Marcus Censorinus, were designated to be consuls, a message clear to Parmensis and to all.

At the northern end of the Tellus map the people of Parma whom Parmensis had left behind saw hope in the Treaty of Brundisium. If Antony wanted to confront Octavian in the future, he would not be able to descend the *Via Aemilia* and cross the Rubicon as Caesar had done. Cisalpine Gaul, as well as the Gauls on the other side of the Alps, belonged to Octavian just as it had once belonged to his father.

Sextus, however, was discontented in the south. He thought that at Brundisium he should have replaced Lepidus as the third and notionally equal leg of the triumvirate. Octavian and Antony rejected that, accepting him only as governor of Sicily, Sardinia and Corsica. Discontent turned to anger, directed first at Antony who, in addition to other perceived betrayals, had accepted Sextus's protection for his mother, a sacred trust, and then forgotten it.

After the peace treaty Pompey's son returned to Sicily and did not stay peaceful for long. He defeated an attempt by an ally of Octavian to take back Sardinia. He sailed with his fleet as far up the western coast of Italy to the mouth of the Tiber, blockading food imports and threatening worse. He was not abused for his attacks but hailed by hungry Romans as a blue-cloaked Neptune, god of the sea.

New taxes at Rome brought new riots. The people blamed the triumvirs not Sextus for the enforced austerity. Statues of both Antony and Octavian were felled, any distinction between them gone. Street attacks were indiscriminate. Romans, long disciplined by dictators' rules, rampaged with fire.

As Sextus's popularity rose, he felt that he had not just been cheated at Brundisium but humiliated. He did not have long to wait for his turn to bring the mighty down. In early 39 BC, at Baiae in the bay of Naples new talks began. They quickly faltered but, only a little later, at Cape Misenum, the three triumvirs joined Sextus on his flagship, a floating successor to the island at Bononia, moored by ropes to the shore. This was the place at the centre that he saw as his due.

This time the proceeds of peace were more widely shared between them. The triumvirs agreed that Sextus would add the southern parts of Greece to his naval domain. As long as he kept the corn flowing to Rome, he could become consul in 33, see the liberation of the slaves on his ships, gain rewards in confiscated land for his soldiers and be restored to his father's property except for that part occupied by Antony in Rome. His daughter, Pompeia, would marry the son of Octavian's sister.

Sextus was confident enough to joke while giving up his claim to the family house in the Carinae, the Keels district near the temple of Tellus. The only *carina* he possessed, he said, was the keel of the ship on which he was standing. But many of his supporters could immediately reclaim their homes. The proscription was over. The *Lex Titia*, death sentence for Cicero and so many sympathisers with the assassins, was declared dead. Those who had survived it could return to Rome.

Only Caesar's named assassins would still be hunted. The *Lex Pedia*, aimed exclusively at the killers themselves, remained in force. Sextus had attempted to negotiate exile as their price of forgiveness. Octavian's cousin's law still demanded their heads.

17

KILL EVERY KILLER

Terracina, Leonardo da Vinci (1514–15)

Almost everyone could see gains from the Treaty of Misenum except Parmensis and the surviving assassins. Octavian had conceded to Antony some control of Italy but he had won valuable time, first to appease the people of Rome who had become ever more enraged by hunger, secondly to find a way to deal with Sextus at sea. The streets around the Forum had become perilous for him, packed with civilians who were hardly less important than the army and harder to buy with promises.

Sextus had wasted his best opportunity to help Antony destroy

Octavian. He had failed to uphold any responsibility he felt for the assassins and their ideals, protecting only the victims of a brutally imposed purge. He felt some guilt for his failure to protect Parmensis and any other of Caesar's killers still alive, but he too had added to his popularity at Rome.

He took personal credit for the end of the proscriptions, the permission to return for those decreed mere accomplices in the killing of Caesar. He won back for the exiles only a quarter of the money extorted from them; but this was a success by the standards of the past. More important was the gratitude of thousands – of men and women flocking to the beaches to cheer home the formerly proscribed, of the former supporters of his father, of Messalla and his friends, the merely quiet and wealthy – all without relying on the arbitrary clemency made notorious by Julius Caesar.

Antony could put the fate of Perusia behind him. He felt free to take himself and his new wife to Athens, the base from which he planned to punish the Parthians as Caesar had intended, eject their clients from Syria to Jerusalem, and build the wealth he needed before he could even consider opening hostilities again at home.

In leaving Cassius Parmensis and Turullius still condemned, Antony had added to the continuing threat from Sextus in Sicily to Octavian in Rome. The assassins were as hostile to Caesar's heir as he was to them. That enmity was essential to Antony's sense of safety. Lepidus had been only a light counterweight in Italy. Sextus – with Parmensis in his ranks – was one whose name and power Octavian could not ignore.

Caesar's last surviving killers and Pompey's last surviving son were not equals; but to those who dreamed of a restored republic they shared the same side of history. Sextus's allies still included many leading Romans who had not accepted the chance to return; the young Marcus Licinius Crassus, heir to one of the greatest fortunes in the history of Rome, was just one of them. Together they had motives against Octavian based on precedent and a degree of principle, all much deeper than Antony's desire to defeat a young rival.

In Sicily, however, Sextus had unexpected problems. He too had to struggle with his internal dissent, executing some of his leading officers in a dispute about how far he should risk their common cause to protect Parmensis and the men most sought by Octavian. Parmensis became more than ever aware of his isolation. He was part of Sextus's past, part of any Pompeian's sense of history but to the vast mass of his fellow sailors around Sicily he was a mere problem.

Sextus's support of Parmensis distanced him from the source of his power. The executions weakened his valuable reputation for being the most moderate among mad men, some sort of gentleman in a world of avengers. His enemies in Rome sensed weakness. He had to remain forceful in maintaining his place at the top diplomatic table. When his commander in Sardinia was persuaded by Octavian to switch sides, he had to respond twice – with missiles, fire and mayhem from the sea.

Nor was the dizzying dance of alliance and misalliance, treaties made and abandoned, yet over. The stage was enormous, the performers no less expansive in their own minds. Sextus, hailed as a living Neptune in his modest Sicilian domain, exchanged his cloak of Roman purple for one of deepest dark blue, the shade of the sea god. There were reports of Antony replacing his Herculean pose in the Lupercalia with a Dionysian role on the Acropolis, even accepting Athens itself as a symbolic wife, an archaic ritual of marriage outside the sulphur caves of the Parthenon.

Everyone seeking power played god. In Rome, a city of the sullen rich and underfed, Octavian badly needed his status as the son of the Divine Julius and deployed it, along with *Imperator*, on his coins and wherever he could. The title of a triumvir was a weakening source of authority, seen as a means of personal vendetta rather than vengeance for the Ides of March.

Octavian called for a further meeting with Antony. In the spring of 38 BC, the master of the east, to his irritation and rage, agreed to be summoned back briefly to Brundisium to discuss again what were supposed to be shared concerns in Italy. In Ariminum and dozens of other towns the confiscations were complete. Antony had lost in the process. The winners in the race for land, even those from his own armies, were all the more likely to fight for Octavian in future. The wounds of the losers were unhealed. None of the issues matched his preference for Cleopatra and the war against the Parthians. His generals, though not he himself, had begun to make some dramatic gains in the distant deserts.

Only a year later, as sullenly as though they had lost their lands and livelihoods themselves, the two men had to meet for a third time, to complain once more about each other and about Sextus. In the spring of 37 BC Antony arrived again off Brundisium, this time with three hundred ships, a vast force and a clear threat to Octavian since there seemed no prospect of his taking on Sextus. Octavian's own fleet had been crushed by storms.

After a show of strength, Antony sailed further south. At the same time Maecenas, again Octavian's chief diplomat, was also traveling south, in a more relaxed manner by road, accompanied on the journey by Horace, Varius and Virgil, the poets whom he was already assembling as ornaments, and instruments, of his master's ambitions.

* * *

Horace, still amazed at the turn in his fortunes after fighting on the wrong side at Philippi, was part of the advance party from Rome. His instructions were to meet Maecenas at Terracina fifty miles down the *Via Appia*. This was the road that ran south and east to Brundisium and Tarentum just as the *Via Flamininia* ran north and east to Ariminum. The Appian was the first great Roman road of Italy, the 'queen of roads', mile after marching mile of square-cut stones and squat bridges, straight where it could be, sinuous where it had to be, studded with wider spaces for a cart of wine jars going one way to pass a diplomat's carriage going the other.

The Appian was the oldest way by which Romans aimed to keep Italy together under their rule, a task begun two hundred and fifty years before but still not complete. Italian towns along the route, Formiae, Beneventum and Brundisium itself were prominent places of Italy's unrest under the triumvirs, of violence and anger, political murder, confiscation and revolt.

Horace was not marching. He was barging and ambling. But he was able to see and describe the current state of the country as Parmensis, at sea around Sicily with his ideals from before the Ides of March, could not. Parmensis was trapped in philosophical arguments and disorganised dreams; Horace was adapting to reality. Rome itself was still a place of horror and hunger but, with a bit of mental adjustment, there was hope; or at least Horace hoped for hope. Meanwhile he was looking forward to the company of Maecenas and others of the new great men, even Virgil and some fellow poets.

Egressum! The first word in the world's first piece of recognisably modern travel writing, an inspiration for two thousand years ahead, was almost a whoop-whoop-whoopee. Out of here! He was leaving something bad and seeing what might be better. Horace was also about to describe himself, a nervous, chubby, sore-eyed twenty-six-year-old with a Greek guidebook called 'Italian Miracles' in his hand and a few days of tourism in his calendar.

None of the political roadside sites attracted his attention as a writer. As a student of the times and sometime fighter for Brutus he could hardly have failed to note the site at Bovillae where Publius Clodius Pulcher, one of Caesar's gangsters, Cicero's enemy and Fulvia's then husband, was murdered in a faction fight fifteen years before; nor the lesson from Formiae of Cicero's own murder nine years later and Fulvia's tongue-pricking delight at that.

At prosperous Capua he must have seen the new 25-acre estates of the Philippi veterans. At Beneventum were the same sights, the same distress of the evicted, a disrupted town whose settled history was traced almost to the age of Atreus and Thyestes. But Horace preferred to write of marshland 'crammed with cheating innkeepers and sailors', a place of drunken bargemen, frogs and dragon-flies, catfish and turtles, for which no soldier would have deemed it worth having risked his life. He preferred Terracina's white rock where the main road turned inland from the sea, giving the town its local name, Anxur, to remind his readers of when Italy was not marked out in Latin and ruled by Rome.

As soon as Maecenas had joined his own party, Horace was a poet among politicians. The catering and hospitality improved. But he still noted the city 'perched on far-shining rocks' in a line of linguistic compression that would last through centuries of translation: *inpositum saxis late candentibus Anxur.* Horace was a travel writer trying all the later themes of that art, sex, alcohol, deft observation and personal hygiene. He noted nothing political except the 'see my toga' pomposity of a welcoming local worthy.

Egressum! He was out of all that. At the next stop Virgil joined them too, a cause for celebrating selfless friendship of the Epicurean kind, not for showing sadness at shepherds by the side of the road who had no longer land nor flocks. Perusia had been the place and time for protest. While Maecenas and his aides were debating how best to deal with the continuing consequences of Caesar's assassination – with Sextus and the seaborne survivors of Philippi – Horace was troubled with his eyes and Virgil with his stomach. A hardship was a hangover.

To the south-west the *Via Appia* continued its way to the Adriatic. The climb was steep. The ground rolled over cliffs and gorges, roiling like the sea itself until it reached the highest plains, places of the largest farms, the industrial grazing lands of the very rich which had for the most part avoided confiscation. The fauna was the same as on the Roman road to Parma, bears, wolves, falcons, harriers, Bubo the eagle owl, the always present crows. The flora showed the life from warmer weather, early swelling figs, wild olive and thyme, oily nuts and pink fruits imported by Pompey from the east. Where the thyme and olive flowered together, the ground looked close to fire.

Horace was heading south, towards his home, and at a faster pace than he had begun. Ahead of him was a meeting which would change the balance of power and settle his place on the successful side of history. Around him, between Italy's heel and toe, was a countryside of beauty and chaos. But he was writing sketches of a personal landscape, self-deprecating comedy, stony bread, a lonely bed, a girl who let him down and a stain on the sheets the next morning. When Horace wrote about fire he was mocking a Jewish superstition that incense might be made to melt and smell without added heat. If that were true, it was true whether the Jews believed it or not. If it were not true an Epicurean could have no time for such nonsense.

18

SEXTUS BETRAYED

Lake Avernus, Aeneas and the Cumaean Sibyl, J.M.W. Turner (1814–15)

At Tarentum, where Pompey the Great had once had a great house, the diplomats stopped and the diplomacy began again. Over many painful weeks Antony agreed a gradual betrayal of Sextus – abandoning the honorary assassin but not yet. They stripped him of future honours, including the consulship, but guaranteed his safety from immediate attack. Octavian accepted Antony's demand that the master of Sicily should survive till at least the following year. For Parmensis this was ever more bad news; the best that an optimist could see was a useful pause for prospects to improve.

The diplomatic dancing steps observed by Horace and Virgil were no less intricate than they had been before. Once the negotiation was over, Antony had many competing priorities for the year ahead – in Parthia and in Egypt and at sea. Octavian decided to focus as tightly as possible on his navy. This was simultaneously an incipient civil war and world war, as complex to wage as it was later to understand

Octavian and Antony awarded each other five more years of power without much belief that so many would be possible. The ties between them had been stretched since the reading of Caesar's will, broken at Mutina, rebound at Bononia and Philippi, tested at Perusia and twisted at Misenum and Tarentum. Their last shared threads might still hold but easily might not.

They tried again to bribe Sextus's Roman allies to leave him. Some of those who had returned home after the treaty of Misenum were already back in Sicily. Others never left. Such loyalty to Sextus, or preference for liberty over dictatorship, was newly pronounced a dangerous risk. Pompey's son was an honorary assassin, to be hunted for reward under the *Lex Pedia*, a message proclaimed in special coins to pay their troops.

Sextus responded with his own massive building programme of ships, paid for from the silver mines of Spain and the profits of piracy. He intensified raids north and south of Naples. Antony agreed to send to Octavian more than a hundred ships to counter the new threat. In return he was promised four legions. Lepidus, neglected but a force still in his own mind, sent fourteen legions to southern Italy from Africa.

Despite these reinforcements Octavian doubted his ability to remove Sextus from the board game of civil war. Military imagination was required. Mere reinforcement was not enough. Agrippa, the victor at Perusia but only nine years ago his fellow student in Greece, took on the task of shifting the balance, of building a new navy for Octavian. It was an undertaking that demanded extraordinary certainty that it would work and be worthwhile, the kind of certainty that Octavian alone had made his own.

The chosen ground was twenty miles north-west of Naples, the *Campi Phlegraei*, fields of fire, bubbling ponds, steaming sand and stinking lakes. The waters were hot enough to boil eggs, sulphurous, sickening. It seemed an unlikely place to rebuild a navy.

The dominant sight in the sky was Mount Vesuvius, not feared then as a volcano. The last time of fire from the vine-covered mountain was almost two centuries before, when it was Hannibal's armies, not rival generals of Rome, who were rampaging through Italy. Perusia was being besieged then by the forces of Carthage, backed by Boii who drank from Roman skulls; Ariminum was a cavalry base for a war which threatened Roman extinction. Throughout all the intervening years between 217 and 35 BC a reeking acrid air had hung over the flat lands behind Cape Misenum.

The *Campi Phlegraei* repelled casual visitors. This was the heart of Italy's magic coast on the Tellus map, the realms of Homer, the entrances to the underworld and beyond. The fields of fire were not the kind that the veterans of Philippi would favour. The black soil was fine for growing grapes where the chemicals flavoured the wine but useless for most human purposes bar prophecy. At the edges of the fields were the holiday villas of warlords and Epicurean philosophers, Caesar's family and Cicero's. But inland and invisible from the sea were the caves where a general might come in normal times only to discuss his future with an intoxicated seer.

This was where modern Italy and mythological Greece came closest together, where a survivor of the war at Troy might slip in amongst the dead, reminisce, learn what in life he had not known. Lake Avernus, named in Greek as the place where no bird would fly, was the water between two worlds. Those who knew Athens recognised the same scent on the Acropolis, the same air without birds. Agrippa knew Avernus as a secret place where no one would watch and anything might be made to happen, a camp for slave labour and for dreams.

Well-known tales from Homer's *Odyssey* haunted the whole long coast from Naples to Sicily and Tarentum, the sites of the Sirens and Scylla and Charybdis, the killing of the cattle of the Sun, the blinding of the Cyclops and the sea god's curse. From his journey to the dead Odysseus had earnt how to escape that curse, to walk with an oar so far from the sea that no one even knew it was an oar, to plant his unrecognised piece of wood as a gift where the sea god's writ did not yet run. Avernus was where a Roman too might see his own future.

For a year after the dealing at Tarentum Agrippa disappeared into this sulphurous hinterland. Out of sight of Sextus's most shore-hugging spy ships, he ordered the lake sides stripped of black-leaved trees. He moved thousands of tons of earth. Sacred groves were felled despite the protests of their priests. A statue celebrating Odysseus's voyage was seen to sweat in outrage. Slaves dug a canal and two tunnels, creating a system of harbours called Portus Iulius after the new god, Julius Caesar, in whose name all was to be fought.

Agrippa built a heavy fleet with new weapons for new tactics against the son of Pompey, whom he saw as the ludicrously self-styled god of the Roman sea, hardly more than a pirate protecting Caesar's killers. Thousands of the captives of war were freed to become oarsmen. Shallow smoking pools for the first time joined the sea. Hercules himself, it was claimed, had tried and failed to do as much. Earliest history and the latest engineering were as one.

The ingenuity of Agrippa – and his call on every resource that Octavian could give him – created a new naval weapon and a stretch of inland sea where it was put to the test. Legionaries were trained to fire harpoons from catapults, to pull enemy ships alongside as though they were fish on hooks. The new *harpax*, known by its Greek name, the robber, would open the way for the beaked iron boarding ramps which the Romans called *corvi* the crows. Used together the sea would become land. This would be magic of a very material kind. When Agrippa came to write his own history, he protested that he had gained too little credit for it.

Octavian himself waited in Rome, watching anxiously for news from the Italian towns. Antony was hoping to rebuild his fortune in the east. Sextus was counting his gains and losses and finding the losses more. Politicians on all sides felt the force from the Fields of Fire.

Poets felt it too. Horace's musings on the journey to the

conference at Tarentum came at the start of an extraordinary literary life. Brutus's young friend at Philippi prospered mightily with
Maecenas, writing subtle patriotic odes and letters in verse with wry
comments on his contemporaries, his former colleague, Parmensis,
among them. For Parmensis himself Tarentum would be a memorable milestone on his own long journey on behalf of the assassins.

* * *

After the diplomatic parties had left the low instep of Italy the trust
between their masters fell further. Antony returned to the challenging eastern campaigns which Octavian wanted to fail. Octavian
was challenged too, though on the smaller stages of Ariminum,
Cremona, Mutina and Beneventum. As soon as he could he would
add Sicily to that list. He had Agrippa's new fleet and Antony's
promise of support but neither had been tested under stress.

Victory against Sextus, the honorary assassin and self-styled
Neptune, might be dangerous, even if achieved. Pompey's son was
a popular figure on whom many, both rich and poor, had pinned
their trust. Weakened by his concessions at the conference table and
the departure from Sicily of so many of the proscribed, he nonetheless had huge credit at Rome as an honourable politician. He
had lost experienced commanders but, backed by supporters of his
father, by enemies of Caesar, by two surviving assassins, by freed
slaves and the dispossessed of Smyrna, Xanthus and Rhodes, Sextus
Pompeius was still the man who had long defeated his adversaries'
hopes.

Not till the summer of 36 BC did Octavian make his move. His
opening steps were political, personal and poetic. He offered further favours to those returning from Sicily to Rome under the terms
of the Misenum treaty. He ensured that everyone around the Forum
knew how Sextus was being abandoned by his allies and friends.
He paraded the returning exiles' loyalty to Rome and to their own
self-interest. He paraded his own commitment by divorcing his
wife, Scribonia, who was from Sextus's family.

Gradually the poets of Tarentum were deployed too, gently nudged into setting an appropriate mood amongst their readers. In the fourth of his *Epodes*, a collection of explosive squibs against various targets, garlic, social upstarts and rivals, Horace ended his dissection of a pompous millionaire with an urbane question why it was worth sending heavy ships against a pirate like Sextus (elegantly unnamed) when such parvenu trash were doing so well at home.

Finally, with all best preparations in place but with no securer knowledge of Antony's troubles in Parthia than Antony had of his in Italy, Octavian ordered the task of retaking Sicily. Agrippa had his high, heavy beaked assault ships. He had their new weapons. He had his transports and triremes for supply and for blockading the supplies of his adversary. He still had to assess the risk of using them.

This was a challenge much more complex than the battles of Philippi. Even to sail around the Sicilian coast required a skill that could not be learnt on Lake Avernus. To readers and writers – to Horace and Virgil and to Parmensis on the other side of the conflict – the narrow Straits of Messina were the most notorious waters of the magic coast. In the *Odyssey* they stood between the journey to the dead and the killing of the Sun God's cattle. They were the home of Scylla, the rival in love whom Circe, seductress and magician, had turned into a dragon, and of Charybdis the whirlpool, monsters that sucked and grabbed sailors as they passed, offering a choice of death but nothing kinder.

Moving from poetry to the military, the strait was no easier to navigate. Its main current ran from south to north while a weaker current ran in the reverse direction, the two on most days alternating every six hours, the water levels falling sharply during the main current, tearing tangling weed from the sea bed, throwing upwards fish with bottle eyes and glowing gills. Ghosts the size of giants held the shores. Even those most immune from the madness of the spirit world would see them.

Followers of Epicurus had an explanation of ghosts based on light and air and the floating of filmy particles from the surface of material objects. At sea there were always more of the superstitious than the scientific. The straits were every night thronged with high flying birds, signals of wind, weather and fortune. Over Avernus there had been none; over Messina flew the buzzards, falcons and eagles on their way to Mutina, Parma, the Alps and far beyond.

Octavian made his own sacrificial offerings to the god of the sea, asking for waters without waves. He planned assaults on the side of Sicily opposite the straits and simultaneously on each of the island's other two sides. It was to be a rare joint enterprise by the triumvirs, Agrippa's fleet operating for Octavian from the north, some of Antony's ships from the south-east and Lepidus's army landing in the south-west.

The planning was better than the practice. They immediately lost ships to storms, to Sextus's superior skill and their own inexperience. On a single July day in the straits Agrippa lost half his fleet. The month named after Julius Caesar could not, as Octavian had hoped, be the date of defeat for Pompey's son. Caesar's heir had to call again on the smoking factories of the Naples fields, retreating to ports filled with the hungry and the angry who blamed him for the war being fought at all.

Money meant to reward army veterans had to go on fighters in the navy. Sextus had a seemingly limitless supply of his own silver coins, each one stamped to show his control over Sicily with the image of Scylla herself. He had solid support in Tauromenium, the town tumbling into the sea beneath Mount Etna. Octavian won some early victories when Agrippa was able to use his new techniques of naval warfare, his heavier hulls and the iron gangplanks along which his soldiers could charge. But he lost at least as much as he won. For months the new war was messy, indecisive, and ever more unpopular.

When reports from Sicily reached Antony he objected to the failure as best as he could. The campaign was out of his control, too much effort, too many losses, too little influence for him over its progress. The returning news for Octavian from Parthia was ominous. Antony claimed to be doing well, imitating Caesar in style. A desert victory for him while Sextus was still undefeated would be a disaster for Caesar's heir.

Octavian's troubles around Sicily increased. He gave up even trying to save his own reputation, deserting his forces at Tauromenium, lowering his ship's flag to avoid capture, ordering his troops to show courage while seeking a safe hiding place as he had at Philippi. Frightened and feeble, he reached Messalla's camp on shore only by moving between different rowing boats to confuse his pursuers. That was the moment when Parmensis might reasonably have seen the end he had been seeking.

But Octavian put his personal humiliations behind him, expanding his efforts all the more, in rhetoric throughout Italy and inducements in the lakes of Avernus. Sextus was a pirate, he argued, not a policer of the seas for Rome. Real pirates were captured and tortured, readily implicating Sextus, knowing the answers that might save their lives or speed their deaths.

Abuse of Sextus could not, however, achieve enough. Octavian returned to his most consistently successful role as the avenger of Caesar's assassination. Cassius Parmensis and Decimus Turullius were identified again as assassins who could not be allowed to live.

Octavian had loyalist officers who made his case – more effectively than poets within legions where little new poetry was read. Prominent among them was Lucius Cornificius, the accuser of Brutus's empty chair in the court which tried the assassins under the *Lex Pedia*, a hectoring man known for riding home from parties on an elephant, hard to ignore. Cornificius and his men suffered acute hardship and hunger but stayed loyal.

Gradually the advantage shifted. Octavian had recruited a new Tenth Legion, promising high pay and more pay later, giving it the number of one of Caesar's most renowned bands of fighters. It took the name *Fretensis* after the *Freta Messinae*, the straits of ghosts and birds. Many of Octavian's veteran legionaries, though discharged and fattening pigs on acorns in Parma, returned to the ranks, proudly loyal for cash and the cause of the assassinated Caesar.

Octavian could also rely on Lepidus's African legions, though less so on Lepidus himself. In skirmish after skirmish, it was the force of the soldiers, some thirty legions in all, that mattered more. Assault after assault, when the troops gained Sicilian land for Octavian they held it for him.

Sextus soon controlled little more of Sicily than the territory opposite his huge fleet arrayed off Naulochus on the north-east coast looking up towards Naples. Tauromenium fell. Messana, a major city on the Charybdis side of the strait, was under siege and set to fall. He tried to suborn Lepidus to his side but failed. He had either to risk a massive sea battle, on a scale unprecedented in Roman history, or sail away.

For Octavian there was even higher risk. Antony would ruthlessly exploit his failure. Antony and Sextus could work together as he and Sextus never could. He had the weight of Agrippa's new ships and the *harpax* and the *corvus*, the combined grappling hook and gangplank. But they had not been severely tried. Sextus had the old naval skills of the Rhodians and the coastal cities of Greece, the triremes and the hard-learnt arts of sliding behind an enemy's line, accelerating on the turn, dipping a prow beneath a wave to crush the hull and the rowers behind it.

Both men accepted the risk. New dice were cast. A battle fought by almost a thousand ships did not happen by accident. It had to be planned, its terms and timing agreed. It might have been a war of one kind of naval skill, dashing and darting through wind and wave, or of another, grappling and grinding hulls into platforms in a sheltered bay.

Sextus's bet was the wrong bet. Each side formed in a long line, one wing on the shore side, the other stretching far out to sea in the waveless waters of Naulochus bay. The *harpax* of Lake Avernus was a devastating weapon. Parmensis and his fellow captains, whenever they successfully came up behind Octavian's ships in the best Rhodian manner, faced downward fire from a catapult launching long iron hooks on ropes too far away to be cut. Hundreds of them were reeled in like fish.

Agrippa was able to stretch his line and come around and behind in force, a classic military tactic for many a victorious Roman army on land. He forced Sextus's ships closer to each other and to the shore. Manoeuvrability and speed meant nothing. When the battle ground was an undulating platform of wood, more land than sea, morale, confidence and commitment made the greater difference.

At the end of the September day Sextus had only seventeen ships afloat, fighting and able to flee. Naulochus bay, never more defying its Greek name, the Ship-shelterer, was strewn with smashed hulls and small boats seeking the more prominent survivors. Sicilian shipwrights readied themselves to repair and rebuild but Pompey's son and Caesar's assassin had gone even before the sea was clear. It was they who had to abandon their men as Octavian had done only weeks before, damaging their own reputations as they fled.

Sextus and Parmensis sailed away first to Sicilian Messana, and then to Cephallenia, to site after site from the story of Odysseus. Maybe the lesson of the *Odyssey* was always an encouragement to a literary sailor. It was the source of so much story. It had sea monsters and storms, gods and magicians, travels to the fantastic and the dead but it never had a proper end.

Odysseus, after being pursued so long at sea, returned home as himself an avenger. He shot dead with his giant bow the suitors of his faithful wife. He hanged the maids who had shared the suitors' beds. None of them was afraid until the last desperate hour because none had anticipated his return.

But, after his vengeance, the hero forgot the call of fate. He did not voyage inland to propitiate the sea god in a place where no one knew of oars, ships and the sea. He did not do what the prophet among the dead had told him to do. The poem simply stopped in implausible reconciliation. In Cephallenia, high in the Ionian Sea, a sea story could restart whenever a poet wished.

* * *

Homeric reflection was for losers – or for winners long after they had won and the landscape of civil war was reclaimed by myth.

Octavian took no pause after the Battle of Naulochus. He avenged the slights to his authority by punishing Sextus's loyal towns; hundreds of men from Tauromenium were deported. Slaves without masters were impaled to discourage insurrection on lands powered by slavery. The whole island lost the citizen rights that Caesar may or may not have granted to them in his will, the truth depending on whether Antony was reading or inventing. Octavian had quickly to take over Sextus's Sicilian legions. His next campaign, he knew, would not be long in coming.

Lepidus, his mostly absent fellow triumvir, made one last attempt to claim his equality with Octavian, marching to Messana and demanding from Agrippa that the surrender be made to himself, the senior man on the spot. Agrippa refused. Lepidus retaliated by allowing his own legions to sack an ancient city that had been secure since the defeat of Carthage.

This left the neglected triumvir with not only some hundred thousand men under arms but many that were unusually grateful, for cash and bronzes and citizens to be ransomed and enslaved. Pushed to the side lines at Brundisium, Misenum and Tarentum, Lepidus was suddenly in his most powerful position since the pact of Bononia. The triumvir with the least personal hatred of the assassins was back where he could make a difference.

Neither the mood nor the power lasted for long. An attempt to follow with further demands for his own advancement brought irritation from Agrippa, then incredulity, then anger. When Octavian arrived he walked into Messana, confident of his reception, with only a small personal bodyguard. After nervous discussions, a few scuffles, there began an unstoppable defection to Caesar's heir before an end to even the pretence that there was a triumvirate. Marcus Aemilius Lepidus, always honoured more for his historic family than himself, still dignified with Caesar's title, Pontifex Maximus, left for retirement a little further north in Circeii, close to where Cicero was murdered, a town famous for its oysters. Antony learnt of the three becoming two only after the subtraction had been made.

For Sextus the battle of Naulochus was a catastrophe but he acted for a while as though it were a mere reverse. He knew about reverses. His had been a life of them, of rises and falls like the sea itself. He was an Odyssean. He had his daughter with him, not yet and never to be married to Octavian's nephew, a reminder to him instead of his journey with his own father after defeat. He had allies in the islands; he could learn from Agrippa's tactics; he could fit long scythes to cut the ropes of the grabbing iron. There was always something new in a navy. He could rebuild his fleet, watch and wait and hope to fight another day.

With him still were senior figures who called themselves Pompeians, surviving assassins, followers of his father and killers of his father's rival. Threatened more than ever by Octavian's success as an avenger, they had nowhere else to go. With Caesar's heir so dangerous in the ascendant, he might join Antony, who was struggling in Parthia, it was said, even be welcomed by him. Or he might stay independent, or do both, or appear to do both. Parmensis had the same choices.

A MAN WITH A WHITE FACE

Octavian's legions wanted the defeat of Sextus to be the light at the end of the tunnel of war. The more successfully their commander appeared as a winner, the more immediately they wanted their money and their farms. They feared that the best land might go to the earliest claimants. The last would get nothing bar the empty promises of prosperity for everyone that came at the end of every fighting season. They were becoming restless.

Loyalty still flowed from rewards as well as Caesar's name. Octavian faced the most dangerous mutinies of his path to power. He had to make his own careful balance between the propaganda of peace and the near certainty that he would at some point need his best forces to fight Antony. As so often before, he had returned to Rome to mundane reflections, nothing Homeric in any way.

He mixed threats and promises. Some men were persuaded to stay in the ranks in expectation of even greater gains than before. He made payments in cash, a rarity for rewards of any size. He identified more land in Cisalpine Gaul. The men of the Tenth Legion, newly renamed the *Legio Fretensis,* the legion of the straits, were offered farms around Cremona and Mantua, twenty miles north of Parma.

Horace's dearest companion on the journey to Tarentum, the poet Virgil, became one of those who lost his fields. His home was 'too close to wretched Cremona'; it had survived the first round of confiscations after Philippi but not the next after Sextus's defeat. No soldier in the winter of 36 BC took much notice of cries in verse.

Sextus himself was meanwhile keeping watch on both remaining triumvirs. Their problems were still his opportunities. While

Octavian faced mutiny in Italy, Antony faced the much bigger challenge to his reputation from Parthia. News emerged only slowly from the battlefields where he had hoped to avenge Crassus and Cassius, outdo Caesar, and match the feats of Alexander the Great: but, once the story was clearer, the military reputation of Mark Antony, honed in Gaul, at Mutina and at Philippi, fell sharply.

Antony had maybe known what Caesar had intended. If he had, his old master's blend of speed and patience had eluded him. He made a too rapid advance, a too hasty decision to leave heavy siege equipment to follow, a tactic that Caesar had successfully used in Gaul but was a huge risk, and a desperate winter retreat in which a third of his army died.

Octavian, insecurely based in Italy, was using every means of propaganda to discredit his rival in the east, blaming him both as a war-monger and failed warrior, a threat to civil peace and a man personally obsessed with the interests of Cleopatra in Egypt, a hostile foreign queen. The facts from Parthia were an unusually clear and decisive help. His added ambition was to manoeuvre Antony into finishing the battle of Naulochus by executing the assassins who had sailed away, however deludedly, to continue their fight.

Sextus, still hoping for some sort of alliance with Antony, did not see himself as deluded. Despite his own depleted forces he was hoping for favourable terms from a man who in Parthia had fallen even further below his ambition than Sextus had himself. Antony, he thought, had surely to see that he might soon need all the support he could get. If Octavian could send Lepidus to enforced retirement on an oyster farm, he might offer the same ultimatum to a second weakened triumvir.

Exhausted and disappointed, Antony took Sextus's bait. The two defeated men agreed to meet at Mytilene on the northern Aegean island of Lesbos. For Sextus it was a journey with no happy memories, back up the coast to the city where he and his step-mother had met his father after Pharsalus thirteen years before. Pompey the Great had been forced to gamble all on a single day; so too had his son. Pompey the Great had been executed to please Caesar. Sextus did not wish Caesar's heir to have the same pleasure. Parmensis was ever more necessary to him to evoke the glory of the Ides of March.

Neither Antony nor Sextus recognised the full depths to which each had fallen. Sextus's lack of realism was the greater, a last failure for the last military captain of the assassins' cause. Antony had done badly but, ship for ship and man for man, not as badly as Sextus and not at all as badly as Sextus imagined. Pompey's son, born close to power, knowing little but obedience whether from pirate bands or armies of Rome, was cut off from views that he did not want to hear.

The loser at Naulochus felt unreasonably confident. He began intrigues with exiled Parthians, hoping to strengthen his position by diplomacy. His defeated father had once considered the same course of retaking Rome from a base inside its greatest enemy. Antony did not like even the possibility of this time the Pompeian thought becoming fact. He responded by pursuing rather than parleying.

Sextus hastily left Lesbos and sailed through the straits and seas separating Europe from Asia, still, as he perceived himself, in the diplomatic game. He did not want to stop. He was a great man of the sea, a romantic in a war of realists, a continuer of war and a continuer of its stories. If he was an Odysseus in Sicily, he could be an Argonaut in search of the Golden Fleece on the way to the Black Sea.

The last honorary assassin reached Nicomedia in the farthest north-east of European water. The Roman governor of Asia had no instructions to oppose him and he landed unopposed, hoping that the triumvirs would be divided over his fate, even that in his own interest he might exacerbate those divisions to restore his lost past. By intimidation and the power of his name he extended his control to nearby Lampsacus and Nicaea too, seeking allies, wherever he might find them, for those who had survived the Sicilian disaster. He assembled three legions and a corps of cavalry. More survivors gradually joined him.

Even in Rome there were signals in his favour. Octavian was wary of ordering Sextus's death. On the Palatine hill and in the Forum he could see the popularity of Pompey's son and the opprobrium that might fall on his executioner.

Antony, his eyes still on the east, was less wary; he did not know – or perhaps did not want to know. He commanded a senior man from his staff, Marcus Titius, to hunt down Sextus before he could treat with Rome's Parthian enemies. The choice revived the name of Publius Titius, proposer of the proscriptions. The blustering Antony of before the Ides of March was back; the tactician was absent.

Antony hoped to distance himself from his own order by sailing back to Cleopatra in Alexandria. He already knew that a final clash with Octavian, if it had to happen, could be financed only from the treasury of Egypt. Sextus was, in every way, less important to him than a sexual relationship based on infinite money for infinite power.

Titius, notoriously ghostlike in appearance from a skin disease, was a solid loyalist in Antony's cause, a nephew of Plancus and himself a veteran of the Parthian campaign. He had been a beneficiary of Sextus's clemency in Sicily: Sextus might trust him to repay the favour.

Sextus did not take the chance of clemency. Gratitude in politics was ever unpredictable, the lesson of Caesar all too fresh He burnt his ships and for the first time in a decade became a man of the land, leading his daughter and his few remaining supporters away from the sea that had so long been his domain.

White-faced Titius followed. Sextus could not defend himself for long. He offered his surrender to a Roman officer who might better, he thought, respect the only surviving son of Pompey the Great. He asked that he be delivered to Antony in Egypt. Rebuffed in both requests, he attempted a night march back to the coast to burn Titius's fleet.

When his plan was betrayed he fled further inland into yet more alien territory, to Midaeon, a hundred miles of thick forest, shrub land and desert south of the Black Sea coast. Sextus was going to where no one would know a famous sailor, or maybe any sailor at all.

He had not given up. He could still hope for at least a gentle old age, the kind that Odysseus, after all his troubles, had been promised if he took a blind prophet's underworld advice, if he carried an oar to where it would not be recognised for what it was, where it might be mistaken for a threshing tool for corn and become a shrine to the sea god far from any sea. Octavian's vengeance too might surely, similarly, somehow be escaped. Still accompanied by his daughter, Pompeia, and pleased to be only an honorary assassin, Sextus took the long road inland. Parmensis meanwhile stayed afloat.

In Midaeon the local rulers were adept at finding the winning side in Roman wars. King Amyntas, a former royal secretary with a minor throne of his own, was one of many who lived by wit and good intelligence. He had marched his men briefly with Brutus and Cassius, had defected to Antony before Philippi and had not abandoned him yet. Amyntas saw Sextus as a man of the past, formally an outlaw without legal rights, a former sailor beached and at his mercy. He handed him to Titius who did not risk keeping him alive for long.

Sextus Pompeius was the second honorary assassin to be hunted to his death, as important in the second part of the assassins' story as Cicero had been in the first. Pompey's son was killed, as his father had been, on sands far from home. His end lacked the theatrical extravagance and epic detail that accompanied Pompey the Great into the future literature of hostility to the Caesars. Parmensis never became his poet. Pompeia's fate, no longer to be married to Octavian's sister's son, Marcellus, was not recorded at all.

The one remaining issue was whether Sextus's head was what Titius's masters had wanted, or had said that they wanted. The execution became quickly a question of credit or blame between Octavian and Antony who were themselves almost at war. Maybe there had been clear and urgent cause. Maybe Sextus had been on his way to Armenia, a successor to Labienus, the embarrassing Roman general who had died as an *imperator* in Parthia, attempting to destroy the armies in which he had so long served. Or maybe there had been no cause and Sextus had not been on the Parthian road. Titius soon learnt the risks of vengeance at a time when the warlords' official message for the people was the bringing of peace.

Both in Alexandria and Rome there were cries of innocence. Antony's supporters claimed that a letter sent to forestall the execution had not arrived in time. Octavian, delighting even more in the killer than in the death itself, said that he himself would have spared Sextus but that Antony had not.

Titius, the man with the white-spotted face and the name associated with the terror, was blamed by everyone who wanted to avoid the blame themselves. When he sponsored games in Pompey's theatre he was booed out of the best seats.

Parmensis sailed back down the Aegean. He was running out of places and people to run to.

* * *

In Italy, and no longer in competition with Pompey's son, Octavian might perhaps have forgotten Parmensis. He was beginning to promote himself as a healer whose years of vengeance were past, a man of family piety, successful avenger of his father, father of the nation and bringer of an end to civil war. To help him he had Antony, who in Alexandria with Cleopatra could increasingly be presented as an alien Egyptian, and his poets, Virgil, Varius and Horace, those who had been on his side since Maecenas brought them on the journey to Tarentum.

None of these writers was biddable as a military officer might be. None was a simple propagandist. Two were among the greatest poets of all time, eliding great deeds into great art, not reliably to the favour of the deeds. Varius, the third, was placed among their ranks during his life. Virgil and Horace were their own men, but also and gratefully Octavian's men, loyal to what seemed in Rome to be the most certain source of peace.

Virgil, like Parmensis, was from war-blasted Cisalpine Gaul, from Mantua, not far inland from the soldiers of Parma. He remembered the confiscation of his family land, reminding audiences for his *Eclogues* of the rural lives lost to men seizing farms for their services at Mutina, Philippi and Perusia. But among Virgil's many arts was his way to transform violence into hope. Octavian had no more influential ambassador.

The tenth *Eclogue,* a passionate idyll of love defeating despair, was dedicated to Cornelius Gallus, also from Cisalpine Gaul, a politician, soldier and a poet who was perhaps the most open supporter of Octavian. The fourth *Eclogue* hailed a child as a symbol of a new age. Many would argue about who the child was meant to be. Octavian was content with the mere recognition that the coming age would be new.

Virgil's *Georgics*, firm in his mind well before civil war was over, was a long hymn to the national unity of Italy. In the literary disguise of an agricultural instruction book, he showed the natural beauty of Italian soil worked by willing hands, adding the ingenuity of Agrippa's Port Julius and the new salt sea in Lake Avernus, offering a multi-coloured commentary on the map in the temple of Tellus.

Meanwhile, Varius, the second traveller to Tarentum, was writing a new Roman epic, a pioneer before Virgil made that art his own. Varius wrote panegyric too, with Octavian and Agrippa his beneficiaries, and plays on Greek themes. He was an Epicurean, as were all Maecenas's poets to varying degrees, and wrote a long poem *On Death*. Virgil in the ninth of his *Eclogues* had the highest praise for Varius alongside Helvius Cinna, the poet who by his own death alone, torn apart in mistake for a plotter, was already fixed in the history of Caesar's assassination.

In 35 BC Horace had already begun writing elegant social satires, soft explosions of outrage and a wry kind of autobiography, lightly re-examining his own life and encouraging others to do the same. His journey with Varius and Virgil was just the start of his literary and political peace-keeping. In making light of his escape from Philippi, his wings clipped and his *parmula,* his little round shield, abandoned, he set a lifetime's tone of gratitude to fortune and great men, to Maecenas and Octavian above all.

Horace, however, was bolder than Virgil in remembering those who had opposed, and were still opposing, Octavian's supremacy. He alone mentioned Sextus, albeit for his piratical pretence to be a sea god, his burnt ships powered by treacherous slaves and his menace to Rome that was firmly, safely and thankfully in the past.

He gently remembered Cassius Parmensis too, as an Etruscan, as a man whose prolific output was like 'a rushing river', the piles of his work a perfect funeral pyre. Horace wondered whether his old friend Tibullus, a poet backed by Cassius's friend, Messalla, and independent of Octavian's court, was in some way trying to out-do the 'little works' of the last assassin. Surely Tibullus would be better employed strolling peacefully in the woods, having thoughts more suitable for someone wise and good, wondering whether wis-dom and goodness were different and, if so, how. Both Sextus and Parmensis, uncompromising or missing the chance to compromise, were supposed to sink beneath the waves of the new literary age; Horace kept them a little alive.

20

PARMENSIS'S LAST STAND

Mark Antony as Alexander the Great (c40 BC)

Parmensis might have trusted in the forgetfulness of Octavian and retired as soon as Sextus was dead. Hiding places, however, were few and the head of the last assassin (it was not clear whether Turullius were alive still or not) would always be a trophy to those who fought as Caesar's troops. Octavian would never forget or forgive. Parmensis chose to stay at war if war would still have him.

He can have had few illusions about Mark Antony either. Caesar's avenger for nine years, though dragged away from the compromise at Tellus against his better judgement, had come to revel in vendetta. Antony had ordered the death of Decimus; his ally, Dolabella, had tortured Trebonius; he had delighted at the severed head of Cicero, hunted through the tents of the defeated at Philippi and sent Brutus's head as a trophy to Rome.

But Antony was the better prospect. He was the one surviving obstacle between Octavian and the absolute power that the assassins, for all their differences, had most consistently opposed. Antony had been a pragmatist on the Ides of March when Octavian was still a student. If Octavian were defeated, dead in their coming battle, Antony might return to reason again. Uncertain how wise would be an offer to serve under Antony, and even whether it would be accepted, Parmensis still made the only choice that he could see.

It would not have surprised Parmensis if Antony had turned his offer down. An assassin as his enemy's ally was just one more way for Octavian to rally Rome for the memory of Caesar. Octavian was using every possible tonic for the troops. Brutus's head had been lost at sea and was unavailable.

There was nothing of substance for Antony that Parmensis had to offer. Cleopatra's fleet hardly needed his ships, nor their army his tiny number of men. The wealth of Egypt was rapidly repairing the losses of the Parthian campaign. Antony had arguably a greater need of an influential poet since the propaganda war, amongst readers of poetry at least, was strongly favouring Octavian. But, abusive verse was becoming somewhat old-fashioned. Parmensis's manner of satire lacked the subtlety necessary for an autocrat's court. He had been a long time away at sea.

Parmensis's poems were another reason why Octavian would hate him. His were not just the jibes of war. He had taunted the heir of Caesar for the lies about himself necessary for future peace. He had mocked his less than aristocratic ancestry, his illegitimacy to be anything other than the leader of a coup. Parmensis's Octavian was not descended from the goddess, Venus, in the scented groves of Cyprus. He was the grandson of a baker and a money lender, a man with hands still dirty from short-changing his customers, who had kneaded his mother in some bakery in Aricia on the *Via Appia*.

Maybe all that abuse had been a mistake. Horace's was the modern gentler style. His readers knew a different imagined world, a different Aricia that began his satire on the journey to the peace conference at Tarentum. *Egressum magna me accepit Aricia Roma,*

Aricia welcomed me on my way out of mighty Rome, the first stop on the first diplomatic journey of his new life. This Aricia did not offer whores from the back of a bread shop. There was nothing in Parmensis's poem that matched the literary spirit, let alone the politics, of Octavian's Maecenas.

Antony was hardly using art to help himself. His own latest contribution to the propaganda war had been to defend himself on personal charges that had been much made by Cicero and much repeated by Octavian. His peculiar pamphlet, *De inebrietate sua*, On his own drunkenness, had to deny his excess devotion to the god Dionysus as well as to other oriental deities. Parmensis might have helped with that but his only recorded advice to Antony, possibly delivered in verse, was where to find the best healing spa waters for his gout.

The time was too late for literature. Naval experience was not, however, so lightly to be dismissed. Few had witnessed directly the revolution at Naulochus and escaped to pass on the lessons. Parmensis had built fleets before. He could be useful at sea and the sea was where he had become comfortable for almost a decade. While his celebrity as an assassin might be a problem, it might also help Antony's aim for the widest possible coalition of Octavian's enemies.

Antony's position was strong. His confidence was growing. It was surprising how fast. There was even talk of a second attack on Parthia before the next phase of the civil war. He was already marshalling troops for the return trip east. A victory over Rome's greatest foreign enemy would bring money, a hardening of his troops and a rebuttal, better than any essay on drunkenness, to Octavian's charge that he had himself become a foreigner at Cleopatra's court.

This charge of no longer being a Roman was the most damaging of all. But Antony knew and was countering it. He was taking contrary advice to that of Cleopatra, a good sign from a headstrong man, and he was letting that be known. His officers included powerful figures separate from the Egyptian queen. After due reflection he left Parthia to his varyingly loyal client kings and turned his own mind solely to the campaign against Octavian. However and whenever this happened, it would be both at land and sea and Parmensis aimed to be there.

* * *

Other supporters of Antony were emboldened by what seemed his new statesmanship. Octavian, by contrast, was struggling. The legal basis of the triumvirate had expired and in Rome he had to face a form of opposition from what seemed a distant age, from the independent consuls of 32 BC. One of them was Domitius Ahenobarbus, the blockader of Brundisium after Philippi who after Perusia had shifted to Antony; the second was Gaius Sosius, whom Antony had made governor of Syria, one of his most loyal allies.

Ahenobarbus used his authority as consul to allow his fellow senators a long and respectful debate to ratify Antony's achievements. Sosius delivered a direct attack on an absent Octavian, forcing him to return to the senate under military protection and take a throne between the consuls, starkly recalling Caesar's assassination.

Octavian had to show again the dictatorial character he had hoped to bury in his past. Sosius and Ahenobarbus, fearing violence against themselves, found it prudent to leave Rome for Ephesus, where Antony established a senate in exile for the several hundred who followed them. Ships and sailors took the same route from all around the Aegean Sea.

Seaside Ephesus became the empire's second capital, its great bay sheltering transports and triremes, its Greek theatre housing Antony's new Roman government and its ancient Harbour Street newly thronged with men and messages. Its temple of Artemis had once been the site of the most merciless killing of Roman women and children on the orders of Mithradates. Fifty years on, its tall steps and columns gave sanctuary to one army of Romans about to be ranged against another. Every arrival passed the dog-shaped island of Samos, its nose pointing down to the sea named for the fall of Icarus, the boy who flew too close to the sun. Soon Ephesus was full.

Samos too became packed with the sailors of eight hundred ships and the hundred thousand men whom Antony and Cleopatra were marshalling to cross to Greece by sea. The task of supply was once more immense. Among the cargoes for the navy were food and fighting-towers for archers, wine and winches for catapults, raised platforms and decks, grappling hooks and scythes to counter the hooks of their enemy.

The ships in the three harbours of Samos were mixed in purpose and origin, shaped and sized as though for many different buyers in a naval yard. Some were familiar to Ahenobarbus and Parmensis, slim fighters and swollen tubs ballasted with rocks and oil. Others were floating palaces powered by multiple banks of oars, the ceremonial survivors of Cleopatra's ancestors and their island allies, as awesome (it was hoped) as they were hard to steer.

New ships were built and others repaired. Decimus Turullius caused offence by cutting down a grove sacred to the healing god, Aesculapius, on Cos, the island of wine and quince blossom ointments close to Rhodes. The rowers trained in the open sea. Teams from far across Asia and the Black Sea, from Egypt to Sicily, practised manoeuvres in the tiny patch of the Aegean between Smyrna, where Trebonius had been the first assassin to die, and Miletus, closer still to the south, where Titius had taken Sextus on his final voyage.

Messengers made daily trips to Rome. There was no blockade. Food for propaganda became the most valuable cargo for export. Antony and Cleopatra were celebrating in the style to which they had notoriously become accustomed. Any gaps in the stories of their feasts and dances were filled by lurid reports from those who sought Octavian's favour.

More frightening stories from Samos concerned the destination of Antony's fleet, fears that it might be aimed at Italy itself. The most potent gossip was of disagreement among Antony's Roman allies about the role of Cleopatra, whether she should stay on the campaign or return home.

Neither in Samos nor Rome was the story clear. The army commanders, it was said, believed that she should stay. They were anxious enough whether their Roman troops would fight fellow Romans loyal to the heir of Caesar; they wanted no extra uncertainty about whether the Egyptian forces would fight without their own goddess queen. Cleopatra had put her signature to a bribe to the head of Antony's land forces, Publius Canidius Crassus, payable to his family in perpetuity, to ensure that he was unwavering in her own view of the military balance.

Ahenobarbus and the navy captains argued instead that she should leave. Her fleet was impressive in port but untried in recent action, her giant galleons better designed to intimidate than to fight the new navy that Agrippa was drawing every day from his sulphurous factories at Lake Avernus. She was an autocrat, a breed which made bad leaders at sea. Her sailors were slavish, looking more closely for a raised royal flag, as though it were an eyebrow, than at the ships of the enemy.

Such oriental failings, a commonplace of Roman rhetoric, were central to Octavian's rhetorical onslaught. Every cliché of Roman fear of the foreign was deployed. Antony had few who could fight back. The alternate senate at Ephesus, though an embarrassment for Octavian, meant several hundred fewer defenders for Antony in the senate itself. The towns of Italy pledged their loyalty to Octavian in a rare commitment of faith.

Ahenobarbus travelled to Rome. He saw for himself the wounds which Octavian, heavily armed with outrage, was delivering to a naked target. Plancus and Titius, still blamed for the death of Sextus and keen to make no more mistakes, heard the same news and prepared to change sides. All sensed who was winning the distant war of propaganda.

Crassus argued the case for Cleopatra from the head of Antony's army. He saw both practicality and profit in her staying. Profit and practicality prevailed. Ahenobarbus conceded. The queen of Egypt stayed with the campaign as it slowly crossed the Aegean Sea. Its new headquarters were to be in Athens. From there Antony cut another link with Rome by divorcing his third wife, Octavia, Octavian's sister: the marriage that symbolised the peace treaty after Perusia was as dead as peace itself.

False news was becoming ever more potent as war, this time between former triumvirs, drew closer. There was never a military possibility that Antony and his fleet could move west rather than east. They could not invade Italy. Parmensis knew that. Anyone who had ever fought at sea knew that.

Not even on the magic side of the country, from Scylla to the Fields of Fire, were there ports for an opposed landing by such a force. The real-world harbours of Brundisium and Tarentum were securely held by Octavian. But in Rome the fear of invasion remained. Few people had studied the map in the temple of Tellus, or any other map.

Octavian fanned popular ignorance to ensure the loyalty of fear. Only the defectors, Plancus and Titius, with a mere few followers, could sail away from Antony and Cleopatra and land in Italy. When they did they brought more reports for Octavian of eastern threat and excess.

Parmensis had no option but to stay with Antony. Octavian welcomed Plancus and Titius, as propaganda tools if nothing else. But, before the final battle for Caesar's legacy, he could not have embraced – or even spared – his last assassin.

The war for legitimacy was still, however, in the balance at Rome. Some fighters with words were more successful than others. Cassius's last companion, Messalla, moved his allegiance smoothly to Octavian and accepted the consulship. Plancus wanted the same advancement but revealed himself unreliable even as a persuader.

Plancus had been Antony's secretary and the organiser, it was said, of some of Cleopatra's most exotic parties, presiding naked, his body painted blue, with reeds around his head and a fish tail. He had awarded Cleopatra the prize for drinking the most expensive wine when she had dissolved a huge pearl, once owned by Mithradates, in her cup. He mocked Antony in the senate for offences in which, to his more sceptical hearers, he had been enthusiastically engaged himself.

Octavian had to recognise that Plancus was a mere follower of the wind and everyone knew it. The general who had abandoned Lucius Antonius on the *Via Flaminia*, in sight of Ferusia, had turned again. That was hardly much endorsement of his latest new master. Titius had still to explain his own excess of enthusiasm to execute the son of the fondly remembered Pompey.

Recognising the weakness of eye-witness accounts from men like these, Octavian took out one more weapon in his war of stories. Breaking law and precedent, he extracted Antony's will from the secret vaults of the Vestal Virgins in the Forum. In a parody of Antony's reading of Caesar's will (both documents owing as much to the reader as the writer), Octavian revealed Antony's wish to be buried in Alexandria rather than Rome and his large legacies to Cleopatra's children.

21

A BATTLE THAT NEVER WAS

The Battle of Actium, Lorenzo a Castro (1672)

In Athens, two years later, everyone had a view on what had gone wrong for Antony and Cleopatra at the battle of Actium. Both had been too careless, too cowardly. Or perhaps she had been hasty and cowardly and he had not. Or he had been louche and greedy and she had wanted to take her treasure ship home. Or maybe it was the other way around. Those who had shared their parties had quickly learnt to adjust their memories. Surely Octavian had been too strong all along? Everyone was for Octavian when he was the undisputed leader of the Roman world.

Actium was the last battle for Cassius Parmensis. It was already famous as the last battle of the civil wars although, as Parmensis and every other sailor knew, the war was over weeks before the promontory of Actium became a battle's name. In the schools of rhetoric they called this a *prolepsis*, a future written in the present tense. Antony was a dead man walking. He was defeated while still preparing to fight.

The final judgement between Caesar's rival heirs was made at sea but not, as at Naulochus, in a crowded bay by the robber, the grabber and the rams of Rhodes. Antony lost because Agrippa held for Octavian the ports and open water that Antony did not. There were as many accounts in Athens as there were defeated men. But the outlines of the stories – and always the outcome – were the same.

Before leaving Rome for Greece Octavian had identified a bit of bare city ground, designated it to be Egypt, and watched while a soldier hurled a spear against enemy sand. This was said to be an ancient tradition although no sign of its antiquity ever survived. Octavian, whose father was not his father, was becoming ever bolder in the use of tradition to disguise what was new.

Agrippa then began the real war. Messalla, who in his last battle at Philippi had swapped philosophy with Gaius Cassius, became one of his captains. The sea around Corcyra, the northern Greek island best placed between Italy and Greece, became the first site for fighting where no fighting took place. Antony and Cleopatra waited there to prevent Agrippa's crossing. Agrippa tricked Antony into thinking that his fleet had already crossed, then seized Corcyra himself when they had left for Actium some sixty miles to the south.

From Corcyra's harbours Agrippa's triremes could cover Octavian's troop transports as they sailed, with barely any impedance, from Brundisium and Tarentum to mainland Greece. With devastating speed, the skill that made him Caesar's closest military heir, Agrippa also took Leucas, the island twenty miles further south of Actium, and other smaller harbour towns. He protected himself as far away as Corinth. Octavian landed his forces just five miles away from his enemy, built a wall between his camp and the sea, and took a position, more exposed than Antony's but easier for supply. From there he could watch and wait.

The army of Antony and Cleopatra was larger than that of Octavian. Their ships were more numerous too and heavier, their crews better paid from the travelling treasury of Egypt. Antony's reputation as a master of tactics stretched back longer than that of Agrippa and had never been threatened by Octavian himself. Antony had the seemingly stronger position for his ships and his army, protected behind the straits that led to Ambracia Bay.

But, as every story-teller agreed, the army was barely used and the bay was not the protection it had seemed. Its waters were warm, sickly and shallow. Slow-flying flamingoes chased sullen coots and kingfishers through insect clouds. Disease spread. The troops were dependent on supply from the land side where food of any kind was scarce.

There had been a vigorous argument about tactics; every gossip in Athens knew about that, happy to repeat it to new listeners. Antony and Cleopatra might have forced the principal battle on land where they could have better commanded the timing and the place. Or they could have marched inland, as Caesar had done before the battle of Pharsalus, abandoning their own fleet but forcing the enemy too to abandon the coast, to follow and fight far away from their protected ports.

Instead they did neither. They stayed in the deepest parts of Ambracia Bay, behind the narrow straits at Actium, and looked out through the marshes to sea. While Antony was away seeking fresh food and reinforcements for his army, one of his admirals, accompanied by the ships of a local king, attempted to break the blockade and was beaten back by Agrippa. That was perhaps the critical point.

From then onwards, as the survivors later reported to themselves and to anyone else who would hear, Antony's star started to descend. His troops, hungry and thirsty, began to die. His mercenaries defected or retreated. Prominent Romans, Ahenobarbus to the fore, joined Plancus and Titius and switched their support to Octavian. Cleopatra took the blame from those who stayed.

Pale-faced vultures flapped like sails in the sky. The army was weakening with sickness from the swamps. Its field commander, Crassus, whom Cleopatra had bribed with perpetual tax-free rights over Egyptian oil and wine, began to earn his shared role as villain in the survivors' eyes. He was already planning his escape to Alexandria if the worst became even worse.

By the time that Antony began what became known throughout the Roman world as the battle of Actium, much of his naval advantage was gone. He had fewer ships; he had to burn those that he could not man. He had to make a grim choice between abandoning his army, which was also Cleopatra's army, and his navy, which even more was Cleopatra's domain. In a decision which, even two years on, consumed the debaters of Athens, he favoured his ships. Parmensis and Turullius watched this last rhetorical victory in the battle between sea and land and prepared to fight for the man who, in what seemed a different age, had tried to crown Caesar king.

Even when siding with his navy, the critics said, Antony saw his best chance as merely to escape. He had loaded on board his money chests of pay for his men; he had ordered sails to be carried, cluttering the decks and weighing down the hulls. Neither decision was one which an admiral would make before a sea battle that he expected to fight. Antony was maybe ready in his mind; in wind, waves and storm anything could happen; a loser might become a winner. But he was much readier to flee.

Or, as others argued, his preparations had been a ploy, not an acceptance of defeat but a way to pretend defeatism. His overloaded navy still had his best possible chance of victory. He might have cut Octavian's lines of supply from home. Octavian's army would then be the one left isolated in Greece, with no option but to fight whenever Antony saw the highest possibility of success. Arguments such as these were more heated – and much longer lasting – than the battle itself.

On the chosen early September day Antony's ships slipped safely from the straits, forming into three squadrons in a long single line. Parmensis was just one captain among hundreds, scenting the slightest shift in a breeze, ordering rowers, legionaries and engineers. Cleopatra's personal ships provided a second line in the rear. A mile ahead of them were Agrippa's ships in a longer arc from shore to shore.

There could be no element of surprise. Just as at Naulochus, exactly five years before, the arrangements were almost formal. The sailors on each side watched the preparations of the other, the packing of hulls with men and machines, as many as 150,000 rowers, marines and legionaries in all. The straight mile between them became a ragged two or three as each side aimed to sail around the other in the best style of the Rhodians.

At Actium there were more manoeuvres than rammings. The sea was like the setting for a dance. Each side had legionaries trained in the same Roman way. Each knew what the other could do. Octavian had his loyal Tenth Legion with the grapnel hook in its insignia but there was no clear advantage to either in grappling a ship close and turning sea into land.

Catapults launched fiery arrows. The wind blew quietly down the coast and fanned the few that found their mark. There was fierce fighting where fighting occurred, enough for Antony's line to fall a little back, barely even the smallest signal of what could have happened if the battle had continued.

At that point, for reasons forever debated, the ships of Cleopatra burst through both Antony's and Agrippa's lines. Under full sail, with the north-west wind behind them, they were not set for turning to fight. Their rams pointed only away. The battle zone was soon at their backs.

Antony followed with some fifty ships to which he was able to send his own signal to follow in retreat. They planned no stop before the sandy shallows of Egypt. Within a few minutes the war which Agrippa had so long and meticulously prepared was won. Within a few hours the army of Antony and Cleopatra, waiting for news beyond the marshlands, had learnt that it must either march inland or surrender.

The troops risked surrender to the heir of Julius Caesar rather than retreat through miles of barren fields, a barrier whose horrors they knew. The sailors did the same. The final act was merely a tying of loose ends and a last blast of theatre.

Octavian suddenly had more troops than he wanted or than anyone could want. He accepted his unnecessary reinforcements with grace. He had already made his plans. An unnecessary army was a dangerous thing. He sent as many men as possible away for settlement in Gaul. Their destination was not around Parma, which was only for the provenly reliable, but in Further Gaul, far enough away for safety, near enough to civilization to encourage proper gratitude.

Parmensis, his death certain under the rule of the victor, his life far from secure in unknown Egypt, retreated into Greece. Turullius began a journey that would end on the island of Cos. Within a week the last surrender had been made; the confused followers of one Roman warlord had fitted into the final civil war army of the only other. Actium's vultures swooped for carrion elsewhere. Ambracia Bay was left to its flamingoes.

Octavian sailed to Antony's former base in Samos. He was beset there not by enemies but by former enemies desperate to change sides. He returned briefly to Brundisium where his supporters were rather less enthusiastic, celebrating only when the latest batch of veterans received their promised land. Antony's men had to be paid too. Rather than risk another war along the *Via Aemilia*, the *Via Flaminia* and the *Via Appia*, Octavian decided to borrow and buy rather than steal. The treasury of Egypt would soon pay the bill.

In July, he sailed to Alexandria where Antony made him a deluded offer of single combat as though they were ancient Greek heroes at Troy. Cleopatra, in the more reasonable manner of a monarch, tried to negotiate for her treasure, threatening to burn it and her children, suggesting that one or more of them might retain her royal rights as a client of Rome. Octavian stayed at a distance. He received the surrender of the self-interested and the suicide of Antony and Cleopatra themselves. The reign of the Ptolemies ended. The treasure survived.

This was no longer a crisis, only a drama and the stuff of future dramas. Octavian ordered the execution of Caesarion, Cleopatra's son by Julius Caesar, Antyllus, Antony's heir by Fulvia and their army commander Crassus whose family lost its perpetual export rights. He arrayed a mass of regalia for his triumph, hoped to outdo Pompey if he could, promised his poet Cornelius Gallus the new post of prefect of Egypt, and returned, rather slowly some thought, to Rome. The two last assassins, accustomed to the vengeance of his climb to power, waited upon his mood at its summit.

* * *

Actium and its aftermath, the battle that barely happened, became in every way the ideal battle of words. There was as little loss of Roman life as there was ample evidence of oriental reluctance to fight. Everyone was happy to remember such battles. Writers looked forward to helping them, the poets first

Parmensis, still condemned to death, was the worst placed but at least he lived to write again, the best that he could hope for and with the added hope that he himself might be forgotten. He escaped fast by land through Greece. Famous places faded behind him, Ambracia, Acarnania, Aetolia, Delphi, Corinth. The further he travelled from Actium and the closer to Athens, the more the countryside relaxed from Roman war zone to a more reliable antiquity.

Gallus, by contrast, his poetic reputation soaring with his patron's success, received the richest playground in the Roman world, so rich that its governor had to report to Octavian alone. Varius, hardly less honoured, received a commission from Octavian for a play to mark the anniversary of the great unforgettable victory, a version of *Thyestes*. Horace and Virgil took on the task of ensuring that Actium was never forgotten by any reader of poetry anywhere.

Only a few years before, even with Sextus gone, Horace had wondered *quando repostum Caecubum bibam*, when could he and Maecenas drink their best wine? Now, after Actium, *nunc est bibendum*: this was the time for everyone to drink and dance now that the queen who threatened Italy was dead, a drunken monster forced to flee from her burning fleet like a dove before a hawk. The propaganda of the period before the final battle was made rousing poetry for the people of Rome.

Horace's message became more subtle as his poem continued, showing sympathy for the Egyptian queen, a shift from contempt to compassion, antagonism to admiration. She did not fear the sword as women do. Neither did she run away to secret shores. Instead she dared to see her ruined power with peaceful face, to clasp fierce serpents to her veins, more ferocious in the death she chose than as a warrior, as though scorning to be led away in her enemy's ships, no longer a queen, a mere woman in a triumph.

This sharp shift in tone moved its readers from the moment the poem was written. It was as popular in Athens as in Rome. But it was the kind of poetic clemency that can go only to the humiliated. For Horace it was one of his quickest and most quoted odes; for Octavian it was perfect.

Virgil's version of Actium was more direct. After the *Georgics*, in which the great victory loomed only lightly, he had begun composing the *Aeneid*. This was to be an epic for the future. Just as Aeneas had been the founder of old Rome, so Octavian, the poem's first audience, was the founder of the new. The goddess Venus, the venerated ancestor of Caesar, was the link between them. Parmensis's version – the kneading of female flesh in the back of bakeries -was consigned to footnotes of biography.

The Aeneas of the *Aeneid* would face some of the same trials as Odysseus, narrowly avoiding the passage through Scylla and Charybdis, finding prophecy in the darkness below Lake Avernus. Like Achilles in the *Iliad* he would also have a mighty decorated shield, a gift of his goddess mother, with Actium at its centre, the victor high on his ship above the foaming waves, light pouring from his eyes, Cleopatra, blind to the snakes in her future and attended by a god dog.

Maecenas was the master of these poetic enterprises, their early audience, encouragement and financier. He also became an early ruler of Rome on the absent Octavian's behalf, supervising a new temple and senate house in the Forum in Julius Caesar's name, mopping up any last areas of resistance.

Propertius the love poet, bitter critic of Octavian after Perusia, was careful to praise Maecenas's loyalty and modest use of absolute power. Compared to Maecenas's ploughing of the swollen seas, a poet, he wrote, was merely dallying by a little stream. Protesting maybe too much, Propertius became the crudest in crying out that Cleopatra was an enemy whore queen, worn out by her own attendants, at the same time invoking the myth of virtuous Lucretia: 'What was it worth to have shattered the Tarquins' axes if now we had to endure this woman?'.

There were a few last security details for Maecenas to resolve. For one of these a soldier called Quintus Attius Varus was sent to Athens on a very personal assignment. He was not a poet soldier although he would be sometime confused with Varius the poet. He was not in a hurry. His only task was to find the right man.

More immediately, the son of Lepidus, it was said, was planning an assassination of the new Caesar. This Lepidus was also married to a grand-daughter of Servilia, Brutus's mother. Maecenas took no chances on the truth or otherwise of such a plot, a dangerously neat closing of the history book that had begun fourteen years before.

He had arranged for his master to have a personal power of legal pardon at Rome, a 'Vote of Athena' as it was called after the eventual resolution of Thyestes' curse, the goddess forgiving the last murderer in the chain of family vengeance. This pardon was not used for Lepidus. Brutus's niece killed herself after the execution of her husband.

22

TURULLIUS, CUTTER
OF TREES

Decimus Turullius, assassin, sailor, aide to Tillius Cimber and master of turning metals into coins was on his way to Cos, the island of banks, perfume and wine close to Rhodes. Much of Turullius's resources had come from the extortion of the people of those islands on behalf of Brutus and Cassius and, most recently, of Antony whom he had joined after Sextus's death. The masts of his ships for Antony's navy had come from Cos. He had both friends and enemies in the islands of the south-eastern Aegean.

Not far away, sailing quietly between Ephesus and Pergamum, Octavian had only friends, many of whom wanted to be worshippers too. He allowed the dedication of temples to himself only for those who were not Roman citizens. Romans abroad had to be satisfied with worship of the city itself and the divinity of Julius Caesar.

Octavian had Turullius hunted down in Cos. The island was in any case worth a victor's visit. In its treasuries the Egyptians sometimes banked their gold. The victor of Actium might claim on Cleopatra's deposits. As well as quince and marjoram for the scent-makers of Rome here was also a sacred grove of trees, a home of the healing god, Asclepius. Turullius had felled some of them to make his ships.

This was hardly a capital offence. The Romans were unpredictable about protecting holy sites, particularly those of other people. Sometimes a wood was a temple; sometimes, as for Agrippa at Avernus, it was just a wood. Julius Caesar, it was said, had once made oars and masts near Massilia from a grove so sacred that not even its priests ever entered it.

Antony and Turullius had not cared where their fleet at Actium had found its timber. After Actium Octavian made a show of caring very much. It was a time for respect and peace to as many men as possible. Executing Turullius on Cos was almost his last act of revenge for the spirit of his father. It also set a tone of piety, long absent, in the islands of Greece and Asia. Decimus Turullius was the eighteenth assassin to die for his role on the Ides of March.

23

THE LAST ASSASSIN

Orestes Pursued by the Furies, William-Adolphe Bouguereau (1852)

Parmensis was in Athens. A year after Actium his nearest groves of trees were the groves of Plato's Academe, the place of idealists which Epicurus had rejected. He was one of many survivors of Rome's civil wars but, after the death of Turullius, he was the only surviving assassin of Julius Caesar. Among the surging bands of refugees there was much talk of the best place to seek clemency, safety and even future success. But it was hard to say where Parmensis might go. His opportunities were the most severely restricted of any man's.

Maps for a fugitive barely existed at this time, even in Athens. There was no guide to the Mediterranean like that to Italy in the temple of Tellus. Agrippa would soon begin to change that, as he changed so much else for Octavian. Meanwhile Parmensis had to rely on what he knew.

Egypt was vast and empty. It was run by a poet but Gallus's loyalty was not first to fellow writers, even one who had once shared his home in Cisalpine Gaul. He was a man on the make. Some asked whether he was even much of a poet anyway. His works were in the Athenian libraries, a bit too polished and perfect, not the most popular. *Uno tellures diuidit amne duas,* with one stream it divides two lands, the formal balance of the *uno* and the *duas,* the *tellures* and the *amne,* the one and the two, the land and the river with *dividit* dividing them all. Away from Maecenas's court the reviews were mixed.

Gallus's river was the Hypanis, separating Europe from Asia north of the Black Sea. That area itself might be an option for Parmensis but only a certain sort of Roman would consider exile as far away as that. He could take a peaceful journey by sea, perhaps a poetic journey following that first ship, the Argo and its sailors' quest for the Golden Fleece, a myth even in the time of Odysseus. Maybe but a man from Parma, accustomed to Rome and Athens, would not want to be there for long.

He needed somewhere nearer, more civilised and governed by someone at least moderately sympathetic to the assassins' side. Syria might have been a possibility. Once Dolabella's and Cassius's, it was under the command of the surviving son of Cicero, the boy who had been almost as much trouble to his father as Dolabella, his sister's husband, had been.

But young Marcus Tullius Cicero, though bold and famously fond of a drink (he had once thrown a glass of wine at Agrippa), was unlikely to rescue an assassin who had last fought for Antony. He was high on the winning side. He had announced Antony's defeat and death to the crowd in the Forum from the very *rostra,* the captured ships' prows, where his father's tongue and hands had been nailed.

Gaul was the great back garden to Parmensis's old home. Messalla, friend of Cassius, the young Cicero and of Horace and other poets too, was on his way west to the source of Julius Caesar's power. An urbane diplomat and quiet defender of old senatorial values, he was unlikely to be noisier in their defeat. After Actium he had Antony's house on the Palatine Hill that Pompey had once possessed.

Macedonia would soon be in the hands of Marcus Licinius Crassus, one of Parmensis's fellow sailors in the cause of Sextus Pompeius. He too had followed the path from Sextus to Antony but the young Crassus, grandson of Julius Caesar's banker and rival, was determinedly seeking advancement in Octavian's new world, just as Horace was doing the same.

It was two years since he had seen Tillius Cimber. If the man who began the assassination was anywhere alive, his chosen place might be a place of safety. Tillius had been a fixer, a man who got things done, a doer who would reward a shipbuilding poet. He could give a good party. But he had probably died at Philippi, his brother too. His sure existence was only in the poems of Horace, as a symbol of why Epicurus was right and raw ambition the greatest threat to a man's mind.

Horace was done with any ambition except in words and simple comfort. *Quo tibi, Tilli, sumere depositum clavum fierique tribuno?* What was the point, Tillius, of your bothering to go back into politics when you had safely left it? Envy follows the uniforms of office. People ask who you are, where you are from. You have nothing to say. So said the fortunate Horace in the satire that followed his life-changing journey to Tarentum.

Horace would be an unlikely helper for Parmensis, whatever the interest of one writer in another. He no longer took that kind of risk. He preferred to praise Pollio for his stories of Caesar tossing the dice before crossing the Rubicon. He would gently embarrass Plancus by reminding him of Rhodes and Ephesus and Corinth and other tourist spots so recently places of war, reminiscing about his treacherous past in the manner of a guide suggesting a holiday at home. *Laudabunt alii claram Rhodon aut Mytilenen aut Epheson bimarisve Corinthi*: Others will praise glorious Rhodes or Mytilene or Corinth of the two seas; let me instead praise the domestic pleasures of life. That was Horace's new interest in the past.

Plancus and Pollio, like Messalla, were slithering up the rungs of Octavian's new Rome. Horace was an equally masterly artist of survival, a sympathiser but not a protector. Virgil and Horace praised Messalla's critical acumen and Pollio's poems and tragedies. Pollio's writings condemned Cicero, civil war and personal bitterness in politics; to Epicureans of the next generation this would become a convenient and uncontroversial truth. In victory everyone wanted the same freedom from 'the power of a faction', the calming words that Octavian, the regime's writer as well as its ruler, used himself when he was summing up his life.

Virgil would be hardly more use to Parmensis than would Horace. He did not have a province or place in politics either. He too was merely a poet, politically helpful but useless to a fellow poet in need. In his *Aeneid* he was taking the black and white world of Homer and colouring it in for that world which Octavian was reimagining. The new Rome's foundations were laid, prime among them Pollio's plans for Rome's first public library of literature, approved poets preferred.

Nor was Varro the librarian, map-maker and critic any more likely to help. Even at his advanced and prosperous age he was busily completing the journey from Pompey via Caesar to Caesar's heir. His anxiety was over his work to define the arts into 'disciplines', the influential cares of a fortunate man.

Beyond the reach of Rome the kingdom of Parthia, where Sextus had been maybe heading before his capture, was still a potential haven. Pompey himself had considered exile there. Various Roman renegades had prospered where the elder Crassus had lost his life, his head used as a prop in a royal performance of a play by Euripides, his mouth filled with molten gold. The Parthians were keen to acquire political intelligence and military expertise but theirs was a desert land. They were far away and they did not fight at sea.

There was no point in even thinking of a return to Parma, as much a part of Octavian's new domain as Parthia was not. With help from Rome, from new settlers and citizens, the miserable Parmenses were rebuilding their shattered town, reinforcing their river banks for commerce not defence, planning a bridge of strong stone arches, planting orchards whose fruits would include annual feasts for their fellow citizens, a legacy of financial confidence for as far ahead as they could imagine. Parmensis, enemy-in-chief of the new regime, would never be welcomed back. Thyestes' ghastly return home was fresh from his pen. He would be killed there if he was lucky.

In the heat hazes of summer Parmensis was reluctant to leave Athens. He had as good a chance of avoiding Caesar's avenger there as anywhere else. He could look out gratefully over the great sea at the sweet sight of others' struggles, *suave, mari magno*, as Lucretius had described, a most suitable motto for the walls of a seaside villa.

The day winds blew cool towards the land. He had his plays and poetry, his perilous satires and his painstaking tragedies. He had reasons to fear but no reason to be uncomfortable. In Athens there were supporters of every cause, even the most lost. He had been hunted for thirteen years and was still alive to read Homer, repeat the mantras of Epicurus, visit the remains of the philosopher's garden and write tragedy.

In Athenian daylight he could remind himself that 'death is nothing to me', that 'what is dust does not perceive, and what does not perceive is nothing to me', that 'death brings neither pleasure nor pain' and that 'the only thing that is bad for me is pain'. In the darkness it was harder. At night, after the wind turned towards the sea and the scent of the flowers fell, he had begun to imagine a massive dark intruder, dishevelled and bearded, who would sever his head.

Quis istam faciem lanipedis senis torquens? Who was that sinister figure at the gate, twisting his face, his feet wrapped in wool against cold or gout? That was a decent line of Latin, slightly wrong long syllables, limping in metre to match its subject, a part of his new *Thyestes*, a picture of one brother waiting to pile vengeance upon another. *Lanipedis* meant wool-wrapped feet; *planipedis* might be better, bare-footed. There were more of the second than the first among the refugees of Rome's wars.

Whenever Parmensis saw the monster he called his slaves and asked if anyone else had seen it. Each time they said no. He returned to sleep. There were dried leaves and flowers, pungent aniseed and other seeds, for nightmares. There was the familiar scent of sulphur. He slept. He saw the intruder again. He called for a lamp. He called his slaves to stay beside him. The black fear returned.

Might he be pardoned? In the realm of art the cycle of murder that began with Thyestes banqueting on his children, that had encompassed the deaths of Atreus's son, Agamemnon, his grand-daughter, Iphigeneia, Agamemnon's wife, Clytemnestra, and her lover, had ended in Athens with Athena pardoning Orestes, the last murderer in the family line. That was the Vote of Athena that Octavian had been given but not used. There was still time.

When Quintus Attius Varus found his prey at home, with his library behind the barred door in the parched garden, the manuscript of the first Roman *Thyestes* was there too. Some said that he took it back to Rome along with the head of Caesar's last assassin and gave it to his near namesake, Varius, the pet poet of Octavian, who had his well-paid commission to celebrate the Battle of Actium. Thyestes the loser would make a perfect Mark Antony.

Others said that the story of the theft was not true, that Varius's version was all his own work. Cassius Parmensis was the nineteenth and last assassin of Julius Caesar to die.

SOURCES

Trebonius was the first assassin to die, Parmensis the last. The historian who first outlined *The Last Assassin* so crisply was called Velleius Paterculus, not a very well-known name. He wrote a short history of Rome in his spare time from fighting Parthians and Gauls. He was born only a decade after Parmensis's death, close enough to know from contemporaries what had happened; his grandfather, a friend of Brutus, had killed himself after the destruction of Perusia. He was damned by the faint praise of posterity (and even of his own time) for squeezing the maximum period of years into the smallest possible space.

Valerius Maximus, the source for Parmensis's dramatic death dream, also wrote short books but was much more successful at it. Unlike Velleius he had no other known profession or income and collected stories from wherever he could find them, grouping them under popular headings, Chastity, Cruelty and Omens. Most were Roman, rather fewer Greek, and all were helpful for public speakers in provincial places far from a library. Under Omens he placed the ghost of the dishevelled black giant that came to Cassius Parmensis before Varus arrived from Rome.

In maintaining their future reputations both men were unfortunate to be subjects of the Emperor Tiberius, the adopted son of the Emperor Augustus, the name that was taken by Octavian when he had won absolute power. Tiberius was less skilful than Augustus in concealing his tyranny, a failing which affected the reputation of almost everything that happened in his reign. The historians of his 'silver age', popular or not, became as disreputable as the sex parties around his swimming pools.

Velleius also lied from time to time and was exposed for that. He made mistakes. He saw Virgil as no better than any other hack who celebrated the great victory of Actium. He could not appeal to successors who preferred historians to write like scientists. He had a rhetorical style in which he too much pleaded to be believed. He began his history with Atreus and Odysseus and ended it with the equally heroic emperor of his own time.

He had many good qualities too. He took part in many of the events that he described, a distinction desirable for being an historian in antiquity and sometimes since. Velleius fought his foreign wars alongside another Gaius Julius Caesar, the son of Agrippa and Octavian's daughter, Julia. His uncle had helped Agrippa to prosecute the empty chair of Gaius Cassius under the *Lex Pedia*. His sons became consuls. He was of the class that could legitimately apply their experience to the past. He knew what later men did not know and, most importantly, his work survived, unlike that of Pollio and other participants who tried to set their own judgements into history.

Velleius was right. Trebonius was the first assassin to die and Cassius Parmensis the last. Possibly Turullius was last but to argue that would be perverse in the face of a clear statement from a man of many virtues whose vice was to eulogise a tyrant who had learnt vengeance from his adopted father if not enough else.

Octavian's own vengeance was not so reliably recorded by Velleius. 'Not one of those who had borne arms against him was put to death by him, or by his order', he wrote, anticipating Tiberius's filial approval. 'It was the cruelty of Antony that ended the life of Decimus Brutus. In the case of Sextus Pompeius, though Caesar was his conqueror, it was likewise Antony who deprived him of his life'. Others, writing in safer later times, took a very different view of Octavian's clemency.

Valerius Maximus avoided such sensitive topics. Parmensis's

ghost appeared first in *Factorum ac dictorum memorabilium libri IX*, Nine books of memorable deeds and sayings, by a man without the protection of wealth and power. Valerius had only one connection to the combatants of the civil wars, a Sextus Pompeius who was not the son of Pompey the Great but a very distant cousin. He had no privileged position of knowledge except being able to read the kind of books by other people that did not always last long.

His own book did last, vying in the Middle Ages only with the bible. It flattered his emperor but also introduced readers in faraway places and future times to the fear of a condemned man haunted by his history. Valerius described Cassius Parmensis on his last Athenian nights. He gave a glimpse of the terrified, of a man who had trained himself not to be afraid of death, or thought he had.

Valerius and Velleius were lesser guides close to great events. Cicero and Caesar, whose letters and reports were essential sources, were part of those events and have always dominated the story however it is told. To both men their words were part of their wars. Other sources, variously lesser and greater, had to vie for their own share of attention.

Easiest to forget have been those who were once popular historians but could later be read only in the tiniest fragments. Take the writer called only Cornutus, probably son of the city praetor who killed himself when Octavian reached Rome after Mutina, once a great filler of halls when he read his work aloud, surviving here only by recording the redness of the banks of the Rubicon. There were dozens of such 'probably men', gradually recorded in pages of learned scholarship, remembered like Parmensis by splinters alone.

The greatest independent historians of the civil wars, Appian and Cassius Dio, gained their reputation not least by extended survival, the most essential quality for a source, each new reader exaggerating their reach, a virtuous circle of success. Both men wrote from a greater distance away in time. Both became necessary for telling the story of the assassins, difficult at various points to reconcile with one another but not so much as to destroy the credibility of either.

Appian was a Greek from Alexandria, born more than a century after the death of Cleopatra. Egypt had been Roman ever since. Gallus the poet had not lasted long as Augustus's prefect, succumbing to the common disease of Egyptian rulers to have his name inscribed on the pyramids, to be worshipped as well as obeyed. His successors fared better. Appian was one of many enthusiastic Greeks who were Roman in Egypt, a provincial agent of the Emperor.

His history of Rome dutifully began with its kings and ended with the successes of his own time. He borrowed from Pollio and Messalla, whose works became fragments despite their power, as well as from Julius Caesar himself. He had sympathy for Antony as Alexandria's adopted son, and for Gaius Cassius among the assassins, but he never showed the slightest doubt that rule by one Roman was the right way for the world to be ruled

Cassius Dio was also a Greek who loved Rome, less interested than Appian in philosophy, more in the calculations of power. He was from Bithynia, born in distant Nicaea below the Black Sea, about a further hundred years from the triumph of Octavian. He was much grander than Appian, a politician as well as a writer, a man of power who shared the consulship with emperors, a Greek-Roman rather in the way that a man might call himself today a Greek-American, rich, Greek-speaking, proud of his home land but prouder still of being a Roman senator and the son of a senator.

This Cassius Dio, or Dio Cassius, as he is just as often called, could switch his identities as though they were codes, looking always east for preference, preferring, he said, to write for a wolf or a bear than for anyone west of the Rhine. This made him a somewhat caustic historian when he reached his pages on Roman Britain but a reasonable guide to the civil wars, well disposed to Octavian, hostile to Cicero, in both cases quite consistently so.

He was also a stylish writer, the best of all our sources, although, like Velleius, he was perhaps a little too fond of his style. He became close to the Emperor Septimius Severus, a ruler peculiarly prey to spirits, ghosts and superstitions of every kind. The combination of art and politics made him an unusually bold explorer of others' fears.

Truth, in his view, did not need to be reserved for facts. Fantasy in its place was fine. Successful fortune-tellers and insatiable women became some of his most useful tools. Dio honed his technique early in his literary life, discovering that dreams and portents prophesying the ascent of an emperor were popular, most of all if the dreams were the emperor's own.

After that he 'never looked back', as we might say, or as we might say more accurately, he looked back into the past with ever greater confidence. His History of Rome took over eighty volumes, the events after the assassination of Caesar coming just after the half way point.

Dio is essential for anyone who wants to chart the story of the assassins, to reconstruct a journey for Dolabella in pursuit of Trebonius, to follow Antony and Decimus along the *Via Flaminia*, to decide what Gaius Cassius did or did not do in Rhodes and whether or not Brutus paraded only his female prisoners before the walls of Patara or the men too. Valerius Maximus may sometimes be checked against him: only Dio and he deliver the detail that Gaius Cassius stole every object of value from Rhodes bar the Chariot of the Sun God that the Rhodians every year drove off a cliff.

Dio says little else about Gaius Cassius in Rhodes whereas for Appian it is an event worthy of pages. Dio gives a brief account of Brutus humbly addressing the people of Rome after Caesar's assassination; Appian describes him praising himself and his fellow killers at some length. Comparing and comprehending these two ancient historians, making allowances for ignorance and bias and both, is what those people do who are also called ancient historians.

For Cassius Dio his writing was a self-imposed task for a luxury retirement in Capua on the *Via Appia*. He did not feel the need to travel too closely to the places he described. His aim was to deploy the arts of the great Greek historians on the only subject that was worthier than their own, to tell the story of how Rome had become so great – with an intermittent sub-text of why the mutability of fortune had sometimes intervened. It was a task that no one would attempt again for a millennium-and-a-half.

PROLOGUE

Valerius Maximus. *Factorum ac dictorum memorabilium libri IX (Nine Books of Memorable Deeds and Sayings)* 1.7.7

ONE

Parmenses Miserrimos: Cicero *Ad Familiares (Letters to friends)* 1 XIIIb. On pioneer rewards for Parma and Mutina: Livy XXXIX 55,7. Shades of purple: Plutarch *Cato Minor*. 6.3. Boius and boia: Plautus *Captivi* 888. Red Rubicon: Cornutus Fr 1. Epicurus: *Kyriae Doxae*

TWO

Politics of the Cassii: Cic. *Philippics* 2.26. Cassius and Caesar: Plut. *Brutus* 9.1, 6.5 *Caesar* 62.6. Previous assassination attempt: Cic. *Phil.* 2. 26.

On Cassius as date trader: Aurelius Victor *De viris illustribus (On Famous Men)* 82

Cassius as instigator and Brutus as persuader: Plut. *Brut.* 10. Cassius Dio *Roman History* 41.14.1. Caesar's honours: Plut. *Caes.* 57-61. Antony offering the crown: Plut. *Caes.* 61-5

Brutus's obstinacy: Cic. *Ad Atticum (Letters to Atticus)*. 14.1.2. Plut. *Brut.* 6 7-8. Brutus as possibly Caesar's son: Suetonius, *Divus Julius (The Deified Julius)* 82. Dio 44.19.5. Cic. *Brutus* 324. Brutus's family tree: Cic. *Ad.* 13. 40. 1. Brutus as money lender: Cic. *Ad Att.* 5.21.10-12

Servilia and Caesar: Plut. *Brut.* 5.2 *Cato Min.* 4.2 Suet. *Div Jul.* 50.2. Appian *Bella Civilia (Civil Wars)* C 2. 112. Labeo and Brutus: Plut. *Brut.* 12.4 51.2

Crassus's columns on the Palatine: Val. Max. 914 Pliny. *Naturalis Historia (Natural History)* 72-5. Basilus's anger: Cass. Dio 43.47.5. Ligarius's resentment: Plut. *Brut.* 11. Galba's lost consulship:

Hirtius *Gallic War* 8.50.4 Suet. *Galba* 3.2, financial dispute with
Caesar, Val. Max 6.2.11 Cic. *Ad Fam.* 6.18.3. Cassius's lions: Plut.
Brut. 8. 6

Concern over value of offices under Caesar: Nicolaus of Damascus
Life of Augustus 63-4 App. BC 2.111 Cass. Dio 44.1.1. On
Epicureans, peace and politics: Seneca *De Otio (On Leisure)* 3.2

THREE

Cornelia and her children: Plin. *NH.* 7.57

Cicero and history of Rome: Cic. *Ad Att.* 2.12.13 Plut. *Cic.* 41.1, on
inexperienced Epicureans Cic. *De Re Publica (The Republic)*
Prologue, on Cicero as too intellectual to join the plot, Plut. *Brut.*
12.1-2

Cicero, Quintus and Lucretius: Cic. *Ad Quintum fratrem (Letters
to His Brother, Quintus)* 2.94: on protecting Epicurus's garden
Cic. *Ad Fam.* 13. 1. 3-4. Cassius on morality and epicurean peace:
Cic. *Ad Fam.* 15. 19. 2-3 Statilius and Favonius: Plut. *Brut.* 12.
3-4. Decimus's closeness to Caesar: App. *BC.* 2.111. Servilia and
Porcia: Cic. *Ad Att.* 13.22.4

Cato and citizenship for Parma: M. Porcius Cato Fr 56. Porcia's
thigh wound: Plut. *Brut.* 13.2.11. Val. Max. 3.2.15

Recruitment methods: Plut. *Brut.* 12. 3-8. Resentment at Caesar's
promotion of former enemies: Nic. Dam. *Augustus* 2. Trebonius's
previous assassination plan: Plut. *Antony* 13.2. Cic. *Phil.* 2.34

Brutus's claimed link to Junius Brutus: Plut. *Brut.* 1.4 5.2 8.2. Brutus
sparing Antony: Cic. *Ad Att.* 15.11.2. Calpurnia's dream: Velleius
Paterculus. *Historiae (History of Rome)* 2.5.72. Cass. Dio 44.17.3

FOUR

Pearls and golden moon: Plut. *Pompey.* 45, 1. Plin. *NH.* 37.14.18.
Statues of gods: Plin. *NH.* 7.34 35,114. Pompey as butcher kid: Val.
Max. 6.2. Personal hatred preventing betrayal: Nic. Dam. *Aug.* 66

Twenty-three wounds: Plut. *Caes.* 26. Even you my son: Suet. *Div.*

Jul. 82. L. Minucius Basilus: Cass. Dio. 43, 47, 5. Gloom after the assassination: Plin. *NH.* 298. Lepidus on Tiber island: Cass. Dio. 44.22.2. Brutus's first speech: Cass. Dio. 44.21.1 App. *BC.* 2. 122

Cicero on worthlessness of Antony's words: Cic. *Phil* 2. 89, on prophetic signs Cic. *De Divinatione*

Nocte intempesta: Varro. *De Lingua Latina (On the Latin Language)* 6. 6-7 and 7.72. Parmensis as author of Brutus and Thyestes: Quintilian *Institutio Oratoria (Rules of Oratory)* V.II.2

FIVE

Decimus as military innovator: Caes. *De Bello Gallico (Gallic War)* 3.11.14-15, at Massilia, Caes. *Bellum Civile (Civil War)* 1.36 57-8. 2.22, as Caesar's heir, Suet. *Div. Jul.* 83.2 Plut. *Caes.* 64.1

Matius warns Cicero of war: *Cic. Ad Att.* 14.2. Antony's funeral speech: Suet. *Div. Jul.* 84.2 Cic. *Ad Att.* 14.10.1. Brutus's promise to troops App. *BC.* 2.140. 581; 3, 2, 5

SIX

Octavius's family: Suet. *Aug.* 1 ff. Cicero and Epicurus: Cic. *Ad Att.* 14.20.5. Choice of play for Brutus's games: Cic. *Ad Att.* 16.5.1

Antium conference: Cic. *Ad Att.* 15.1, Decimus's defeatism: Cic. *Ad Fam.* XI. I, IV. Brutus's testament: Vell. Pat. 2, 62,3. Andromache's farewell to Hector: Homer *Iliad* 6. 429ff. Octavian's temporary coalition: Cass. Dio. 45,11,1

Pontius and Servilia: Cic. *Ad Att.* 14.21.3. Brutus into exile: Cic. *Tusculanae Disputationes (Tusculan Disputations)* 5, 107

SEVEN

Whereabouts of Cassius: Cic. *Ad Fam.* 12.2. Torture of Trebonius: Cic *Phil.* 11. 3.7 App. *BC.* 3. 24-6. Epicureans on painful death: Sen. *Epistulae Morales ad Lucilium (Moral Epistles)* 30 1-3, 14

EIGHT

Cicero and the banquet invitation: Cic. *Ad Fam.*12.4.1. Decimus's force inside Mutina: App. *BC.* 3.49. Decimus's mother: Sallust *Bellum Catilinae* 25. Hirtius leaves Rome: Cass. Dio 46.35.7. App. *BC.* 3.65. Pansa's scouts: App. *BC.* 3.67. Galba on Forum Gallorum: Cic. *Ad Fam* 10.30. Hirtius comes to Pansa's aid: Cic. *Ad Fam.* 10.30. 4

Battle of Mutina: App. *BC.* 3. 68. 281. Octavian rescuing Hirtius's body: App. *BC.* 3.71. Antony abandons Mutina: *App BC.* 3.72. Accusation of Octavian killing Hirtius: Suet *Aug* 11, citing Aquilius Niger Fr 1. Octavian's troops unwilling to help Decimus: Cic. *Ad Fam.* 11.10.4. Antony in retreat: Cic. *Ad Fam.* 10.34.1

Lepidus and Antony: App. *BC.* 3, 83, 341 ff. Octavian and the consulship: App. *BC* 3. 88. 361. Decimus to Cicero: Cic. *Ad Fam.* XI. IV –XIIIb. Suicide of Cornutus: App. *BC.* 3.92.381

NINE

Parmensis to Cicero: Cic. *Ad Fam.* 12. 13.*cedant arma togae* Quint. *IO.* 11.24. Decimus to Cicero: Cic. *Ad Fam.* XI, XXVI. Suicide of Dolabella: App. *BC.* 4 60-62, Cass. Dio 47.30

TEN

Cicero on the consulship, Cic. *Phil.* 14.15, *Ad Fam.* 1.4a.4. App. *BC* 3.82. 337ff, Cass. Dio 46.42.2 Plut. *Cic.* 45

Pedian court for Cassius: Vell. Pat. 2, 69, 5, and for Brutus, Plut. *Brut.* 27. Ten years pay for Octavian's troops: App. *BC.* 3,94 Death of Pedius: App. *BC* 4,6, 26

Etruscan soothsayer: App. *BC.* 4.4.15. Fulvia having nothing female but her sex: Vell. Pat. 2. 74. Plotius revealed by his perfume: Plin. *NH.* 13.25. Spirit escaping through hole in head: Petronius *Satyricon* 62.5

Antony replacing names of those spared: Cass. Dio 47 13.1 8.5.

Varro's escape: App. *BC* 4, 47. Another Varro: Cass. Dio 47.11.2. Varro cites Parmensis's *Brutus*: Varro *DLL* 6. 6-7, 7.72. Cales saves Sittius: App. *BC* 4.47. Death of Basilus: App. *BC* 3, 98,409

Parmensis as author of *Brutus* and *Thyestes*: Quint. *IO* V.II.24. Theft of Thyestes: Scholiast on Horace: *Quintus Varus ab Augusto missus, ut eum interficeret, studentem repperit, et perempto eo scrinium cum libris tulit, [ubi multae trag<o>ediae inuentae sint, inter quas Horestis et Tiestis]. Vnde multi crediderunt Thiesten Cassi Parmensis fuisse.*

ELEVEN

Death of Gaius: Cass. Dio. 47.24.4 Plut. *Brut.* 28.1. Conference at Smyrna: Plut. *Brut.* 28.3-7. App. *BC.* 4.63. Brutus at Xanthus: Plut. *Brut* 30.6-31.7 App. *BC.* 4, 76-80 Cass. Dio, 47.34. 1-3. Divisions at Sardis: Plut. *Brut* 34.2. Cass. Dio 47. 35. 1. Caesar deified: Cass. Dio 47. 18.3 -19.3. Fire at Xanthus App. *BC.* 4.80

TWELVE

Turullius as Cimber's aide: Cic. *Ad Fam.* 12.13. Cassius at Melas: App. *BC.* 4. 12. 89 ff. Cassius's seniority: App. *BC.* 4.89.376 Plut. *Brut.* 29.1. Messalla's family: Hor. *Sat.* 1.10.8

Cassius compared to Pompey: App. *B.C.* 4.124.520. Messalla's admiration for Cassius: Tacitus *Annales* 4.43.4. Cimber at sea: App. *BC* 4.13.102. Brutus's ghosts: Plut. *Brut.* 36.7. 48.1 App. *BC* 4.134. Naval defeat for triumvirs in Adriatic: App. *BC* 4 15.115, Cass. Dio 47.47.4. Plut. *Brut.* 47. Scale of the forces at Philippi: App. *BC* 4.108. 454. First move uncertainty: Plut. *Brut.* 41.3. App. *BC* 4.111. Cicero's obsession with Antony: Sen. *Suasoriae.* 6.23. Cassius's suicide: Plut. *Brut.* 43. 4-9 Vell. Pat. 2.70.2-3; Val. Max. 6.8.4

THIRTEEN

Statilius and Epicurean argument: Cic. *Rep.* 1.10 Sen *De Otio* 3.2.

Brutus diverts river: Cass. Dio 47.47.3, orders looting, Plut. *Brut*
46.1-2 App. *BC.* 4. 118

An Ethiopian at the gates: App. *BC.* 4.134. Octavian in the marshes.:
Plin. *NH.* 7.147-8 Agrippa *De Vita Sua* Fr. 2. Brutus and virtue:
Cass. Dio 47.49.2. Brutus's quote from Medea: Euripides *Medea*
332

Messsalla's surrender to Antony: App. *BC.* 4 38. Octavian's executions: Suet. *Aug* 13.12. Death of Favonius: Cass. Dio 47. 49.4

FOURTEEN

Brutality of Octavian: Suet. *Aug.* 13. Brutus's head lost at sea: Cass.
Dio 47.49.2. Rejections of surrender after Philippi: Vell. Pat. 2.71.1
App. *BC.* 5.2

No money to pay for land: App. *BC.* 5.15. Fears of Sextus's strength:
App. *BC.* 5.55.230. Sextus' tutor Aristodemus: Strabo *Geography*
14. 1, 48, 650. Sextus with Pompey and Cornelia: Lucan *Pharsalia*
8. 238. Caesar receives Pompey's head: Cass, Dio. 42.8.1 Val. Max.
5.1.10 Luc. *Phars.* 9. 1035-43

FIFTEEN

Land riots in Italy: App. *BC.* 4. 25. 104. Fulvia's role: App. *BC.* 5 19.75.
Cass. Dio. 48.28.3. Lucius's fears on behalf of Antony: App. *BC.*
5.14.55. Antony's knowledge of events in Italy: App. *BC.* 5.21.83.
60.25.1 Cass. Dio 48.27.1. Conflicting reports of human sacrifice:
Suet. *Aug.* 15.1. Cass. Dio 48.14.4 App. *BC.* 5 48. 201-2

SIXTEEN

Virgil: *miles habebit barbarus* Virgil *Eclogues* 1.71. Propertius.
1.21. Antony's loss of Gallic legions: Cass. Dio 48.20.3 App. *BC.*
5.26.103. Labienus as Parthian: Cass. Dio. 48. 26.5.

Sextus on Brundisium pact: App. *BC.* 5. 67, on Misenum pact, App.
BC. 5. 70-2. Popular anger after Brundisium: Cass. Dio 48.3L6

SEVENTEEN

Crowds welcome back the proscribed: Cass. Dio. 48.37. Octavian struggles against unpopularity at Rome: App. *BC.* 5.92. Sextus's dark blue cloak: App. *BC.* 5.100. Octavian's fleet crushed by storms: App. *BC.* 5. 92. Antony's marriage to Athens: Cass. Dio 48. 39.2. Horace's journey to Brundisum: Horace. *Satires* 1.5

EIGHTEEN

Antony unable to help Sextus: App. *BC.* 5.93. Avernus construction: Strabo *Geog.* 5.4.5 Florus *Epitome* 2.18.6. Athens and Avernus: Lucretius. *De Rerum Natura (On the Nature of Things)* 6.749

Protest at desecration of sacred groves: Cass. Dio 48-50 Servius on *Georgics* 2.162. Agrippa's lack of credit for success: Agrippa *De Vita Sua.* Fr 1. Storms halve Octavian's fleet: App. *BC.* 5.98

Octavian misses July date for battle: App. *BC.* 5.97, hides at Tauromenium, App. *BC.* 5. 110. Harpax at Naulochus: *App.* BC. 5.106, 119. Punishment of Sicilian towns: App. *BC.* 5.129. Pompeia escapes with Sextus: Cass. Dio 49.11. 1

NINETEEN

Mutinies after Naulochus: Cass. Dio 49.13 App. *BC.* 5. 128. 528. Sextus in Nicomedia: App. *BC.* 5. 137, burns his own ships, App. *BC.* 5.139

Horace on Parmensis writing like a river in flood: Hor. *Sat.* 1.10.61, and on Tibullus emulating Parmensis, *Hor. Epistles.* 1.4.3

TWENTY

Turullius on Cos: Val. Max. 1.1.19. Cos for quince and marjoram: Pliny *NH.* 13.5. Parmensis on Octavian: Suet. *Aug.* 4, on advice for curing gout, Pliny *NH.* 31.8

TWENTY-ONE

Messalla joins Agrippa at sea: Plut. *Brut.* 40.11 App. *BC.* 4.38.161. Antony sends inland for mercenaries: Cass. Dio L.13.4. Defection of mercenary kings: Hor. *Ep.* 9 17-18. Antony abandons his army: Plut. *Ant.* 66-68

TWENTY-TWO

Turullius with Antony: Cass. Dio 51.8 2-3, dies, Val. Max. 1.1.19. Caesar at Massilia: Lucan. *BC.* 3, 399-452

TWENTY-THREE

Messalla and Antony's house: Cass. Dio 53. 27.5. Horace and Virgil on Pollio: Pliny *Epist.* 5.3.5 Hor. *Sat.* 1.10 42-43, Virg. *Ec.* 3. 86. Epicureans following Pollio: Aufidius Bassus, cited by Sen. *Suas.* 6.23. Pollio as library builder: Plin. *NH.* 35.10, not at Actium, Vell. Pat. 2.86.3

Augustus on factions: *Res Gestae* 1. 4. Opposition to Octavian enduring in Athens: Cass. Dio. 54.7.23. The sweet sight of the sea: Lucr. *DRN.* 2.1 *Quis istam:* Quint. *IO* 5.2.24. Varus and Varius; Porphyrio on Hor. *Ep.* 1.4.3

BIBLIOGRAPHY

Adams J. N. (2003) *Bilingualism and the Latin Language* (Cambridge)

Adams J. N. (1982) *The Latin Sexual Vocabulary* (Duckworth)

Barbieri M.E. and Manzelli V. (2006) *Emilio Romagna* (Libreria del Stato)

Beard M. (2015) *SPQR* (Profile)

Beard M. (2007) *The Roman Triumph* (Harvard)

Balsdon J.P.V.D (1979) *Romans and Aliens* (Duckworth)

Bradley M. (2009) *Colour and Meaning in Ancient Rome* (Cambridge)

Bradley M. (ed) (2015) *Smell and the Ancient Senses* (Routledge)

Catarsi M. (2007) *Parma e Fidenza in Forme et tempi dell'urbanizzazione nella Cisalpina (All'insegno del Giglio)*

Coarelli P. (2007) *Rome and Environs, an Archaeological Guide* (California)

Cooley A. (2009) *Res Gestae Divi Augusti* (Cambridge)

Cornell T.J. (ed) (2013) *The Fragments of Roman Historians* (Oxford)

Donahue J.F. (2017) *The Roman Community at Table during the Principate* (Michigan)

Edwards C. (2007) *Death in Ancient Rome* (Yale)

Epstein D.F. (1987) 'Caesar's Personal Enemies on the Ides of March' (*Latomus* 46)

Garnsey P. (1999) *Food and Society in Classical Antiquity* (Cambridge)

Gowers E. (1994) 'Horace Satires 1.5 An Inconsequential Journey' (Cambridge)

Gowing A.M. (1990) 'Appian and Cassius' Speech before Philippi' in Phoenix 44 (Class Ass of Canada)

Grazzi L. (1972) *Parma Romana (Banca del Monte di Parma)*

Henderson J. (1998) *Fighting for Rome* (Cambridge)

Jacobs P.W. and Conlin D.A. (2014) *Campus Martius* (Cambridge)

McClellan A.M. (2019) *Abused Bodies in Roman Epic* (Cambridge)

Mahy T. (2009) 'After the Daggers: Politics and Persuasion after the Assassination of Caesar' (PhD diss. University of St Andrews)

Millar F. (1964) *A Study of Cassius Dio* (Oxford)

Millar F. (1998) *The Crowd in Rome in the Late Republic* (Ann Arbor)

Pitassi M. (2009) *The Navies of Rome* (Boydell Press)

Powell A. and Welch K. (eds) (2002) *Sextus Pompeius* (Duckworth)

Rawson E. (1983) 'Cassius and Brutus: The Memory of the Liberators' in J.D. Smart, I.S. Moxon and A.J. Woodman (eds)

Rice E.E. (ed) (1996) *The Sea and History* (Sutton)

Richlin A. (2002) 'Cicero's Head' in Porter J.L. (ed) *Constructions of the Classical Body* (Michigan)

Sedley D. (1997) 'The Ethics of Brutus and Cassius' (JRS 87)

Southern P. (1998) *Mark Antony* (Tempus)

Syme R. (1939) *The Roman Revolution* (Oxford)

Talbot R.J.A (ed) (2000) *Barrington Atlas of the Greek and Roman World* (Princeton)

Tempest K. (2017) *Brutus* (Yale)

Treggiari S. (2019) *Servilia and Her Family* (Oxford)

Welch K. (2012) *Magnus Pius* (Swansea)

Williams J.H.C. (2001) *Beyond the Rubicon* (Oxford)

Wiseman T.P. (2008) *Unwritten Rome* (Exeter)

Wiseman T.P. (2009) *Remembering the Roman People* (Oxford)

Woolf G. (2006) *Et Tu, Brute?* (London)

Zucchelli B. (2003) *Il poeta Cassio Parmense e Parma romana* (Battei)

ACKNOWLEDGEMENTS

To Mary Beard, Joanna Evans, Holly Harley, Caroline Michel, Llewelyn Morgan, Ruth Scurr, Andrew Sillett, David Smith, Paul Webb

ILLUSTRATIONS

INDEX